CLUBHOUSE CONFIDENTIAL

CLUBHOUSE
CONFIDENTIAL

A Yankee Bat Boy's Insider Tale of Wild
Nights, Gambling, and Good Times
with Modern Baseball's Greatest Team

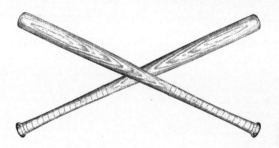

LUIS "SQUEEGEE" CASTILLO

with
WILLIAM CANE

St. Martin's Press ⋈ New York

CLUBHOUSE CONFIDENTIAL. Copyright © 2011 by Luis Castillo and William Cane.
All rights reserved. Printed in the United States of America. For information, address
St. Martin's Press, 175 Fifth Avenue, New York, N.Y. 10010.

www.stmartins.com

Library of Congress Cataloging-in-Publication Data (TK)

ISBN 978-0-312-64542-7

First Edition: August 2011

10 9 8 7 6 5 4 3 2 1

For Tina Lewis and the Bleacher Creatures

At old Yankee Stadium,

Where it all started

One summer day

Not so long ago.

And for my family—

My mother, Milagros Reyes,

My father, Luis A. Castillo,

And my wife, Margarita Pacheco.

Without their love and support,

This book would not have been possible.

And for my children, Luis A. Castillo III, and George Santiago,

So that they can share firsthand in my experience as a Yankee bat boy.

Contents

CLUBHOUSE CONFIDENTIAL

1

Clash of the Titans
Roger Clemens

What is wrong with this guy! A giant of a man stands pressing his face up against the New York Yankees' clubhouse mirror, cheeks puffed out until they look like they're about to explode. When he leans back there's a smudge of oil where his nose touched the glass. Baseball cap in hand, he's breathing like he just walked up a flight of stairs, but the game hasn't even started.

He steps back and I see it's Roger Clemens. He's pitching today. He screws his cap tight onto his head. His eyes rake over the clubhouse and he begins pacing back and forth. Roger is massive through the chest, nearly the size of two average men, his legs cut and muscular as he turns and exits through the tunnel leading up to the field. I can hear him breathing, the echo of each breath magnified in the runway.

At first I was worried about him, but then I started worrying about *them*—the batters going up against him. For it dawned on me that this was a new side of Clemens, one I hadn't seen yet. This was a side of Clemens that you see only if you happen to be in the clubhouse during the minutes before he goes out to take the mound. He had been getting ready, in his own unique way, going through a personal ritual in preparation for the ordeal of pitching. He had been working himself up into a state . . . and I felt sorry for the batters who would face him.

Part of my job at Yankee Stadium included picking up bats and balls for players. During games I was responsible for patrolling the area between home plate and first base. Even now I remember how I hustled to get upstairs, eager to see what Clemens would do after that warm-up.

By the time he took the mound on July 8, 2000, the fans were buzzing and the air was tense with anticipation. It was over eighty degrees in the sun, but the sweat drizzling down Clemens's face didn't seem to bother him. Longtime interleague rivals were facing one another: Yankees vs. Mets. The fans roared with each pitch and each swing of the bat. Still, Clemens never let the roar of the crowd distract him. No, he had that focus going, and I knew why. He had psyched himself up for it. His fastballs popped into the catcher's mitt with a sound like gunshots. *Bang! . . . Bang! . . . Bang!* He was pacing himself, breathing hard, but pacing himself for the big confrontation to come.

Everyone was looking forward to it, too. Because Mets catcher Mike Piazza had racked up an impressive record against Clemens. In fact, he came to the plate that night with an intimidating score of .583 against the Rocket—including three home runs and a double. People in the know said Clemens resented Piazza's success against him.

When Piazza approached home plate, he swung the bat a few

times and the crowd came alive. Then there was the windup and the pitch—*a high fastball headed directly at the batter's face!* You could hear a sharp gasp from the crowd. Piazza had no more than a fraction of a second to react. His right foot was already off the ground because he had launched into the swing, preventing him from getting enough twisting force to turn his body away. He only had time to move his head a few inches to avoid a direct blow between the eyes. The baseball—unleashed, some said, with an intention to hit him—smashed into the upper crown of Piazza's blue helmet, directly above his left ear.

For a moment the massive body of the Mets catcher shook, as if uncertain what to do. The echo of the *Craaaaaackkkkkkkkkkkk!* that the ball made upon impact with his batting helmet could be heard all the way down in the Yankees' dugout. The Yankees players and coaches leaped to their feet to see what had happened. A few seconds later, the powerhouse who had faced Clemens with such confidence and dignity crumpled and fell, collapsing over home plate.

A hush fell over the crowd and for a few scary minutes all 50,000 spectators seemed to be thinking the same thing: this is a hell of a dangerous sport. Then, as the fallen player was helped off the field, the mood changed. The buzz of conversation spread in waves. Everybody was talking about it! The legendary Mets catcher had suffered a concussion and had to be taken out of the game.

The Mets players were on top of the dugout yelling at Clemens.

"You're an asshole!"

"You're fucked up!"

Players were upset and reacting. The Yankees were jabbering

back at the Mets, too. It was a free-for-all where everybody wanted to put in his two cents.

Roger Clemens was saying, "I didn't mean to do it," and backing away from the Mets players. Before you knew what had happened, the inning was over and he disappeared back into the shelter of the clubhouse. A few minutes later, he sent over Brian McNamee to tell the Mets and Mike Piazza "I didn't mean to do it." Brian McNamee was the Yankees personal trainer who later submitted sworn testimony that he injected Clemens with steroids over a dozen times. That may seem like an odd choice for a personal messenger from Clemens to Piazza, but it shows how close Clemens and McNamee were in 2000.

The response from the Mets was predictable: Tell that asshole that he's a complete jerk. He *meant* to do that. He's a headhunter.

But in reality I thought that Clemens felt bad, and I was convinced that he knew that he had made a mistake. I was in the players' lounge and I saw how upset he was when he came inside. The media wasn't there to cover this behind-the-scenes part of the story. He was walking around in the clubhouse and talking to himself out loud, cursing at himself, telling Mel Stottlemyre what had happened, wringing his hands, acting moody, and looking like a man who had just made a major error. The Yankees used to feel the same way the Mets felt when Clemens was pitching against us and hitting *our* players. We were annoyed because he seemed to be running away from his responsibility by going into hiding in the clubhouse after his inning of pitching. When he's out of sight you don't know what he's thinking because you can't observe how he's reacting, and naturally the Yankees had been upset when he hit one of our guys. But when we saw his reaction—in the Yankees' clubhouse, when he was finally on our side—we realized that he was acting like a nervous man. He was muttering sorry comments like, "I didn't mean to do it!"

Three months later things got even worse. It was Game 2 of the World Series between the Yankees and the Mets. More than anything else, what fans had come to see that October night was the rematch between Clemens and Piazza. By now these two had a history between them that went deeper than statistics and numbers. It was a history of blood and violence, and fans came to the arena to see how it would unfold.

In quick succession, Clemens struck out the first two Mets batters, Timo Perez and Edgardo Alfonzo, which brought up the main event: Mike Piazza. When he stepped up to the plate— the future Hall of Fame Mets catcher facing the future Hall of Fame Yankees pitcher—I happened to be on bat boy duties that day and was in the dugout. Piazza looked relaxed and ready for business, swinging the bat around to show off his massive arm and neck muscles. The Rocket was looking intense and focused on the mound, psyched and ready to rumble. Roger's face was red, the muscles of his arms clearly visible in the lights. He was concentrating and breathing hard, just as he had done on that day three months before, when he had psyched himself up in the clubhouse. He was here to face his rival and finish this business between them.

The Mets catcher took a few warm-up swings and stepped into the batter's box. An air of excitement and anticipation snapped through the crowd, and you knew what they were thinking. There wasn't one man, woman, or child whose eyes weren't trained on the green diamond. The chatter wasn't the usual noise you hear at

Yankee Stadium; tonight it was mixed with hope . . . and a real sense of fear.

After three sizzling pitches by Clemens—and two missed swings by Piazza—the count stood at one ball, two strikes. There was a brief pause. A cool breeze ruffled the long brown hair visible behind Piazza's helmet. Clemens got set, nodded at the catcher, and wound up for the pitch. Piazza raised his bat a few inches higher and got ready to swing. In the next instant, Clemens unleashed an inside fastball and Piazza swung hard and connected, the ball striking the bat close to his hands. *Smuuuuuuuunk!* I looked up. *What in the name of Babe Ruth was that!* It wasn't the typical sound of ball hitting bat, which I knew so well I could hear it in my sleep. *Pop!* It's supposed to sound like a goddamn *Pop!* This was something entirely different.

The ball was hit foul, but upon impact Piazza's bat splintered into three pieces of different length. He had already started running toward first. While he was on the move, a small piece of bat landed behind home plate and a second piece flew out toward foul territory. But the largest fragment, the barrel, tumbled end over end toward the pitcher's mound, where Roger Clemens was standing. It moved so fast that it looked like a white blur. Roger's reaction was instantaneous. He actually fielded the *bat*, picking up the piece of barrel, which he apparently thought was the ball, and then—upon realizing his mistake—flung it into foul territory . . . almost hitting Mike Piazza in the process!

In the next moment, all hell broke loose.

But before I tell you about that, I have to add a comment from my perspective down on the field. None of the fans could see Clemens as clearly as I could. I had never noticed an expression like that on his face. In fact, he looked disgusted, and to me that was one of the most telling things about the whole incident—that look of disgust, as if he had been dragged down into some kind of dirty business by having come in contact with the bat.

Piazza, who had also been confused by the splintering bat, couldn't believe what had just happened. He was convinced that Clemens had thrown the bat at him! He slowed and moved off course, approaching Clemens, saying, "What's your problem?" A gentleman through and through, restraining himself from harsher words, Piazza must have been thinking, What the fuck's going on? First you hit me with a baseball and now you throw a *bat* at me!

Not acknowledging Piazza, Clemens walked toward the home plate umpire and said, "Give me a ball."

But there was no way Clemens could walk away from this one. That carelessly flung piece of bat had started a big to-do that would have an impact on Roger and the rest of the team for months afterward. Both benches poured onto the field, cleared of all players. Everyone was fussing and cursing. Umpire Charlie Reliford stepped forward to keep Clemens and Piazza apart.

With noticeable control of his emotions, Piazza returned to the batter's box and the game continued. But as soon as the inning was over, some spectators booed, and Clemens did a speed walk toward his dugout, apparently eager to escape all the commotion.

From an insider perspective, having worked with Roger, I can tell you what really happened—and why. The whole thing was the result of his competitiveness. It was his intimidation factor against other teams. As if he were saying, "If you step into that batter's box you're going against *Roger Clemens* . . . You're not going against an average Joe." But there's another side to it also, in addition to his competitiveness and his desire to win. Everybody knows the facts about what happened that day on the field, but nobody in the media knows what happened when Clemens went downstairs into the clubhouse and felt guilty. He was nervous backstage. You could see it. He was holding his head, he was on his chair in the locker room, he was in the trainer's room, he was back and forth all over the place, as if he couldn't find a spot where he could get away from himself and what he had done. He was walking around and he wasn't acting like himself. Those incidents—when he hit Piazza in the head, and when he threw the bat—put him off his game. Suddenly, Roger wasn't acting like a warrior anymore, he was acting like a little girl, and he was moaning, "Oh, my God, what did I do!"

It's never as black and white with Roger Clemens as the media might lead you to believe. He's more than an aggressive headhunter who thinks only of himself and his reputation. You can't understand him unless you consider both sides of his personality—the raw aggression as well as the contrition and guilt. This combination of opposites is what makes the real Roger Clemens.

Before every game the Yankees air the national anthem, and all the players stand on the field. Sometimes, though, a player is late getting to the ball park. To remedy this problem, Joe Torre made up a rule:

IF YOU'RE LATE

FOR THE NATIONAL ANTHEM

YOU PAY A FINE OF $100

It was the manager's way of creating unity and making sure that everyone was on time and responsible. He would use this money at the end of the year to take the coaches out to dinner.

On off days, when he wasn't pitching, Roger might get a massage and order something to eat. So when he came back to work he was still in a relaxed frame of mind. Sometimes there would be a memo posted up on the door of the clubhouse to let players know what time they had to report in front of the dugout for the national anthem. Roger Clemens would be late a good 80 percent of the time.

When he arrived late, he would go into Torre's office in full uniform like a schoolboy reporting to the principal's office. He would leave three hundred-dollar bills on the manager's desk, and then he would take his time walking up to the dugout. After the national anthem was over he would approach Torre.

"Hey, Mr. T, I left three hundred bucks on top of your table. I know a couple of other guys were late so I'll pay for them, too."

Joe Torre would give him a sour look.

"Don't make that a habit."

But the funny thing is that having to pay these big fines never seemed to teach Clemens a lesson. He was like a lot of the athletes I've known: they're late more often than the average person. I don't know why that might be, unless maybe it's because they're so confident of their physical stamina that they think they can get to places faster than they really can. Clemens's lateness might be a sign of arrogance, but it might just as easily be a sign of overconfidence. One thing I know for sure is that it was this kind of confidence that made Clemens such a menace on the field.

Torre would shake his head.

"I'll let you off this time," he would say. "But next time you *have* to be here. Don't make this a regular thing because then everybody will get used to it and just leave money on top of my desk and won't take the rule seriously."

Forget the impression you may have of Roger Clemens as an aggressive, inconsiderate person. Not only was he considerate enough to pay for teammates who were late, but if you were in the same room with him, like I was hundreds of times, you'd see that he was a friendly guy with an almost sweet disposition. Yes, he was competitive during games, but when he was off the field he was like your fun-loving kid brother. That's the best description I can give of him. Like your little brother. You'd have loved him.

There's no question that inside Clemens lives a little kid just waiting to come out and have fun. Take, for example, what happened one fall day in September 2003. It's always a tradition in baseball on each team where the rookies—guys playing their first full season in Major League Baseball—get hazed during their first year. It's called Rookie Dress-Up Day. This practical joke is scheduled for the last road trip in September. Rob Cucuzza, the Yankees' equipment manager, searches the Internet weeks in advance and orders costumes. I would see Robbie sitting at his desk, hair uncombed, sleeves rolled up, focusing on the task of finding something crazy-looking. People thought he was working. He would spend hours setting up this prank, and Clemens would take a more active role in the planning than other players. He used to walk into the office sometimes when I was in there, and say, "How's the costumes coming along? Did you guys get them yet?" Robbie would show Clemens a couple of pictures of what he was considering.

"Yeah," Clemens would say. "Let's get this one! I like that! It's awesome." This would go on for weeks until finally the costumes were ordered.

On this particular day the costumes were ready, hidden in Rob Cucuzza's office. The rookies didn't know anything about it. They were playing the game, unaware of what was in store for them. During the seventh inning, the other players told the bat boys to hide the rookies' street clothes.

Hideki Matsui had a weird-looking outfit waiting for him— a full-length leopard-skin coat. There was also a cane, a wide-brimmed hat, and a gold cap for his tooth.

When the game was over, Matsui returned to the clubhouse and took his shower. Then he started looking for his clothes. He was frowning because he couldn't find them. That's when he noticed the costume on his chair. His eyebrows went up and his lips twisted into a frown.

His interpreter approached and put a hand on his shoulder.

"Hideki, you gotta put this on. It's a tradition."

But the Japanese slugger didn't understand. They don't do this in Japan. It took a little while before they could explain it to him. Then a tiny smile spread across his lips. He picked up the shiny black pants. Clemens was videotaping everything with his camcorder. Matsui started getting dressed, with reporters and photographers snapping away. The designated hitter slipped on the leopard-skin coat and topped it all off with the hat. Clemens motioned for me to approach.

"Squeegee, put on some Elvis."

Once the music started playing, Clemens urged his teammate

to do a dance. Matsui grinned, and the fake gold tooth popped out. He waved the cane in the air and started tap dancing. Roger was recording it all, and the laughs in the clubhouse were louder than the music.

Later, Clemens was shooting video from the team bus that takes players to the airport. Matsui was still signing autographs in the pimp outfit, as it came to be known. Holding his camcorder in one hand, Roger was kneeling on the backseat, leaning so far forward he almost fell out the window. Weeks of planning and anticipation had paid off. He seemed to be enjoying it more than anybody. It was the kid in Clemens.

I have to slip in a quick explanation here about how I came by this next bit of information about Clemens or otherwise you might not think I'm on the level. But the fact is I did a lot of running around for the Yankees. I was their unofficial personal assistant. And it took a good deal of legwork and organizing. None of it was in my contract either. But before long, because of the trust the players placed in me, I even saw some of them committing crimes.

This one takes place at three P.M., when no one's looking. That's good. Good for three New York Yankees players, I mean. They glance left and right, walking on tiptoe. At all costs, they don't want anybody to notice what they're doing. Most of all, they don't want to be caught by George Steinbrenner or the front office.

They're in the clubhouse on a regular game day, but they're not supposed to be here doing what they're doing. In fact, the "crime" they have planned has escaped notice from management for years. But it *still* goes on.

As an accomplice to this crime, I can tell you what they did and why they did it. The information I'm sharing has never before been revealed in print.

The man in the lead is Roger Clemens. Standing six foot four, he's in full uniform. He doesn't want to run into trouble today, so he makes sure no one sees him as he moves through the clubhouse, down the long white and blue hallway of old Yankee Stadium and into the storage room. There's a fine layer of sweat on his forehead and upper lip. No one can say that Roger Clemens isn't conscientious. He's worried sick that he's going to be caught.

This is the guy who used to hit Jeter with baseballs. Once upon a time he used to rub people on the team the wrong way. In fact, the Yankees weren't big fans of his before he joined the team. But after we got him with a blockbuster trade—giving up David Wells, Homer Bush, and Graeme Lloyd to the Blue Jays—and once Roger came on board, things changed like magic and he was welcomed like a brother into a fraternity. The prank he's playing today is like a fraternity prank, too, almost as if he and the other Yankees with him are trying to push their luck and see what mischief they can get into without getting in trouble.

Chad Curtis is behind him, a short sturdy guy with a fresh scent of talcum powder coming off him. An excellent outfielder, Chad is light on his feet as he walks with short steps after Clemens. Just before entering the storage room, he glances behind him to make sure nobody is watching. I was the bat boy who had helped arrange this crime and I knew very well that these guys weren't supposed to be here. And yet, here they were.

Ramiro Mendoza tags along after the others, hoping for some fun and excitement, no doubt. He isn't usually the kind of guy to get mixed up in something like this, yet he marches along behind Chad and Roger, looking for all the world like he's worried sick.

Rumors were that Clemens was a high-maintenance guy. I didn't know who he was before he showed up with the Yankees, but now I was helping him commit this misdemeanor at Yankee Stadium. We had entered a big room in the basement of the clubhouse. These players were coming into the storage room to get an illegal haircut. Illegal because it was against regulations for a barber to be in the clubhouse. There was no barber chair in there; no counter with combs and scissors. We just had a metal stool in the middle of a bunch of boxes, a small little stool for these big guys to sit on, one by one, as they got their haircut. You never see the storage room on television or in news photos. We had decided that this was the safest place because we weren't likely to be discovered. The barber was Martin Chavez, my barber from the Bronx.

"How did *your* barber get mixed up in this monkey business?" friends ask me. Even today I have to smile when I think about how it started. It came out of the blue.

One day I arrived at work with thin sideburns and a pencil mustache. My boss, Rob Cucuzza, looked me over.

"Wow, that's cool. Who cuts your hair?"

"My barber from the neighborhood."

"Tell him to come in on an off day and cut *my* hair."

"Are you sure, Robbie?"

"Yeah, but I don't want that line you have. I just want the top done and that's it."

Now I was committed, at least to helping *him*. So I brought in Martin, my Mexican barber, who doesn't know anything about baseball—he's a soccer man. He didn't know who these guys were and he wasn't interested in autographs. Before you know it, Robbie got his haircut in the storage room, and was staring into the mirror as if my barber had worked some kind of magic on him.

A light went on in Robbie's eyes and he said, "Listen, I got a great gig for you. What do you think about cutting players' hair?"

That's how it started. I would call Martin whenever they needed him. He was thirty-five and still working for his dad, who was proprietor of the family barbershop. It turns out this gig changed his life. He would leave his clients at the drop of a dime when I would call him to give haircuts to Reggie Jackson, Roger Clemens, David Justice, and Andy Pettitte. He didn't know who these guys were, but he knew he was going to make more money in a couple of hours than he typically made in a week.

There were times when Roger would want to look good before an important game. He would stand in front of a mirror, putting gel on his hair, poking the strands to get stand-up hairs for a spiky look. He would put on more gel and water and look at himself from every angle, trying to turn around to see the back. I would notice him and think, Oh, my God, this guy is obsessed with himself.

But people all said the same thing: They loved his haircut.

Little did they know it was my barber who made him look good. It was because these players aren't like the average person. They can't walk into a barbershop and wait their turn because they would get harassed. Using my barber was their way of staying away from the public and getting a favor done at the stadium.

One afternoon on an off day I was at home and my cell phone rang. I didn't know it was Andy Pettitte. I thought it was a wrong number, some guy talking in a high-pitched voice, saying, "Hey, Squeegee."

I'm thinking, Who the heck is *this*?

"It's me, Andy."

He sounded totally different over the phone.

"Come on, man," I said. "You're playing with me."

"No, no, this is for real. What's up, Squeeg?" He sounded like he was in a rush. "Hey, listen, can you tell your barber I need to see him and to bring his tools and meet me at the stadium?"

"Are you serious?"

"Yeah, yeah. I'm gonna be there in about another hour. Tell him to meet me at the stadium."

So I called Chavez and said, "What are you doing right now? Drop everything. You have to go with me to the stadium."

Fifteen minutes later he picked me up in his car and we were on our way to do this job. Now Martin found himself cutting Andy Pettitte's hair. Pettitte was telling him, just like Clemens, "Listen, I want my hair like this, see? I don't want it too low, you know? Because it won't make me look like Andy. And I gotta have it high, understand? I just want it trimmed, okay? Just a little bit trimmed. Don't take off too much."

I'll never forget working with Roger Clemens and being just a few yards from him while he was pitching. The hum of his fastball was a beautiful sound. I'll always remember how he looked when he wound up for the delivery and devastated batters from every team we faced. But most of all, I'll never forget the first afternoon Roger had his hair cut by my barber. I turned to Martin and said:

"Do you know whose hair you just cut?"

"No."

"You just gave a haircut to Roger Clemens."

Roger feeds on this shit.

Martin was just trying to learn. He turned to Roger and smiled. "I hear you pretty good pitcher."

2

Welcome to the Clubhouse
How I Became a Bat Boy

People always ask how an ordinary kid from the Bronx ever got to be in a position to see Clemens throw the bat at Piazza, and how I came to work with the Yankees for eight years as a bat boy. The answer is rather embarrassing.

It all started with my going to a baseball game at the old Yankee Stadium in the summer of 1997, a game that changed my life in a way no fifteen-year-old could ever in a million years have imagined. As I entered the bleachers I had no idea what lay ahead, no clue how the next few minutes were going to rip me out of my everyday world and put me into baseball history. After all, I had no connection with the Yankees organization. How could a kid like me, who was just going to see a game, ever be part of that? No way! The possibility never crossed my mind.

I entered the bleachers with my friend Max. There weren't that many people sitting in our section, maybe twenty or thirty. Despite the fact that my ticket was for the back row, I went down to the first row of seats, my heart hammering in my chest, not knowing whether someone might shout, "Stop! You don't belong here!" Suddenly I had a front-row seat to the New York Yankees! At my side, Max smiled like a devil. We considered these bleacher seats the best spot in the house because you can see every play in the game. It was my love of baseball that made me move forward that day, and it was that act that changed my life and made the rest of my boyhood so different from that of all my friends.

Darryl Strawberry is practicing his swing. Other players are warming up, and I'm right there, smack-dab in the middle of it! As I look at Strawberry, the fans around me start to fade away. The seats around me disappear, and all I see is Strawberry swinging his bat. I'm so focused on what he's doing that I never notice that someone is approaching me from behind.

"Hey, kid!"

For a moment I'm too stunned to turn. They can't mean *me*, can they?

It's actually the voice of a woman.

"Hey, you. That's *my* seat."

I get up. I'm going to apologize to her. I'm going to tell her I'm sorry. I love the game so much that I just had to take the chance, and I'm going to be nice and friendly to her. But before I can say a word, my friend lets his mouth get the better of him. "What the fuck do you want, lady? Leave us the hell alone!" My God, Max is such an idiot. I wish I could clap a hand over his mouth and shut him up before he gets us into trouble, but it's already too late. As soon as he curses at her, the woman turns pale, does an about-face, and marches away. Max smiles at me, but I'm in no mood for smiling back because of his mouth. Before we can even sit down again and think about relaxing, a security guard approaches. I realize right away that we're in trouble. "This isn't your seat," he says. "It's illegal to sit here this afternoon. Where's your ticket?"

The woman is in her mid-forties and she's wearing a plaid scarf, her bleached red hair flying in the wind. Her narrow eyes stare at me, flicking over to the game, then up to the big official who is questioning me and Max. "Kid, this ticket doesn't give you permission to be in this seat," the guard says. "This ticket is for back there." He's pointing. But my embarrassment prevents me from uttering a word. Max is still muttering under his breath as we're escorted by the officer up the aisle and out of the seating area, down a corridor past the concession stands, past the beer taps and the lines of fans, and out to the exit. That's where he tells us, "You can't see the game today. You lost your right to do that by moving up and cursing at Tina, and you guys have to leave the park."

Leave the park! From my high hopes and dreams to *this* outcome! I'm so crushed and embarrassed by it all that I can only walk away, shaking my head.

Luckily I live only a twenty-minute walk from Yankee Stadium. But I don't feel lucky now. I've been struck with the worst thing that can happen to a boy like me: I've been kicked out of Yankee Stadium. What will I tell my dad and my older brothers and sisters? How will I explain to my mother that I got kicked out before the game even started? Max begins complaining: "That bitch!" But I don't want to hear it; not now. Not after what happened. Not after getting kicked out of my dream ball park. I just want to get out of there, I'm so depressed.

———

The next day I went back without my friend. I guess I have a friendly way about me. I've always gotten along well with people, all types of people. So I had no doubt about what I was going to do.

It's another beautiful afternoon, and as soon as I arrive I climb up to the bleachers and look down. Sure enough, there she is, sitting right in front—the woman the guard referred to as "Tina." Her reddish hair is hard to miss in the crowd. Cap in hand, I approach and stand waiting at her side until she notices me, but as soon as she recognizes me her face goes pale. "I'm sorry," I say. I say it quickly so she knows I'm not here to annoy her. I continue apologizing like crazy. "My friend is a loudmouth. I don't know why he blew up like that. But he had no right to speak to you that way. And I want to apologize on behalf of both of us for the way he behaved yesterday." As I speak, her face relaxes and the color comes back into her cheeks. She asks who I am. I tell her my name and that I live close to Yankee Stadium and that I love baseball. "I love baseball, too," she says. "But these seats are off-limits except for the regulars. You were in the late Ali Ramirez's seat, the man who founded this section, God rest his soul. That's why I got so angry. We keep that seat vacant in his memory." A twinkle comes into her clear blue eyes, and she sits back in her seat. "By the way, I'm Tina Lewis. They call me Queen of the Bleachers." Then she asked what I wanted to do when I grew up. I laughed and admitted that I had always wanted to be part of the New York Yankees. I told her that I had thought of being a bat boy. At this, she said, "It's not easy to get a job like that. Do you know they get thousands of applications every year? But I'll let you in on a secret. I know someone on the team: Sonny Hight, the vice president for administration. You send *him* a letter and that's the way to get the ball rolling. You're a lot different from your friend, you know that? You're sincere and kind. If you write Sonny a letter and mention my name it might help."

I went home that day elated. Now I had a tip that might get me a hearing with the Yankees' equipment manager. I wrote that letter, too. I showed it to my big sister and she checked my spelling and grammar and then I mailed it off. In the letter I said I wanted to be a bat boy and that I was a baseball fan. I also said that I would work hard and that I was fifteen.

After I dropped the letter in the mailbox I kind of forgot about it. It was still such a long shot that I went about my business with no real hope of anything happening. But a few days later I got a letter back from Sonny Hight explaining that the requirements for becoming a bat boy were good grades in school and being a model citizen. Naturally I was excited to receive a letter like that, and I started studying hard to improve my grades. A few weeks later I received a letter inviting me to come for an interview.

I didn't tell my parents because I was nervous and I thought I'd look silly if I went for an interview and then didn't get the job. So I put on my jacket and tie, combed my hair, and snuck out without anyone seeing me.

The interview lasted an hour. They asked me about school, my family, and baseball. Did I know how to play? Did I know the rules? Did I realize that working as a bat boy would require a big-time commitment? (I was soon to find out just *how* big a commitment it really was.) I answered that I was in love with the game. I told them I knew the rules inside out since I played in a semi-professional baseball league as a pitcher. I said that I would be honored to devote all my free time to the job, and that since

I lived only a few minutes from the ball park it would be easy for me to report to work.

Then I went home and waited. I waited three months. I never thought anything would happen from the interview. But I did have hopes occasionally. When you're fifteen, three months is an eternity. And then finally a letter came. When I opened it I didn't know what to expect. I thought they were going to say no. But the first sentence took my breath away: "Congratulations on being inducted into the New York Yankees organization as a bat boy for the 1998 season."

I had to sit down, I was so excited my knees were trembling. I read it again to make sure I had it right. But the words were still there. No matter how many times I read them they didn't go away: I had gotten the job! They wanted me to be a bat boy for the Yankees! I was going to be right there with the team. Talk about a life-changing letter. And, sure enough, my life would never be the same.

Opening Day 1998 is my first day on the job and I arrive at Yankee Stadium not knowing what to expect. I walk through the empty concession area, headed toward the clubhouse, looking for Rob Cucuzza. I've been instructed to report at 10:00 A.M. and already it's 9:55. I turn into the hallway and go down a flight of steps.

Inside the lower level of the old Yankee Stadium the hallway is white and blue. My footsteps echo as I walk. I come to a door marked YANKEE CLUBHOUSE and knock. No answer. I stand waiting for a few minutes. Finally two young men amble down the hallway. They're bat boys, and they point me in the direction of

Joe Torre's office. "Down there," they say. Already I'm late and it's my first day.

When I get to Rob Cucuzza, my lateness doesn't even become an issue. He's all business. A short man in his late thirties, with a high forehead and sleepy-looking eyes, he tells me what to do. "Get your uniform from the locker room. Bring it to the dressing area and get dressed. Then come back and find me and we'll get you started." Before I turn to go, he breaks into a grin.

"Welcome to the team."

Oh, my God, I'm thinking. *It's true!*

I move quickly, aware that I'm late. Soon I will become very familiar with this man, Rob Cucuzza, who is in charge of the uniforms that all the players and team members wear. This includes all the well-known baseball players as well as the bat boys, coaches, and even the manager. Everything worn by a Yankee is stored in this enormous clothes room, and carefully categorized by size, function, and player.

I take my uniform and go down a long white and blue hall into the clubhouse, which is what the locker room is called. There's a lot of activity inside the large room, with about a dozen players getting dressed, but no one pays any attention to me. I've been instructed to use the far end where the bat boys have their lockers.

I open the box that Rob gave me. I'm excited to see the jersey with the official NY Yankees logo. My mother would be proud to see me now. I'm going to remember to tell her all about this moment. I rip off my shirt and pull on the jersey. My pants come off next and I step into the Yankees pinstripe white pants. The socks come on next. Then the shoes. I go over to the mirror. Is that really me, Luis Castillo, in a Yankees uniform? I'm smiling like a man on top of the world. My crew cut looks good, my brown eyes are sparkling, and I must say I look terrific. Suddenly I'm filled with pride. But then I remember I have work to do.

Before long, a thin teenager with curly brown hair approached and introduced himself as Joe Lee. A former bat boy for the Yankees, he was then a clubhouse assistant. After we shook hands, he said, "You know you can't start working here without being named."

Being named? I followed him back into the clubhouse, and the first player I met was Derek Jeter. I had been in the clubhouse with most of the players already, but the first one I ever talked to was the future captain. Sitting at his locker in his chair, in underwear and a Yankees T-shirt, he was pulling on baseball socks.

He glanced up. "What do you want, Chad?"

I was surprised when he called Joe Lee "Chad."

I turned to my new friend and said, "I thought you were Joe Lee."

"I'll explain later."

I was confused and I was beginning to suspect that they were setting up some kind of practical joke. Standing there in my crumpled uniform—my pants baggy and my jersey bulky because I was skinny—I felt uneasy because now Jeter was looking me up and down. He didn't say anything. I was starting to sweat with worry. Derek Jeter was just staring at me. I admit I was starstruck because it was my first day and I didn't know how to introduce myself.

"Hi," I said. "My name is Luis Castillo."

Jeter frowned, narrowed his eyes, and said, "Nah."

I was thinking, no *what*? Why did he just say no to me? But I didn't say anything, I just stood waiting. Jeter looked me up and down some more. I could feel Joe Lee laughing behind my back.

He was almost falling over he was so amused. I was still standing right in front of Jeter as if I were being inspected.

"That's it!" Jeter said.

What's it? I was wondering.

"Your nickname is Squeegee . . . You *look* like a squeegee." He smiled.

"What!"

"That's tradition," Joe Lee said, putting his arm around my shoulders and leading me away. "He names everybody. As leader of the team he has to give everybody nicknames."

"I got a strange one!" I said. But I never had a chance to ask Derek Jeter why he named me Squeegee. I knew what a squeegee man was, though. They're guys who clean car windows for money, standing in traffic and approaching stopped cars, wearing baggy white jumpers and looking skinny in their clothes. That's how my uniform looked that first day.

At least I had been initiated and was now an official member of the team. From that moment on my life would never be the same. It became almost a dreamlike fantasy—I was able to walk everywhere in Yankee Stadium and see everything the players did. I had permission to go places that no Yankee administrator, no reporter, no fan ever does. The rest of this book will share with you what I saw and heard during the eight years I worked with the New York Yankees. It's a behind-the-scenes peek at some of baseball's superstars. But keep one thing in mind: some of the stories you read may sound too incredible to have really happened . . . yet every word that follows is true.

3

Help!
Andy Pettitte

Ten minutes before game time. Everyone is up on the field except for a tall guy sitting in front of his locker. He's wearing pinstripes but doesn't look like he's ready to play. Knees spread at a forty-five-degree angle, he swallows hard, raises his eyes to heaven, and appears to be seeking help from above.

"I don't know . . ."

He pushes his left hand against his forehead with such force I think he's trying to rip his face off. His fingers run up through his Duck's Ass haircut. I feel like I'm watching a *very* troubled man . . . but this *can't* be a troubled man. It's Andy Pettitte—and he's our starting pitcher.

Mel Stottlemyre appears. Andy gazes up at the pitching coach as if hoping for the answer to a prayer. Mel puts a hand on Andy's shoulder.

"Stick to the plan. Relax."

Andy shakes his head.

"I really don't know . . ."

"Come on."

Andy stands and begins walking up the runway toward the dugout, Mel behind him.

It's the same old story every time. Before he goes out to pitch Andy needs a few comforting words from Mel. It's an aid to him in the final moments before he has to do the thing he's been blessed to do: pitch with a precision that few Major League starting pitchers can match. Yes, he's fast, very fast, but most of all, Andy Pettitte is *precise.* Yet never have I seen a man with such talent so shaken before—and after—games. It seems like the only thing that can calm him on these occasions is a few words from Mel.

"Your pitching coach is almost like your spouse," says Pettitte. "He's someone to go to when you want to gripe and complain. The big thing for me with Mel is that we've been through so much together. He's been through everything I've been through on the mound . . . He's been there, and that's what makes a good pitching coach."

The odd thing is that the more unimportant the game the more he appears to rely on Mel. For big games he's cool and collected, laser focused.

Taller than most other players at six foot five, Pettitte is built like a wobbly house on stilts. His neck is long and lean, his frame virtually two-dimensional when viewed in silhouette, and when he walks, oh, man, there's no mistaking him for anyone else! His head bobs up and down, his arms flop, and you can't imagine that this guy is all precision and mechanically correct because he looks so clumsy. Affectionately nicknamed Donkey by Jeter, he *looks* like he can't pitch but in actuality he's one of the finest in the league. They called him Donkey because, well, because he looked like a donkey, especially when walking.

One day I went into the Yankees gym to deliver a message to Andy. Heavy metal was blaring. He and Roger Clemens were in the middle of an intense workout. Wearing a weight belt inscribed with an NY logo, Andy was doing squats. The barbell on his shoulders was loaded with a stack of fifty-pound weights. Brian Mc-Namee stood behind him in his usual blue shorts and white T-shirt. Roger had on an identical weight belt and was drenched in sweat and red in the face. Andy dropped the weights and wiped his face with a towel.

"Yeah, Squeeg?"

I hated to interrupt, but at least my job kept me in the path of these two guys so that I got to see how close they had become, how friendly they were with their strength and conditioning coach, and how much fun they had together. Not only did they work and train together, they also played together—golf, that is. Fact is, they were so *into* this game that they would ask me to pack golf equipment onto the team truck when they went on the road. If they had to travel on short notice, I would FedEx golf equipment so that it would be ready when they arrived. Half the time you saw Pettitte with Clemens you'd hear them jawing about divots and drivers, putters and fairways. Sometimes they'd be so locked into a discussion about "that Westchase course" or "the way the ball gets into the sand at Palma Ceia" that I couldn't break through their conversation and get their attention.

Sure, we all knew that Andy had a natural talent, but the guy was so dedicated, so hard on himself, such a lover of the game that he drove himself—and me—to the brink of exhaustion on more than one occasion. I'm still asking myself, Whatever happened to that day of rest we were supposed to have after Game 5 of the 2003 World Series? We had flown back from Miami and arrived in New York at 2:30 A.M. Then I had to work until 8:00 A.M. getting all the gear stowed away, putting bats in order, and washing and folding laundry. All the players and coaches had gone home to bed because we had to play Game 6 the next day. I was looking forward to some sleep, too. But by the time I got home and had breakfast it was 9:00 A.M. The sun was shining as I walked into my bedroom.

Rinnnnnnnnnnnnnnnnnnng! My darn cell phone. The kind of ring that doesn't sound good. I wanted to punch the phone, but instead I answered it.

"Hey, Squeeg."

"Yeah?"

"Robbie."

"What's up?"

"Listen, Andy wants to play catch."

"Hunh?"

"You gotta come back."

"Are you serious?"

"Yeah, nobody's here."

"But I haven't had any sleep in two days."

"He asked for *you*."

"Well, okay, tell him I'm on my way, then . . . but I'm tired."

My suit was still on. When my mother heard me calling a taxi, she frowned. "Didn't you just come from work?" I explained that they needed me again. When I got back to the stadium, there were no pitching coaches or bullpen catchers available since everyone was exhausted. Only Gene Monahan and a couple of other trainers were there.

Andy arrived a few minutes later and we got our gloves and went out to the field. Now, you have to picture this: I'm seventeen years old, and I'm trusted by this ace starting pitcher because as a pitcher myself I understand what he's doing. We walk to the outfield and I get ready to begin catching. I squat down like a catcher, but I don't have on catcher's gear. I'm protected only by my glove and reflexes. I know he's going to be throwing real pitches, as fast and as hard as he would in a game.

Andy waves his glove from a three-o'clock to a nine-o'clock position. Just a little motion so that I know a cutter is coming—a fastball that typically tails into the hitter at the last fraction of a second. I know from experience that Andy's cutter moves inside, so I envision the path of the ball in my mind's eye before he unleashes it. (In contrast, Mariano Rivera, the Yankees closer, throws two different cutters, one that moves right, the other left. Andy is a little more predictable with this pitch.)

Zooooooonnnnnnk!

It hits my glove with a force that none of my friends in summer league can ever achieve.

Okay, keep your eyes open! You're tired but you gotta keep alert. Remember, you're catching for Andy Pettitte!

I throw it back.

Andy moves his glove from six o'clock to twelve o'clock. Fastball. He's letting me know he's going to blow it by. I get set for the impact. The windup *aaaaaaaaaaaaannnd* the pitch.

Zaaaaaaaaaaaap!

It sizzles my catching hand. I lob the ball back and get down into my crouch.

Like a prince meeting a queen, he holds his glove out and tips it down from twelve to six. Curveball. This will move *down* with departure off its flight path as it reaches me. So, don't miss it!

Sssssssssssssssssssss!

The ball hisses into my glove, and now we're on a roll. He's getting comfortable. Trusting me to catch whatever he delivers, we're moving a little faster now. No words spoken. It's like a dance—everything silent, balanced, floating, timed to perfection. It amazes me that I can catch his curveball. Most pitchers who throw as hard as Andy won't catch with a bat boy if he doesn't know how to catch because he's afraid he might hurt him. But I never missed a catch, and he liked that. It made me feel good, too, despite the fatigue.

It was almost a superstition with Andy for me to catch him before a game. About 80 percent of the time he would look for me and I would have the honor of catching with him. I actually learned a lot by watching him.

That afternoon he threw about twenty pitches to me. While we were doing that, Roger Clemens arrived, and then the two of them started working out. I went home and slept for twelve hours.

After the series was over Andy signed a baseball for me. I still have it as a memento of our time together. It says:

To Squeegee from Andy
Thanks for all your help

Some players, like Ruben Sierra and Erick Almonte, had vast appetites and would eat anything and everything you put before them. Not Andy. He's a one-food kind of guy. No matter if we went to a restaurant or if he was having lunch or dinner at the stadium, it was always the same darn thing.

"Hey, Mitch," he would say to our resident chef. "Can you fire me up a grilled chicken sandwich with lettuce and tomato?"

That was it. You never heard him ask for a steak or fish. There was an almost laughable consistency about Andy, a set routine in everything he did. Repetition and routine made him feel good.

His peace of mind was easily disturbed, however. For example, he hated finding porn magazines in the bathroom. Guys like David Cone would leave centerfold photos in the bathroom, sometimes I think on purpose to tick him off. Even if there was just a page torn out lying on the floor, you would hear Andy lose it, his voice rising into a high scream.

"Robbie! Hey, Robbie! GET THIS SMUT OFF THE FLOOR. Geez, you know, *any*body might come back here—my kids, a reporter . . . I can't look at this myself, either. Come on, clean this up."

He was very religious, so maybe that's why he reacted the way he did. But sometimes if he had a bad game his religious feelings were at odds with his behavior. He never missed chapel meetings, preaching about the Bible to anybody who would listen, but if he was pulled from a game by the manager he would bolt into the clubhouse and fling his glove against a locker and let out a string of obscenities that would make a trucker blush.

Maybe he had inner demons. Most great athletes do. But he never let them keep him down for long. After a healing dialogue with Mel, Andy would go through the same routine when he was a starting pitcher, especially when we were coming off a losing streak. And it always brought us confidence.

You would see him sitting by his locker, a white towel around his neck, glove in hand, wearing what Joe Girardi called his game face. *That look!* You would swear that Andy was ready to go to war. And that look, we knew, was a good sign: he wasn't worried now. Some pitchers, like El Duque, would pace back and forth, revealing their nervousness. Not Andy. There would be a smell of camphor lifting off his long legs and arms. The trainers had given him a pregame massage to loosen his muscles and prevent injury.

In those days, before 2001, there was a calm in the air before a game, like the eye of a hurricane. Media wasn't allowed in the clubhouse thirty minutes before game time. We would all be in uniform, and everybody had their own job to get ready. Maybe just a few low conversations going on down at the other end of the clubhouse. But around Andy all was quiet, which was reassuring. He inspired confidence, and so did that aroma of liniment. He might have been an old man in a hospital—except for his laser focus. The way he sat preparing himself mentally: that was the look of success and winning. We used to call him Big Game Andy.

Every time we saw him—and smelled that Bengay—we *knew* we were going to win. And you could look up the statistics, too: we *would* win 99.99 percent of the time. When his mental preparation was completed, Big Game Andy would stand, hat tilted down so that you couldn't see his eyes. He would exit like he was just going upstairs to sing a song. No words. Just some low huffing and puffing. It amazed you what a warrior he was! A beautiful sight, too: the dim blue light on his skin, the battleship gray reflecting off the runway walls. Big Game Andy . . . moving in an awkward walk, leaving in his wake the scent of Bengay that told you, We *are* going to win.

Fans never saw this. Never guessed the inner workings of the clubhouse, the energy sparking like static from man to man, coming from the Core Four: Jeter, Posada, Rivera, Pettitte. When Andy was starting pitcher, he didn't have to say a word to energize us. We all felt it, from the pitching staff, to the guys in the lineup, to the utility players—all the way down to the clubbies and bat boys.

"Andy is a big-game pitcher," Jeter would say after Game 4 of the 1998 World Series. "That's the bottom line. Every time you think his back is against the wall, he comes out and he does a per-formance like this. He did it against Texas and he came through again tonight. You can't say enough about him."

But if we were down during a game, and if we didn't come out of that slump, Andy had *another* signature move that he employed to fire us up. He would finish an inning and run to the dugout for his few minutes of rest. Once inside he would take off his hat, huff once with a deep sigh: "Whuuuuuuuf!" and then clean his spikes by knocking the metal cleats against the cement wall with a famil-iar metallic *clink! clink! clink! clink! clink! clink!* to take off the dirt, and then he would look straight down the bench and say: "Come *on*, gang. Let's go!" In response the other players would perk up out of their sadness. "Yeah, let's fucking go!" Posada would say, echo-ing Andy's feelings. I'd be getting the bats ready for the players, and I'd see this energy zing from man to man, lighting them up.

Jeter would be there, listening. Torre would be sitting down, turning his head to look at it, too. Tino Martinez would be behind Andy, clapping his hands, saying "YEAH!"; eyes lit like he was ready to kill. We were like a family and it would fire the team up since now you had your starting pitcher—who usually doesn't say a word because he wants to concentrate on his game plan—goading you on. "Let's put a crooked number up!" Torre would cry.

Robbie made me go down to Tampa during spring training because I was a hard worker. While there, in addition to soaking up some Florida sun and enjoying excursions to Siesta Beach, I had a rare opportunity to run the bases with Andy during pitcher's fielding practice, or PFP, as we called it. It was exciting, too, because the experience was like being in a real Major League Baseball game. About a thousand fans were on hand watching Andy on the mound during simulated game practice sessions, and we would rehearse what he should do in various situations. One of the things we practiced was how he would field the ball when a runner was on first. I would take a lead off first base, pretending to be a runner trying to steal second. But Andy had the best pickoff move in Major League Baseball, the throw to first to get the runner out. A pickoff is a little easier for a lefty like Andy because of the way he's standing to begin with. He begins by pretending he's going to throw to the catcher. First he lifts his right leg as he usually does when throwing home, so the base runner is deceived. But at the last second Andy turns at forty-five degrees and fires the ball to first. *Gotcha!* Oh, man, I could *never* get to second.

I had seen him do it many times in games, but now I was

seeing it up close and personal. Once I tried to slide back to first, but Don Mattingly, the special instructor, came up to me and shook his head.

"What are you trying to do?"

"I was sliding back."

"Hey, I don't want you getting hurt. Just run back."

We ran the play again. I took my lead. Andy made believe he was going to pitch. Don told me to run. Andy lifted his leg and I swear I thought he was going to throw home. Before I knew it, he had thrown to Tino at first, who flipped it to Knobby—Chuck Knoblauch—at second, and he tagged me out. *Zip—zap—bam!* Can't outrun him, can't do nothing against that move.

"Pretty cool, hunh?" Knobby smiled.

I felt like a pro.

We had another play to practice, where I would try to run from second to third. Reader, you may think this is easy when you see guys do it on television, but with the Yankees in the field it's practically impossible, and let me explain why. You never hear what's being said by the players when you watch a game in the stadium or on television. Chuck Knoblauch would be on second, Jeter at shortstop. Andy would get set. Meanwhile Jeter would be talking to me, trying to make me nervous. "Go, go now!" he'd say. He was always jabbering out there. It was funny in a way, but also nerve-racking because he and Knoblauch started talking to me at the same time.

"Go, go!"

"Get back!"

"Now's your chance!"

"Hey!" clapping his glove.

"Go, go, go!"

These are the type of silly things they're saying to guys from the opposing team, too, and it distracts you no end. I was tripping all over my feet just trying to run and not laugh.

During games Andy had energy and aggression enough for two men, but he also displayed calmness under fire and a politeness rarely found in starting pitchers. After a great play by his teammates, he would pump his fist back and forth, especially after a double play by Jeter and first baseman Tino. This was remarkable in a man who rarely showed emotion on the mound. Then, after the inning, Andy would wait by the front of the dugout and thank the player who had helped him by smacking him with his glove on the behind. Once when Andy, Posada, and Jeter were on the David Letterman show, the host jokingly held up a photo of A-Rod squeezing Jeter's butt. It was a funny picture, but these physical ways of expressing congratulations and thanks are everyday occurrences in a high-stakes environment like Major League Baseball; still, Andy was the only pitcher who thanked teammates this way.

Another polite thing he did, one which was more controversial, was how Andy refrained from hitting other players. Many guys won't tell you this publicly, but if the opposing pitcher hits one of your men, they expect *their* pitcher to retaliate by hitting a player from the other team! But Andy didn't like to hit anyone. I'm convinced that it was just his nature. He felt that he didn't have to resort to such aggressive and potentially dangerous tactics. Pitchers like Wells and Clemens wouldn't think twice about moving inside with pitches and taking the risk of clipping guys. Andy's refusal to retaliate might have caused friction on the team because players might have felt he wasn't with them 100 percent and wasn't protecting them. But he never stooped to the level of headhunting, as the practice is called. He had class and calmness in everything he did.

Still, because he was a lefty, his pitches *did* tend to move inside on right-handed batters. So maybe he didn't *have* to hit anyone to intimidate them since they were already intimidated by how close the balls would come to their hands and bodies.

"He's not afraid to challenge you," Jeff Kent would say. A good hitter, and second baseman with the San Francisco Giants, Kent added, "What makes him scary is that he's left-handed and the ball comes in on you."

Everything about Andy was aboveboard. While other players denied using performance enhancing drugs, he came right out and admitted using them a couple of times—but not to get an edge on anyone, just to help his elbow heal faster. Brian McNamee recalls injecting him two to four times with HGH—human growth hormone—during the 2001 season. Using HGH was perfectly legal back then since it wasn't banned until 2005. In contrast, Roger Clemens—who was later accused of using steroids by McNamee in the Mitchell Report—kept denying that he ever used them.

Anyone who worked for the Yankees in those days knows that Pettitte and Clemens were good friends. When you saw one, chances are you would see the other: talking, training, or socializing together. Friendships on the team were common and didn't usually cause difficulties, but some players didn't like the fact that Brian McNamee was associating with Andy and Roger. It's hard to say exactly why, but the general feeling was that McNamee was an outsider, hired by Clemens instead of by the team. McNamee trained Clemens and Pettitte, but he didn't train David Cone or David Wells; in fact, Cone had a particular distaste for McNamee, which he displayed through sarcastic comments whenever he had the opportunity.

"He's on the Mac Program," Cone would say.

One day before a game all the pitchers and a few outfielders sat on the grass to stretch with Jeff Mangold, the team's strength and conditioning coach. Mangold, who looks like a marine with a crew cut, was sitting in the center; circling him were Cone, Clemens, Mike Stanton, Luis Sojo, and six or seven other players. Cone, an active member of the Major League Baseball Players Association, was a player representative—a guy who sided with players against management if there was a dispute. He was looking at everyone and telling jokes as they stretched. McNamee happened to walk by and Cone's face got dark. He didn't like McNamee, and he would use whatever opportunity arose to rip the man. He looked up and opened his mouth, and I could swear he was on the verge of making a sarcastic remark, but on this occasion he didn't because McNamee was gone too fast.

I used to see McNamee in the clubhouse all the time, and he struck me as quiet and reserved. I guess he struck other players the same way, although we didn't know exactly what he was doing. Later he admitted that one of the things he was doing was supplying steroids and other performance-enhancing drugs, although I never saw any transactions. One thing I do remember, however, was how he used to give training and nutritional advice to us even though we didn't ask for it. He would make creatine shakes in the players' lounge, and while doing that he would explain how to get bigger muscles by drinking them and taking protein powder and working out in the gym after the shakes. "You should drink this, not that," he would tell bat boys. I could see by the looks on their faces that some of the players didn't like McNamee hanging around, but the guy who was most annoyed was David Cone. It pissed him off when McNamee even told players he *wasn't* working for what to do. So Cone came up with the sarcastic name "The Mac Program," and whenever you heard him say that you knew he was challenging the man.

McNamee must have felt offended by these sarcastic comments, but he never talked back to Cone, and neither did his all-star clients. Andy and Roger never stood up for McNamee and never told Cone to back down. Sad to say, the two great pitchers had a falling out in later years, with Andy admitting his use of human growth hormone and Roger claiming he never touched human growth hormone or steroids. Their disagreement seems to have wrecked a good friendship.

Despite all his wonderful work for the team, and his calmness once he got out on the mound, the image that sticks with me about Andy is how he would rub his hands on his forehead and pull back his hair, like a man coming apart from internal pressure. Head-to-head with Mel before, during, and after games, it always looked more like psychotherapy than a coaching lesson. In fact, Mel took on the role of babysitter with his ace starter. But it was all part of a winning strategy. Andy leaned on Mel; he admits it himself. But there's no shame in that, especially since he used the confidence he gained to do so many good things for the Yankees.

As Mick Jagger said, "We *all* need someone to lean on."

4

Mr. Charisma
Derek Jeter

From the time I met Derek Jeter in 1998 until the time I left the Yankees in 2005, I came to see him as more than another Joe DiMaggio in the making, more than a talented shortstop with eyes that never missed a thing, and more of a well-rounded person than most fans ever realize, even those who follow all of his achievements with pride.

But some of the things I discovered about Jeter were so unusual that I would never in a million years have imagined that *this* was the man America considered the darling of baseball aficionados. He may come across as mild-mannered and courteous when you see him in interviews on television after a game, or when he's forced to comment on one of his teammates' misbehavior in the news—then he's warm, well-spoken, and even a little humble, in the way every fan wants to see humility in a top player. He appears for all the world to be a perfect example of moderation.

So you could imagine my surprise when I discovered that every time he walked into the clubhouse in his street clothes, he would breeze by the young bat boys, and the fourteen- and fifteen-year-old clubhouse attendants, and greet them with an offhand "How're you doin', biatches!" *Bee-atch-es.* Three syllables of in-your-face gangsta lingo. You'd turn around and say to yourself, Hunh? Was that *Derek Jeter* who waltzed past, the team captain, the man who is—in the public eye—a model of correctness and good taste? Was that the man who just called us a bunch of bee-atch-es, referring to us as if we were a bunch of no-goods? It wasn't a one-time thing, either; it was *every* time he walked into the clubhouse before a game for batting practice. This greeting wasn't meant to annoy anyone; on the contrary, it was intended to be a funny way to start our workday together. As I would come to learn from working with Jeter, however, it was also notable in that it was a reference to men—or, to be precise, in this case, to young men or boys—as if they were females. And as you will see, it actually took me many years of working with the captain to grasp the meaning of this casual line.

By all accounts, his origins were humble and middle-class, and big money wasn't flowing freely when he was a kid. Instead, it was his upbringing as a young man with good relationships with his mother and younger sister that groomed him for the role of captain that he would play with the Yankees, and that, along the way, cultivated in him a sense of responsibility and leadership that is evident in everything he does. His father, who I met numerous times, has a strong aggressive handshake, and a more forceful personality than his mother, who struck everyone as sensitive and considerate. Jeter's sister, who frequently came to the ball park to see her brother play, was also a considerate young woman, probably making her brother more of a sensitive person himself. Jeter's aggression on the field was inherited from his father, but that gentle side is what makes Jeter stand apart from most of the other rough-and-tumble players.

You don't see this if you're sitting in the stands or watching the game on television, but Jeter's way of relating to Joe Torre was another one of his personal traits that struck me as unusual. While other players referred to their soon-to-be legendary manager as "Skip" (for Skipper), or "Joe," or "Godfather," or just said "Hey," Jeter always used a more respectful manner of speaking and called him "Mister T." This wasn't mock deference, either, or excess politeness. It was respectful and somewhat formal, especially coming from the team captain. The relationship between them was like father and son. This elevated way of referring to Torre was nowhere more apparent than at the end of the day, when Jeter would always pop by the manager's office and say, "Good night, Mr. T. We'll see you tomorrow." He had respect for the manager. I could tell that he made Torre feel young.

Another thing I learned about Jeter was that his easygoing sense of humor tended to rub off on the more macho players. I'll never forget the night Jeter went to dinner with Posada and Mariano Rivera in St. Louis. Now, you have to keep in mind that Posada rarely told jokes: he was usually very intense and serious. Joining them at the restaurant on this occasion were Luis Sojo and Rob Cucuzza, the equipment manager. Everyone was at a long rectangular table, Jeter at one end, Mariano at the other. Sitting to Jeter's right and left were Sojo and Rob. Posada was at the other end of the table, to the right of Mariano, and there were two empty seats opposite Posada. At about five minutes to seven, Ruben Sierra and I arrived late, walking up to the table together. Ruben was decked out in a $5,500 rose gold necklace, a $100,000 Jacob the Jeweler diamond-studded watch, and an $89 onyx stick pin in the lapel of his $595 camel hair sport coat. Earlier in the day Ruben had told me that he wanted to show me "the finer things in this world" and that he was going to teach me "how to wear jewelry like a man." In his halting robotic voice, he had said, "You . . . cannot wear . . . that . . . cheap watch." To my amazement he proceeded to take me to Neiman Marcus and three or four upscale Manhattan jewelry stores, buying me the same type of jewelry he had. So that night I, too, was wearing a rose gold necklace with diamonds, worth $600, a rose gold watch with a blue band, and an onyx stick pin in the lapel of my $19.95 Polo shirt. Ruben and I sat in the vacant seats opposite Posada, and as soon as our asses hit the chairs all conversation stopped. Posada looked from me to Ruben and then back again at me. His eyes blinked as if he were processing something difficult to comprehend. Then he turned to the end of the table and said, "Hey, Jeet, look at Squeegee." Everyone put their eyes on me. "It's funny, isn't it?" Posada continued. "Luis looks like a mini Ruben." That did it. It was too much for them! Everyone burst out laughing. Afterward, what struck me was not so much the fact that Posada had made a joke—which was unusual for him—but that his joke sounded just like something you would expect *Jeter* to say. I had the impression that, just as I would not have been wearing that outlandish costume jewelry if Ruben weren't there, Posada would not have made that funny remark if Jeter hadn't been there. Something about Jeter's presence caused his sense of humor to rub off on others. Posada was funnier and more relaxed when his friend was around. And the effect didn't stop there. It radiated out, affecting all the other players on the team.

Now, you have to understand that it wasn't only to dinner dates that Ruben dressed like a pimp. One day he came into the clubhouse wearing a suit and tie and he went to his locker to get changed. But, oh, that suit! Deep purple, verging on mauve, with green chalk stripes that made you dizzy to look at them . . . and to make matters worse, he had attempted to match this fabric with a yellow silk tie and a wide-brimmed white panama hat. In short, he looked like a clown, and of course Jeter noticed. The captain started in on Ruben, jibbing at him with little jokes. "What in hell is *that!*" Jeter began. Ruben said nothing. "Who *dressed* you today?" Jeter asked. Ruben stood up straight and said, "I . . . haff to look . . . stylish." But Jeter knew when he had a good thing going and he began to milk it for all it was worth. He turned to bullpen catcher Mike Borzello and batting practice pitcher Charlie Wonsowicz, who were at adjacent lockers, calling their attention to Ruben: "Hey, guys. Ruben says he has to be stylish, but get a look at that hat! Did you ever see anything like it!" Mike and Charlie turned and smiled. Then Jeter called to other players, ones who were not even close enough to have overheard the conversation. Across the wide clubhouse Jeter's voice rang out, calling one and all to witness the absurdities of Ruben's outfit. "Hey, fellas!" he would say, laughter bubbling over from those nearby. At the far end of the room, players would turn to see what it was all about. "Get a load of this suit," Jeter would say. "He thinks it's *stylish.* Oh, it's stylish, all right—it's the style of a man from a bygone age." The way Jeter would widen it out was one of his trademark tactics. It got everyone involved. It prevented any attempt by Ruben to defend himself. And in the end, too, it lightened the mood in the clubhouse and brought everyone together. By the time it was over, even Ruben would be laughing at himself, enjoying all the attention that Jeter had thrown his way.

Posada was one of Jeter's best buddies yet Jeter never hesitated to make the easily irritated catcher sweat and swear through all the teasing he did. He would comment about his hat, his shoes, his gloves—anything that was out of place, anything that might give him a chance to poke fun at his friend and make him laugh. But Posada was such a serious guy that he didn't know when Jeter was tearing him, and he would almost come to the point of crying when Jeter would lash into him for his soiled uniform or his untied shoes. On and on Jeter would push the poor guy, until you actually started to feel sorry for him . . . but then the whole room would crack up and Posada would realize that there was no ill will intended after all, that it was all in good fun, and that he had been selected for teasing because Jeter *liked* him.

While I was absorbing all these scattered impressions about Jeter as a joker, something happened on July 1, 2004 that changed my mind about him because it illustrated his grit and determination under fire. It was during the twelfth inning of a game against the Red Sox at Yankee Stadium, and we were in a dangerous situation because the Sox had men on second and third, and they were poised to win the game if they could score just one more run. There were two outs when Trot Nixon hit the ball hard and began running for first. With the winning run racing off third and heading home, and only seconds away from winning the game for the Red Sox, Jeter moved.

He seemed to have a sixth sense about where the ball was going as soon as it left Nixon's bat, and he tore off at a fast sprint, moving under the ball as it sailed into left-field foul territory. Raising his glove almost straight overhead he timed it perfectly and made the catch while running full tilt. But he was only twenty feet from the stands and he had so much inertia that he was unable to stop. To prevent himself from crashing into the photojournalists, he leaped into the air and dove over the photographers' pit. He could have careened into fans to break the impact of his fall, but he didn't want to injure anyone, so as his feet lifted off the ground he calculated his flight path, noticing that there was one seat where nobody was sitting. To this empty seat he directed his airborne body, which was now moving up and over the railing. "I knew I couldn't stop," he said later. "If I just jumped over the photographer pit I would run into a fan, but I picked the one seat where there was no fan sitting."

At first the amazed spectators wanted to cheer him and pat him on the back, but when he arose, dazed and covered in blood, their surprise turned to concern. The bruised player now in their midst was walked off the field by a trainer, who held a rag to his face to try to stem the tide of blood. When I saw Jeter enter the clubhouse, flanked by trainer Steve Donohue and Gene Monahan, arms outstretched like Christ, a shiver ran through me. The doctor began stemming the blood dripping from his face and hands, and Jeter sat down and let them work. But later when he heard the loudspeakers announce in the thirteenth inning that the Sox had taken a 4–3 lead, he cried, "Jesus Christ! You let them get *ahead*!" I could practically hear him thinking, How could you let them get a lead after the sacrifice I made!

Before long, though, the Yankees' backup catcher John Flaherty—who was hitting only .150—surprised everyone by belting a line drive down the left-field line to send in the winning run. Jeter's dive into the stands had paid off. It was the highlight of the game, and one of the crowning achievements of his career. The clip of the play is run repeatedly on the YES Network.

So there's no question in my mind that Jeter's easygoing personality traits—the way he joked, teased, and bonded with players— were something extra, almost in contrast to the aggressive fielding that fans had come to expect from the captain.

One day Bill Clinton walked into the clubhouse with four Secret Service agents. This was after he had been out of office a few months, but everyone still acted as if he was the commander in chief. Ruben Sierra was shaking his hand, and other players were saying "Hello, Sir" and being polite as hell with him until Jeter—in full uniform, on his way out to the game—paused just long enough to tease him with a casual remark: "Hey, Mr. President, you staying out of trouble?"

Jeter didn't even stop to have a chat, he continued out to the field. The confused expression on Clinton's face said it all: Here was a man so shot up with confidence that even running into the president didn't make him miss a beat. He was able to poke fun at Clinton as if they had been buddies from day one.

Never one to bother much about putting the big picture together, I simply went about my daily chores with the Yankees, but year after year some impressions started to penetrate into my awareness about Jeter that didn't fit the bill, at least with the way he was usually described by the media. Great, flexible, fast, yes; these were the adjectives you heard when Jeter was the subject, but did that match what I saw in the trainer's room before a game when I would be summoned to help the captain select music? No, then it was a different man I saw: it was a guy who asked, "Squeeg, you know music, you hear what people play on the street, what do you think I should use?" Standing in the little room in full uniform, a bunch of CDs in hand, he would raise his eyebrows and wait for my reply. "Should I use Puff Daddy? Aerosmith? Led Zeppelin?" I told him that none of the above sounded right, and that Black Rob might be better. Jeter would put his CD in the music box, pump his fist, and start dancing to the music. "Listen to *this*!" he'd say. "This is *it*! They don't know about *this*, Squeegee." Steve Donohue, the trainer, would look at me and Jeet, smiling. Jeter would say, "Come on, Cookie"—Steve's nickname—trying to get him to loosen up. After he selected the one he liked, Jeter would tell me to ask the soundman in the booth to play a certain section of the song thirty seconds before he reached home plate. If you're watching the game on television you have to really listen or you won't catch the music. But if you look close you'll notice that Jeter takes his sweet time when walking out to the batter's box, and he's nodding his head in time with the music. "Whoa!" the chorus is going, "Whoa!" and Jeter's head is bopping right along with it. What a sight it was to see him jitterbug around the trainer's room when he discovered that song!

The team captain had what I can only call a streak of nobility in him. It took a while for me to realize it but once I did, I noticed it all the time. For example, after he became captain Robbie suggested putting a capital C over the NY logo on his uniform—the way Jason Varitek, captain of the Red Sox, had one on *his* jersey—

but Jeter refused, and all the players loved him for that. You can also see some of his calm assurance as he rounds the bases and chews bubble gum and chats with players from other teams. These guys, many of them youngsters and rookies who think of the Yankees as the gods of baseball, could then go home and tell their families that they not only *played* against Derek Jeter, but that they actually had a conversation with the man. It's all a game, he seemed to be saying; and, of course, it was. No hard feelings, we're here to do our job, and maybe have a little fun in the process. This pleasant attitude is the kind of disposition a man wishes on himself. It's the way *you* want to be when things don't go right at work, or when your family gets on your nerves, or when misfortune strikes. You want to be smiling that same Jeter smile.

When you get right down to it and you see the curtain swept back fully, you realize that there is in this baseball mastermind a touch of the gentleman that raises him above the roughness that surrounds so much of the sport. You couldn't outfight him, he was too quick and sure-witted on the field for that, or at least he was when I was with the team. But you could irritate him, and this is why I think Alex Rodriguez and he didn't hit it off too well.

Both superstars with big paychecks, the main difference was that Jeter was a leader who was so flexible he could also follow, and A-Rod was a follower who tripped over his feet every time he tried to lead. More than this, Jeter had a playful gentle side that A-Rod lacked. When he joined the team in 2004 A-Rod was a prima donna and had to have everything done for him, even to the point of having clubhouse attendants lay out his clothes on a bench in a specific order. If the clubhouse door was opened sometimes a kid in a wheelchair would come up and ask for an autograph. A-Rod might say, "I can't right now, I gotta get ready for the game." But Jeter would always take time to sign for the kid. The rivalry between them was even visible in the clubhouse because you never saw Jeter sit down beside A-Rod's locker to strike up a conversation with him, as he did with the other players, even those he wasn't close with. The two superstars were watchful of one another and probably a little jealous of the attention the other received.

But I think that you had to see Jeter interact with women to get a complete picture of his character. That's something fans sitting at home never get to see. I saw how kind he was to his mother and sister and how respectful he was of women in general. He pined after some women, too, and felt that he was snubbed by some of them. "There are women that think they're out of your league," he would tell me. But he wasn't going to run after a woman for long if he had a sense that she would snub him. When we went to bars you would find him sitting at a table with his personal trainer and a few other guys, sipping his drink. He would let his eyes play over the crowd, commenting only in the way his gaze lingered here and there on a woman he found attractive or interesting. His preference was for women who had a nice smile and personality. But he never used any tricks of the trade, like other players did, to try to attract these women. There were some players who would go into a room and do things to call attention to themselves, letting all the men know they were Yankees so that the women would start to notice them, too. Jeter never went in for this kind of play-acting. After checking out the scene in a club, he would tell his personal trainer which girl he liked. Very down-to-earth and low-key, he would ask the trainer to go up to the woman and tell her that Derek Jeter wanted to talk with her. Then he would leave the bar first and wait for her. I would often see groups of women giggling and leaving with the trainer, who would lead them to their rendezvous with the captain. In this way, Jeter avoided scandals and gossip and kept his meetings secret.

After we won the 1999 World Series, I was in a bar with Jeter and Chuck Knoblauch, who were surrounded by attractive women in the VIP section. But Jeter didn't put his arms around any of them or try to lead them out, the way other players might. Instead, he surprised me by turning from the women and motioning for me to approach. "Squeeg, come here," he said. When I got to his side he put his arm around *me* and said to the girls, "This is my little brother. I want you to make sure he has a good time." Within seconds I was surrounded by a group of beauties.

There were other players who would leave a bar with a blonde on each arm, but Jeter wasn't like that. I'm sure he liked blondes as much as the next guy, but his manner with women wasn't showy or fake, and when he was with someone he gave her his undivided attention. You might see him sitting side by side with Vanessa Minnillo as if they were good buddies, or with his arm around Mariah Carey as if they were a couple, or, in later years, with a protective arm around Minka Kelly at the ball park as if they were in their own world. All the women he associated with had a friendly style, and I guess this was as important to him as physical beauty. He had a sensitive nature, and this is the kind and considerate side of the man that I discovered after working with him for eight years. I don't think this considerateness takes anything away from his extraordinary athletic ability. In fact, I think it adds to his mystique as a good all-around human being.

5

Look at Me, *Will Ya?*
Alex Rodriguez

One day I went into the Yankees' weight room to deliver a message to reliever Tom "Flash" Gordon. Enrique Wilson, Gary Sheffield, and Jose Contreras were also working out, but you couldn't walk *any*where without feeling that the focus of the entire place was on one guy, who was bench-pressing 320 pounds, the steel bar quivering as he pushed up a stack of fifty-pound weights and then dropped them with a resounding *BLAAAAAAAAMMMM!* It was Alex Rodriguez, of course, and he had the music cranked up to an ear-splitting level.

"Look at me!" he seemed to be screaming after each set.

Then, which isn't all that unusual for a bodybuilder, he would stand before the mirror contemplating his magnificence.

When the average guy goes into a gym, he enjoys the experience because of the rush of adrenaline that makes him feel good . . . but when you get to the level of Alex Rodriguez, who has a real love of punishing his arms and legs until they ache, who lives and breathes for the joy of that physical torture, well, then we're in another world altogether, a world of high octane performance where the body can be fine-tuned until it hums with pent-up energy. In order to accurately describe His Magnificence, however, there's another element that needs to be added into this mix, and that's how A-Rod loved focusing attention on himself, so much so that he seemed to disregard anyone who didn't follow suit.

Maybe the fact that his dad left the family when he was only nine had something to do with it, or the fact that he was raised by his mom (with two older half-siblings). Whatever the reason, this is how he turned out, and this is how he came to the Yankees: a player who craved the limelight more than anyone I ever met. It goes without saying that nearly *everyone* likes attention, but it seemed that *he* needed a fix of Hey-look-it's-A-Rod-isn't-he-wonderful! every day, every hour, every minute. So we all had to adjust. Oh, boy, did we have to adjust! Despite his great stats, it was the beginning of the end, really, in terms of pulling together and team unity . . . and, ironically, winning, too.

In 2001, *Esquire*'s hotshot writer Scott Raab interviewed His Magnificence and included a few choice zingers from the lips of A-Rod, such as the line, "Jeter's been blessed with great talent around him . . . He's never had to lead. He can just go and play and have fun. And he hits second—that's totally different than third and fourth in a lineup. You go into New York, you wanna stop Bernie and O'Neill. You never say, Don't let Derek beat you. He's never your concern."

Amazing, isn't it, what he does to his good friend Derek Jeter in that *Esquire* article! Yes, his good friend. His Magnificence apparently used to sleep over Derek's house whenever he was in town. And you should have seen them in 1998, joking together and talking about how they admired each other as shortstops. But after *Esquire* muddied the water with A-Rod's mistimed remarks about how Jeter was *not* all he was cracked up to be, you got a picture of a man whom ambition and the stress of performing on the field had pushed to a point where he was making careless remarks that didn't sit right with fans—or with his onetime buddy. You got a sense that Alex Rodriguez wanted the spotlight so much that he was even willing to sacrifice friendships for it.

In fact, when His Magnificence arrived you could feel the chill in the air. He single-handedly changed the atmosphere in the clubhouse. I observed how players interacted before A-Rod showed up in 2004, and there was a big difference after he got there. Before his arrival you would see Jeter joking with Bernie Williams, Ruben Sierra, Andy Pettitte, and all the other guys. But when A-Rod moved into his locker at the other end of the clubhouse, you didn't see Jeter pull up a chair and chat with A-Rod, like he did with other players. Okay, he and A-Rod were polite and would say hello, but a truce had been called and they were cool toward one another. It was clear to everybody that Jeter had called this truce for the sake of the team.

Before long, though, A-Rod had splintered the Yankees into two camps. On any given day you'd see one group of players talking with His Magnificence in the field, another group hanging around inside with Jeter. In the past, everybody would be in the clubhouse changing together, and there used to be a communal spirit that fostered unity. But after A-Rod arrived it was like there was a big elephant in the room. It reminded me of the Kobe

Bryant–Shaquille O'Neal feud, which simmered on and off for years between the two Lakers superstars. Eventually, of course, Kobe and Shaq got over it and became close friends again. I was hoping for a reconciliation between A-Rod and Jeet, but it didn't happen during my years with the team.

It may sound strange, and it sure seemed strange to me, but sometimes A-Rod seemed to go out of his way to intentionally try to split things up. Posada's locker happened to be beside A-Rod's, and everyone knew that Posada was good friends with Jeter. So A-Rod took this opportunity to try to kiss ass with Posada, currying his favor and talking him up. He did it to butt in on their friendship, and it was so noticeable that Ruben Sierra commented on it to me, pointing out how A-Rod operated. But Posada never paid any mind to A-Rod; instead, he just let him talk while he (Posada) would be doing his own thing at his locker, such as taping his bat or getting dressed.

Despite his high-maintenance profile, A-Rod *was* a sports hero, there's no question about that. But as sports pundits Tim Delaney and Tim Madigan have observed, he wasn't a charismatic hero, like Derek Jeter, or even a reluctant hero, like Lou Gehrig; instead A-Rod was one of the bad boys of sports, in the same category with people such as Barry Bonds, Dennis Rodman, and Mike Tyson. There's no denying that despite his sore-thumb personality, and how he wasn't able to fit in as one of the guys, Alex Rodriguez did have fans—plenty of them. I'll talk later about how he treated some of his female fans, but first I want to bring up a topic that almost no one—not even baseball writers—discusses adequately, namely, how he changed the dynamics of the Yankees, and how he imitated Derek Jeter while doing that.

Sometimes I would use the team washing machines to do personal laundry for various trainers, and one afternoon I was doing Reggie Jackson's clothes when Reggie came in to give me a tip. He took out a hundred-dollar bill and handed it to me. Then he gave me a big grin and said, "I tip better than A-Rod, right?" I smiled but didn't say a word because whatever I said might get back to A-Rod and cause problems. What struck me as strange, though, was that everything had become A-Rod—even tips from freakin' coaches! Reggie could have said something along the lines of, "I'm a good tipper, hunh?" But no, everything had become A-Rod, A-Rod, A-Rod.

Because A-Rod was the leader or "the man" on other teams—such as Texas and Seattle—he probably felt a need to compete with the leader of the Yankees; but here in New York this was Jeter's team and A-Rod had to take a backseat. Over time, however, A-Rod must have sensed that, despite their rivalry, there were things about Derek Jeter that were *worth* copying. I had to chuckle at how he aped the captain. For example, Jeter and some of the other guys were terrific tippers. Roger Clemens gave me $3,000 at the end of the year. Posada gave me $7,000. A-Rod might come in with $1,400. Sure, it's still a sizable amount, but when he found out that other players were tipping higher, he had to imitate them, and he bumped his tips up. A-Rod was actually a *good* tipper as far as bat boys and clubhouse attendants were concerned. In fact, he had to make sure he was the *best* tipper in the league. It was like a competition with him. He would hear about bat boys and clubhouse attendants getting tips from other players, and he'd come up with more money—just to be the best. He even tipped me $100 a week to make sure there was a creatine shake waiting for him after each home game.

Then there was the music issue, where he found out exactly which track on the CD Jeter was playing, and when Alex went up to bat you heard *the exact same clip from the song* over the stadium loudspeakers. *Excuse me, but has our sound system gone haywire!* That's what fans must have been thinking. I was the one who helped A-Rod arrange that little prank, although I didn't think it was funny; I just thought it was odd and puzzling.

The other thing he imitated about Jeter was his generosity with giveaways. As a spokesperson for Team Jordan, the captain would receive free samples, and then he would use his connection with the company to obtain sneakers for all the bat boys and clubbies. He always asked us what size we wore, too. When A-Rod discovered what Jeter was doing, he got Nike Air Max shoes for us one year. And that was it: one year. Then I guess he forgot about it. I got mine, and they were two sizes too big. I gave them away to a friend. It was a nice gesture on A-Rod's part, don't get me wrong. It was just, well, kind of an imitation. Everyone knows that imitation is the sincerest form of flattery, so despite all the undertones of negativity you hear about the competition between the two, I believe that A-Rod was really complimenting Jeter by doing all these things the way the captain had done them. Even if A-Rod had intended his imitation to be funny—like with the music—it still struck me as a subtle form of respect and flattery.

Before I get into some of the other crazy things that A-Rod did, I have to tell you what happened when he first arrived because it sets the stage for the antics that followed.

I had already been in Yankee uniform for six years when word came that yet another superstar was heading to New York, so I was used to newcomers and how they could temporarily change the dynamics of the club. This time, though, it was Alex Rodriguez, the man whose loud mouth had gotten him into hot water with our team captain, so we were all anticipating the meeting, and I remember well the first time he showed up at spring training— the media frenzy, the lights, the reporters, and especially this one thing that nobody ever talks about, namely, how he requested his own personal assistant. Well, they mention it, but they never explain that *I* was the guy who was told by Robbie to look out for Alex and work as his personal assistant. But when I approached A-Rod he took one look at me and said, "No, I've already got a guy." Turns out that at spring training he preferred to work with a cherubic little fellow who went by the unlikely name of Heat. A pink-cheeked, fifteen-year-old Hispanic bat boy, Heat had the dubious distinction of having become A-Rod's personal slave. Like me, Heat was fluent in Spanish, and A-Rod liked to converse with him in his native tongue. Heat often got abused in a joking way from players for the job he was doing for A-Rod. But on days when Heat wasn't available, A-Rod would request that I act as his personal attendant since I was also bilingual. I would wind up doing the little chores and taking care of the specific tasks that he wished done for him.

It's not an exaggeration to say that Heat was like a slave to A-Rod. No one used that word, of course, but that's what it boiled down to. And no one saw that dynamic, or felt it, more keenly than I did on the days when Heat wasn't there and I had to follow A-Rod's orders. There's a natural closeness that develops between players and bat boys that's reflected in an incident that happened before a three-day vacation we were anticipating. I was sitting in the clubhouse talking with Ruben Sierra, who had become a good friend, when in marched His Magnificence, followed by his toady, Heat. A-Rod paused and looked at Ruben, who said, "What are you going to do for Luigi? He's always helping you." A-Rod said, "I'm taking Luigi to the All-Star Game with me." I was flabbergasted. This was the first I had heard of his plan. It was customary for players to take one or more bat boys or clubhouse attendants with them on vacations, but no one had informed me that I was scheduled to go on a trip with A-Rod, and, to be honest, I wasn't too thrilled about the idea. Thankfully, Ruben didn't let this remark go unchallenged. "No . . . you . . . are . . . not," he said. He may have sounded like a robot, but he was saying words I loved hearing. "Luis . . . is . . . coming with me to . . . Mi . . . ah . . . mi." A-Rod's eyebrows shot up, and he marched out with a smile pasted on his face. But when he and Heat were gone, Ruben shook his head. "You don't . . . need to . . . go with him," he said. "You . . . are going to . . . have fun . . . with . . . me." I wound up going to Miami for three days with Ruben instead.

As time went by I started to feel more comfortable with the fact that A-Rod hadn't chosen me to be his primary personal assistant since if he had I probably wouldn't have developed such close relationships with players like Jeter, O'Neill, and Ruben. Also, Heat got yelled at a lot by Lou Cucuzza Jr.—Robbie's older brother—and I didn't want that happening to me. Lou was in charge of the visiting clubhouse, and he would have fits with Heat because, as A-Rod's personal assistant, Heat was hanging around in our clubhouse even though he had chores to do on the visiting side. Lou would kick Heat out of our clubhouse from time to time, and that's when I became A-Rod's second assistant.

But it wasn't his chumminess with Heat that got the goat of the other players. After all, many of them were friendly with the clubhouse attendants and bat boys, and a good number of them even enjoyed taking us on excursions during their off days. No, what irritated the hell out of these guys was that A-Rod was a high-maintenance player who needed to have things done His Way and no other. I happened to be one of the only people who got to see this side of him from both the outside—as a member of the Yankees organization—and from the inside, as a substitute for Heat when I was designated to be the person who had to satisfy A-Rod's demands.

When I talk about high maintenance I'm not referring to personal attention or emotional connection, the way you might expect it in a relationship. No, Alex wasn't in need of emotional support of any kind; on the contrary, he was self-sufficient, even detached, in his dealings with others. What he needed, however, was attention to all the mundane little things that make life easier for a member of royalty, such as transportation assistance, wardrobe preparation, and other matters of personal service that a clubhouse attendant might provide, all of which went above and beyond the call of duty, so much so that other players would raise their eyebrows when they saw me carrying out his orders, and would even go so far as to tell me to STOP CATERING TO THAT DAMN SELF-CENTERED EGOMANIAC. Ironically, they railed against me for carrying out his orders, but not once did they ever take arms against the man himself, or even bring up the matter with him in a friendly or joking way.

If you follow baseball, I'm sure you've heard the list of demands that His Magnificence made, such as preparing his peanut butter and jelly sandwiches, getting his toothbrush ready after a game, and laying out his clothes. But there are details about these and other matters that have never been revealed before. For example, while other players, even the most wealthy, occasionally took taxis or had a driver drop them off, they usually drove themselves and relished owning and driving expensive cars. Alex, on the other hand, never got behind the wheel. In all the years I knew him, I never once saw him in the driver's seat. Instead, he would sit in the back of a chauffeured limousine and let his personal driver escort him to the stadium, the airport, or wherever he was bringing his royal presence.

When it came to brushing his teeth, he had something of a fetish about it and was always standing in front of the mirror, before, during, and after games. You would see him in the trainer's room checking his smile, making sure there was nothing between his teeth before an interview, an inning, or even before lunch. But the most demanding request he made pertained to his toothpaste. There have been stories published—which are all true—explaining how he required his personal assistant to ready a toothbrush after every game, positioning it on the edge of the sink. But what no one has ever revealed is that he also demanded that the toothbrush be on a certain *part* of the sink, specifically, the edge near the right-hand cold water tap, leaning with bristles up over the basin. The first time he ordered me to do this, I couldn't believe my ears when he said, "And put the toothpaste on it."

What irked me most was that this guy couldn't get *anything* on his own, even if his life depended on it. Chips, coffee, snacks, newspapers, whatever it was, *you* had to get it for him. "Hey, get me some candy . . . Run and bring me a water . . . I need gum, go pick me up some." He couldn't even get his own bat or glove! In contrast, you'd see Jeter carrying three bats and a glove, going out by himself to batting practice, asking no one's help. You knew A-Rod would never do that.

Another well-known habit A-Rod had was eating peanut butter and jelly sandwiches after a game. But what no one has described is that the sandwich had to be made a certain way, sliced in two and placed dead center on a Styrofoam plate so that he would find it waiting on the table when he came inside after the last inning. One day we were on the road in Boston and his assistant, Heat, wasn't around. As Alex jogged off the field, he spotted one of the bat boys from the home team and snapped at him: "Peanut butter and jelly!" The surprised kid looked like he had been slapped.

All baseball players have numerous bats: some heavier, some lighter, some varying in other ways to suit their preferences. Most players look after their own bats, but A-Rod, I soon discovered, was different, demanding that you place *his* bats on the clubhouse floor in a precise order for his inspection. "They have to be lying in front of my locker," he would tell me. "And I want my glove on my chair, and my hat on *top* of my glove—not the other way around. Do you have that?" Sometimes I'd be getting his bats ready, arranging them in front of his locker so that he could choose the ones he wanted, and I'd get another order from him before I even finished, this time regarding tickets. In those days the Yankee organization made six tickets available free of charge to each player, and if they wanted more they had to pay for them. Since A-Rod was a popular player, he always had a lot of people—family, friends, business associates—coming to see him, and he would have to pay for these tickets out of his own pocket so he was very particular about making sure that they got to the right person at the right time. When Heat wasn't around I would have to go upstairs and make sure that A-Rod's guests—which could easily be ten to twelve people—got their tickets from the box office, where they would be waiting (if all went well) with the name of each guest on a master list. If there were any problems, I would have to deliver a personal note from A-Rod to the box office manager and smooth over any mix-ups to make sure that his guests were taken care of before doing any of my routine chores.

Yet another demand he made was that I take care of helping with batting practice in the tunnel under the stadium within the batting cages. I would have to load baseballs into a green Casey 3G pitching machine, which would automatically fire them toward him at the same speed as a pitcher, near 100 m.p.h. The funny thing is I could *never* do this right for him, despite the fact that I wasn't *throwing* the pitches—they were coming out of the gosh-blamed Casey! Even a *machine* couldn't satisfy him, let alone a human being.

Probably the strangest thing we had to do for A-Rod, however, was lay his clothes out on the table so he could get dressed. You might think that an athlete would want to get dressed by himself and would consider it an inconvenience to have someone else messing around with his socks and underwear. Not Alex, though. You had to lay out these items in a predetermined order: socks at the head of the table, followed by undershorts, undershirt, shirt, pants, and then shoes. I had to carry his clothes from his locker to the trainer's room, where he liked to get dressed away from the prying eye of the media. One day I was getting his stuff ready, arranging his socks on the edge of the table like he demanded, and it just so happened that Posada was in the room, getting tape cut off by Steve Donohue. Jeter was sitting on another table talking with them. At first they didn't pay any attention to me since they thought I was just in there doing some errand, but after a while, when they noticed how carefully I was laying out all these clothes on the table, Posada turned to me, his dark brows raised. "Who the heck is that for?" he said. I stopped what I was doing. "Alex," I said. Jeter and Posada burst out laughing. "Geez, would you tell him to walk to his locker himself," Posada said. They left me to finish arranging the clothes, but to my knowledge they never raised the issue with him personally.

There were other issues, however, that they *did* taunt A-Rod about, and they did this so often that they even had a name for their teasing: riding. Posada liked to ride A-Rod about the unusual suits he wore; for example, you would often see Alex come in wearing a three-piece suit, but the style would be bizarre and the shirt mismatched. "Who dressed you!" Posada would say. A-Rod would hold his head high and let out a loud fake laugh: "HAA!-HAA!-HAA!" To his credit, he would sit at his locker and take the riding like a sport. Poor Ruben Sierra, though, was the butt of more jokes than anyone because of his extremely outlandish taste in clothing and jewelry. Jeter used to ride him all the time, so Ruben took satisfaction in hearing players ride A-Rod because it made him feel better about being constantly ridden himself. A-Rod's laugh, though, was hollow and had a ring of falseness to it. It was such an obvious stage laugh that Mike Borzello started calling him A-Fraud because of it. Someone would tell a joke and you would hear the loud "HAA!-HAA!-HAA!" and you knew it was fake emotion. No one else laughed like he did and no one ever thought he was really amused when he laughed. I felt sorry for him. If you can't laugh, geez, something's broken somewhere.

One day Alex was at his locker, and Ruben Sierra and I were nearby. Ruben struck up a conversation with him. "Alex, how you doing?" Alex was wearing a pink shirt, blue jeans, and white sneakers. "Man, I like your clothes," Ruben added. Alex issued his fake laugh: "HAA!-HAA!-HAA!" He knew we were playing around, but he didn't realize how delighted Ruben was that he had finally gotten an opportunity to pay someone back by ribbing him. Ruben tapped me on the arm to tip me off, as if to say, Look, man, I got him going now. "Love that shirt, man," Ruben said. "HAA!-HAA!-HAA!" came A-Rod's familiar reply. Yes, Ruben loved messing with A-Rod, and it did him good to turn the tables like that, too.

Another example of Ruben riding A-Rod stands out in my mind because it happened after Robinson Cano joined the team, and there were high expectations that the young second baseman would be a hot prospect for the Yankees. Despite the fact that he was a professional Major League Baseball player, Cano's salary wasn't that high, and Ruben befriended him, giving him secondhand suits. The two players had the same build, and Ruben owned some suits that fit Cano perfectly. Cano's locker was next to A-Rod's, and before long it became clear that A-Rod wanted to take Cano under his wing, which was unusual since A-Rod never buddied with anybody and remained more of a loner. Ruben figured him out, though. He understood that A-Rod liked to associate with popular guys, almost as a way to appropriate *their* popularity for himself. In fact, A-Rod used to invite Cano to hang around with him, and it was rather obvious what he was doing. One afternoon, Ruben, in a rare but insightful comment, playfully warned A-Rod, "Don't take his shine!"

A-Rod, however, didn't have this kind of pally sense of humor. He was more intense, focused on getting ready for the game. You wouldn't catch him palling around with other players even *after* a game. And he was different in another, childish, way that made players laugh behind his back. When you watch games at home you sometimes see players come into the dugout after they hit a home run and you'll notice them high-fiving their teammates. If you've ever wondered what they're saying while they congratulate one another, it's things like, "Way to go!" or "Good job!" and the like. Not A-Rod. After he hits a home run, he comes into the dugout and brags about it. Usually he's speaking Spanish to one of the other Latino players, and if he hit a home run he wouldn't shut up. "Wow, did you see that I hit a home run!" he'd say. "That pitcher threw me a ball right over the plate and I smashed it over the fence. Did you ever see anything like that before!" The players he was addressing would always be polite, saying things like, "Good work" and "Nice job"; but from the looks on their faces as they turned from him, they were most likely thinking, Shut up, already! All of which solidified my belief that A-Rod's style was less team-oriented than it could have been. In contrast, after having a good at bat or hitting a home run, Jeter might say, "Great game, guys. Let's grind it tomorrow!" A-Rod would constantly remind you how far he hit the ball, or how he had fooled a pitcher and smashed a home run off him.

After working with him, though, I have to say I grew to respect him for his intelligence and knowledge of the game. He would always ask the batting coach questions. "Does he have a slider? How is he after the seventh inning?" He could spit out statistics on pitchers and players from other teams like a computer. He was always in early, working out, preparing. But when he went to hit you felt he wasn't trying to win the *game* as much as trying to increase his own stats. He seemed to be trying to do too much during each at bat, as if he felt the pressure of history on his shoulders. To make matters worse, he let the New York media and fans get under his skin. He never appeared comfortable, despite the fact that he *was* doing well. In 2004 he hit thirty-six home runs. In 2005, he hit forty-eight. Yet nothing seemed to be enough. In comparison, in a five-years period only Babe Ruth hit more home runs than A-Rod's forty-eight. With a record like that, why couldn't A-Rod relax a little?

There were various other odd things about A-Rod that stick out in my mind. One was the way he would often trip over the rug in the clubhouse, as if he were expecting even the floor to be perfect for him. But the strangest thing was the day that he told me to bring baseballs into the batting cage before a game and make him a creatine shake, and then he said, "Could you throw batting practice for me?" After I brought his shake to him, we walked out together onto the field. It was a warm summer day in 2004 and we were exiting through the tunnel toward the outfield in Yankee Stadium. I was carrying some gloves, bottles of water, and other baseball equipment. Alex was carrying a bat and walking slower than usual. He shook his head and turned to me.

"Hey, Luigi." He was speaking Spanish.

I looked up at him; he's half a foot taller.

In a friendly voice he continued, "Why doesn't anybody on this team like me?"

I didn't say anything because I knew he just wanted to vent. After you've been around players you get a sense about which ones like to talk and express their feelings. He was asking the kind of question that doesn't require an answer.

Then, out of the blue, he said, "Do you know if my shirts are selling more than anyone else's on the team?"

I was shocked at the question.

"I don't know," I said.

Here it is, only minutes before a midseason game, and this guy isn't concerned about the team we're facing; instead, he's worried people might not like him because his clothes are selling more or his salary is larger. That's what the greatest living baseball player—as some would call him—was thinking on that summer day. He wasn't thinking about the pitchers he would be up against. He wasn't thinking about how he might hit a home run. He was thinking about money and his reputation. Sometimes you get a good idea about a person's inner feelings from a conversation. Despite his fame, and the constant media coverage, and the attention he got from women, the sense I got was that he was isolated and even a bit friendless. I guess it's true what they say about it being lonely at the top.

Before I go any further I have to tell you a funny little story about A-Rod and coffee. Yes, he was a big coffee drinker, even probably a coffee addict, like so many baseball players. But he was particular, too, about *how* you made his coffee, *when* it was made, *where* it was made, and how it was *delivered* to him. It went like this: Every game day he had to have a cup of coffee drawn from the big coffee machine in the players' lounge, which was off-limits to the media. (There was a sign on the door saying PLAYERS ONLY ADMITTED.) This machine was the one all the players used, and it had a switch that would deposit exactly one sixteen-ounce serving of steaming hot black coffee into a cup. "Dump out half the cup," A-Rod instructed me. "Then stir it nice and good with the red stirrer and bring it to me." I would make it according to directions and then go about my business. What I never did figure out, however, was how he and the other guys who ingested all that caffeine ever got to sleep.

Although A-Rod kept pretty much to himself before and after games, except to go to the gym with other guys, he was fond of going out for a few drinks now and then.

One cool evening we were in Boston and I saw him coming out of the Whiskey Park Bar, near the Public Garden. I happened to be wearing a suit because this was a swank watering hole and I was going to meet a couple of other players, including Bernie Williams, who was sitting inside the right entrance. A-Rod was on his way out, with two blondes on his arms. When he saw me, his eyes lit up and he said, "Wow, look at *you!* I never saw you in a suit." As he passed he reached into the breast pocket of my jacket, and I thought he was rearranging my pocket square. "Have a good night," he said, breezing by with his lovebirds.

Since he was married at the time, I was under the impression that he was walking the ladies out to their car, or perhaps stepping outside to sign some autographs. Because these young women were dressed in a way that revealed a good deal of their very considerable charms, I was sure they would not be out in the cool air for long. Maybe they were simply going to have a cigarette and then come back inside, although this impression couldn't have been correct since they never did return. Perhaps, gentleman that he was, Mr. Rodriguez was planning to escort the young women to their suites, or convey them to their chaperones, although I hadn't noticed any chaperones or limousines out front.

At any rate, when I got to the bar I happened to look down into my breast pocket and was surprised to find two hundred-dollar bills. To this day, I have no idea why he gave me that money. All I know is that he got my attention all right—despite the presence of the two starlets, whom many a young man would have had a hard time not devouring with his eyes. Yes, he got me to look at *him*, and *that* was the real Alex Rodriguez . . . and that will *always* be the real Alex Rodriguez.

6

What the Hell's Everybody So Worked Up About?
David Wells

Big man on the mound today. Crouched down, getting ready for the windup. Left hand snaking below his belt to adjust his crotch, as if he weren't David Wells but Michael Jackson pitching for the Yankees.

Then without warning the left arm whips back and delivers: fast, on target, 95 m.p.h. But the batter knocks it straight out to second, where the Yankees fielder makes a blunder, missing the catch, and allowing the batter-runner to reach first.

A warm breeze fans the flames of the crowd. Wells turns and, in an odd breach of etiquette for a Major League Baseball player, throws his hands up in a gesture so rude to modern eyes that it registers shock all the way back in the dugout, where I'm standing with Joe Torre, watching the action. Torre spits out an insulting comment. "I'm gonna talk to him," he mutters under his breath. "I'm gonna give him a piece of my mind. I've told him about this a hundred times and yet he keeps on doing it."

Torre wipes his lips with his right hand and chokes back resentment. I know why, too. Because Wells has done this many times. When a teammate does something that Wells considers inappropriate, he expresses his disapproval in front of all the spectators, throwing his hands up in the air and making a face, as if to say, "You gotta be kidding me." As if he were above it all, better than them, and never made a mistake himself.

But everyone makes mistakes, and there's an unwritten rule in professional baseball—in fact, in all baseball down to the lowest level—that you save your gripes for after the inning is over and you're alone and out of sight of the crowd in the clubhouse. Then you can go up to the player who made the error and vent, telling him, "You shoulda done this" or "You shoulda done that." In fact, Jeter and Paul O'Neill had confronted Wells about this breach of etiquette, but to no purpose. It was Wells's nature to express himself. He had a short fuse. He was wired. That's what made him David Wells. In my mind, that's what made him a winner, too.

Torre knew that his star pitcher's temperament was brash and out front, but he couldn't deal with it. Fans never noticed, but I saw it all the time in Torre's expression. It annoyed him no end. The uncontrollable nature of Wells would eat away at him. It probably kept him up nights, furious at the guy for the way he brazenly did things *his* way. But that was the New Yorker in Wells. Born and raised in San Francisco, he had more of the New York I-do-things-my-way outlook than most native-born New Yorkers.

In fact, it was his rock-star attitude that threw the Yankee organization into such a panic when dealing with him that they decided to try to tame him. Yes, they tried to throw a collar around his neck in the person of David Cone, who happened to be Wells's best friend on the team. "Come on, Coney," Torre would say. "You gotta talk to this boy and get him to simmer down. You gotta keep an eye on him, keep him out of trouble for the sake of the team." Helpful, smart, total team player David Cone would nod and agree that *something* needed to be done. Whether *he* was the one to do it was another matter, and something he wasn't so sure about. But when the pressure came from Torre and the higher-ups, he caved in and started to play the role of big brother to Wells, going out with him and trying to make sure he got home on time, watching over him, talking with him when no one else could. They shared something, these two . . . They had a certain amount of stardust sprinkled over them, and both would wind up pitching perfect games: Cone a year after Wells's 1998 game. They liked each other, they hung out together, and they laughed and told each other jokes. But that didn't always lead to success in changing Wells. He was a hard one to tame.

That was Torre's dilemma because he knew that Wells had a lively nature, a disposition that rejected all restraint, a wild and uncontrolled fury that, when unleashed from the pitcher's mound, would consistently win fifteen or twenty games a season. Which is why Torre and the Yankee organization would tolerate Wells, take his disorderly behavior, and try to ignore it. Because he won games. That's what really mattered in the long run—not how people felt, or how Wells might embarrass the organization. Winning was all that mattered in those bright and optimistic days, and so Torre was often at odds with himself. "I'll talk to him," he'd say. But talking never did any good with Boomer, and the manager knew it. He also knew that this pitcher was like a wild horse. If you break a wild horse he'll lose a good deal of his power, and that was *not* what you wanted.

Even his look was wild, too: pudgy, overweight, with a curved belly that reminded people of Babe Ruth. That comparison wasn't lost on Wells, either. In fact, he idolized Ruth, as if knowing there was a similarity between them that went more than skin deep. Like Ruth, Wells never trained, or so infrequently that it went unnoticed. Also, like the great slugger, he was roundish and chubby. Managers and trainers thrive on whipping guys like him into shape, believing they can get more mileage out of players who fit a standard athletic mold. I used to hear them talking about "putting him on a diet" or "getting him into the gym at least once a week."

But these attempts to get Wells into shape actually insulted him. He would ask me to buy him something from McDonald's and then he would parade around the clubhouse eating a big hamburger, with lettuce and cheese dripping onto the floor. This sloppiness was his way of paying them back. He would go into the trainer's room while chomping on a foot-long steak and cheese sandwich, slobbering over it and leaving a trail of crumbs in his wake. He loved to eat fatty food in front of managers and trainers, as if he were saying, "You think I'm fat now? You ain't seen nothing yet!"

Boomer, they called him. He had no problem with the nickname. It was a friendly form of referring to him, and he liked it. Despite all the trouble he gave the front office and Torre, he was actually one of the most laid-back members of the team. When you got to know him the way I did, you saw that he was inspired and that his independent nature was a strength, not a problem.

But despite how they complained and moaned, management knew they had a winner with Boomer. He was the 1998 MVP, and was in the 1998 All-Star Game: two distinctions few players achieve.

On May 17, 1998, I was on the field at the old Yankee Stadium for his perfect game against the Minnesota Twins. I was stationed on the right-hand side, out beyond first base, close to where the outfielder stands. From where I was positioned I noticed that Boomer started to develop a mannerism as the game wore on. You didn't see this if you were watching on television because the camera would cut away to other players. But during most of that game my eyes were on David Wells, and I was surprised to see him start to wipe his head more than usual. He had a mannerism where he would take off his hat and run his hand over his hair and then replace the hat. But he usually did this only two or three times in a game. On this particular day, though, he was doing it all the time. I knew, from that changed mannerism, that there was something different about how he felt. As he later admitted, he was getting nervous. The 49,820 fans started to get to him with their buzzing and talking and distracting chatter.

"I kind of wanted them to calm down," he said. "Because they were making me nervous . . . By the end, I could barely grip the ball my hand was shaking so much."

I'll never forget the fly ball hit high to right field. Paul O'Neill went back for it and raised his glove. He was twenty feet away from me when he made the catch. Miraculously the ball seemed to be drawn into that glove as if called there by the cheers of the crowd. At first I was so excited I wanted to laugh, but then I realized that something magical had just occurred. In the instant O'Neill caught that ball, Boomer pumped his fist twice to signal victory. The crowd let out a deep roar of appreciation. I had goose bumps as Paul O'Neill, Jorge Posada, and the other teammates lifted Wells to their shoulders and carried him around the field. The victorious pitcher took off his hat and saluted the fans.

In his memoir, *Perfect I'm Not* (2004), Wells claimed he was half drunk while pitching that game. He later clarified that statement to explain that he was hung over from drinking the night before. From what I knew of him, that's totally believable. He liked the nightlife more than most. But when you're a little less than 100 percent—as he was that day with his hangover—you can sometimes do your best work, maybe because you have less chance to second-guess yourself. Gut instinct took over and Wells was flawless.

Billy Crystal arrived in the clubhouse after the game to get his ticket stub signed. He stepped up to Wells and said, "I got here late. What happened?"

Before long the whole baseball world knew what had happened. David Wells was on a roll. And all through this time he was kind to me, especially on my birthday.

"Listen," he said, "I called the Hooters restaurant and told them you have carte blanche to throw a party. Invite your friends, whoever you want, and enjoy!" That day I invited Joe Lee and other bat boys and clubhouse attendants. We drank, ate, and partied, and then we were informed that we could even take souvenirs home.

"The bill is on David Wells," the waitress said.

It came to almost $2,000. Next day he wanted to know if I had fun. That was important to him because he wanted others to have as much fun as he did.

———

But his fun in New York came to an abrupt and surprising end in 2000 when the Yankees traded him for Roger Clemens. Wells wasn't happy about the trade, but he went to the Toronto Blue Jays and performed miracles for them, going 17–10 and 20–8 in the two years he pitched for the Canadians.

Wells was so good that he was traded back to the Yankees in 2002, and we all looked forward to working with him again. But his return to New York started on a wacky note, typical of the late-night partier. On September 7, 2002, he was in an East Side diner at around 5:00 A.M. when he got into a mix-up with a Yonkers bartender who punched him in the face and knocked out two of his teeth. Despite his reputation as a brawler, Wells was praised by his attorney for showing restraint on that night and not throwing a punch back at his attacker.

"I was so dizzy from being hit," Wells said, "that for a few seconds I didn't even know where I was."

Next day I was in the clubhouse when people started asking, "Where's David Wells?" As game time approached and he was nowhere to be seen, we began worrying that something bad had happened. The following day he showed up and flashed a big smile, pointing to two new white implants. His forehead was bruised and blue, but he was laughing and joking about the incident. Amazingly, his spirits weren't dampened by the fight. Before long a Manhattan jury cleared Wells of wrongdoing, finding his attacker guilty of assault and battery.

After this fight, the Yankee front office put even more pressure on Coney to babysit his teammate. Little did they know what was in store for them.

Within months Wells would drop yet another bombshell on the team, upsetting the administration by writing *Perfect I'm Not*, which contained comments the front office claimed tarnished the image of the club—chief among them Wells's assertion that he had pitched his perfect game half drunk. Another thing he said was that if he "were Mike Piazza, that broken bat would still be shoved up Roger's ass." (A remark which didn't much please Clemens.) Wells also claimed that pitcher Mike Mussina and he didn't see eye to eye and weren't pals, which was quite true. You never saw Wells chatting with Mussina. The fact is that Mike Mussina, although polite, wasn't a very outgoing and sociable guy like David Cone. He had none of Cone's sociability and friendliness. Wells and Cone were buddies, and it's easy to see how that could work since Cone was one of the nicest guys on the team, with always a smile and a friendly word for everyone. Mike Mussina, on the other hand, was more of a one-word guy. He replied if you asked him a direct question but he wouldn't come out of his shell to talk with you. Mussina had let it be known that he thought Boomer was "high maintenance." With this assessment I disagree: Boomer may have been outspoken and rebellious, but he was not, like A-Rod, high maintenance. He was just full of life and energy and he liked doing things his way. But when he came to work he performed, he won games, and you didn't have to baby him or give him special treatment, the way a player like A-Rod demanded.

The Yankees fined Boomer $100,000 for publishing those remarks. They should be ashamed of themselves! As writer and former pitcher Jim Bouton said at the time, "These guys have voluntarily gone into a business where people know that everything that they do or say is subject to being written about. They act as if they're surprised when somebody tells what they do."

The final story I want to share with you happened during the late career of David Wells, and it reveals information that no other reporter or journalist has disclosed. It's about the controversial performance of Wells in Game 5 of the 2003 World Series. You have to remember that this was during a time when the Yankees were in heated negotiations with Wells, whose contract was expiring at the end of the season, and there were allegations that they weren't treating him fairly.

In this particular game, Boomer was the starting pitcher, yet he pitched only one full inning. Then he left the field, complaining about a bad back. Everybody believed he had quit in anger and resentment after the first inning. People actually thought that he had stopped pitching because he was angry with the Yankees organization. Don't for a minute believe it. The real story about what happened that day is very different—and I know because I was there and I saw Wells in the clubhouse. Nobody else heard what he said. But before I tell you about our conversation, let's put Game 5 in context.

The Yankees were down and out and griping about bad luck because they had lost Game 1 to the Marlins. They had won Game 2 thanks to Matsui's first-inning three-run homer, which gave them a lead they would carry to the finish. They had also won Game 3, due to two ninth-inning home runs by Aaron Boone and Bernie Williams. Then they lost Game 4 despite Roger Clemens's good pitching in his last outing with the team. So by the time Game 5 rolled around the count stood at 2–2. David Wells was our starting pitcher, and there was a blood feud going on between the Yankees and the Marlins. It wasn't just important for the Yankees to win that game, it was *necessary*.

Everyone knew that Wells had more than baseball on his mind since contract negotiations were looming. And it was no secret what Wells wanted. He had been traded once before—for Roger Clemens—and he wanted to remain in pinstripes. It was less clear whether the Yankees wanted Wells, and they had announced that they wouldn't negotiate during the World Series.

So Wells comes to work the next day, not knowing where he'll be pitching next year, and I'm in the clubhouse when he walks in. I'm getting autographs for players and everything is going fine. Wells is listening to music, he has his headphones on, and he's apparently in a good mood despite his concerns about his contract. But how can you get inside a guy's head to find out what he's *really* thinking? Simple. You look him in the eye and listen to what he says. He's got no reason to lie to me. Remember, I'm low man on the totem pole. I'm just a bat boy.

An hour later millions of fans watch in astonishment and see Wells drop out of the game after the first inning. Speculation ripples through the ball park. *Why?* Speculation runs through the media. *What happened to him?* Speculation spreads through the entire baseball world. STARTING PITCHER DAVID WELLS DROPS OUT OF GAME 5 OF WORLD SERIES AFTER ONLY ONE INNING. *Why?*

I'll tell you why.

It was the third inning. Everybody was out of the clubhouse. The players were on the field. We were all alone. He was sitting on a chair eating a cheeseburger.

He was holding his back.

"I'm hurt," he said. "I'm seriously hurt."

Here's a guy who can pitch along with the best of them. And he *never* trains. Okay, slight exaggeration, he *almost* never trains. You see other guys in the weight room all the time. In seven years with the Yankees, I never saw David Wells so much as step inside the weight room, let alone pick up a dumbbell. He's a natural talent. He's got a rubber arm. He just never works out the way anybody else does. I know his natural inclination is to take it easy. But when he gets on the mound he's a pitching fury and has nerves of steel. He *wants* to win. Bad. Just as bad as your most enthusiastic fan. Just as bad as the manager and the owner and the most competitive players.

He didn't drop out of that game because he thought the Yankees screwed him in contract talks. He didn't drop out because he thought they had insulted him. He had all the mental concentration he needed. It was a physical injury that did him in. And if I'm any judge of character that's the end of the story right there.

I would be doing a disservice to Wells if I ended the story there, though. That one time I saw him with the backache stands out in my mind because it was the opposite of the way he usually acted and the way I remember him: a fighter, a guy who would speak his mind to anyone, who would be happy to slug it out with any team the Yankees faced.

The image of Boomer sitting there sticks in my mind for

another reason, and I get a little choked up every time I think about it. He idolized Babe Ruth and wore number 33 in honor of the Babe's retired "3." You had to see him alone in the clubhouse that day with the big 33 on his back to realize that he probably wanted more than anything in the world to be back out in the spotlight, challenging our opponents.

Some guys are born to be wild, and I guess Boomer had that untamed spirit all right. There were so many times when he put his raw talent on the line for us that it's hard to believe it ever stopped. So, yeah, he may have been sitting on the sidelines that day, but if you looked close enough you're likely to have seen him the way I did, covered with Yankees stardust.

7

Impure Perfection
David Cone

I have to admit that my idol was David Cone. A true man's man, full of all those "good" vices—love of hard liquor, smoking, and women—that help a man take life by the reins and enjoy it to the fullest. He was friendly to me, too, and had a way with words, always ready to talk and socialize, and personable as hell, with a smile for everyone.

"Hey, kid," he said one day. He was always calling me "kid." We were in the clubhouse and I went over to him. He was sitting in front of his locker.

"Listen, can you do me a favor and find some me some smuts?"

I gave him a blank stare.

"What's *that*?"

"Don't you know?" He laughed. "It's periodicals with pictures of the fair sex in various stages of undress."

The way he spoke I didn't always catch his drift. But he finally made clear to me what he was talking about, and the next day I brought him a few magazines together with a pack of Marlboro Lights. He hadn't asked for the cigarettes, but I had seen them in his locker and, like I said, he was my idol.

When he saw the magazines his eyes lit up. "Great job, kid!" He started paging through them right there in the locker room. I was seventeen and embarrassed at how uninhibited he was, but his behavior also cracked me up. He would comment on the women, too. "Oooooooo-weeee! Look at this girl! . . . My, my, my." He would go on to describe the girls in such graphic terms that I, and other players, would blush. Sometimes he would rip pages out and tack them up in his locker and even leave them on the floor of the bathroom.

Next thing you know, Andy Pettitte is screaming at the top of his lungs. "Robbie! For heaven's sake! Clean this stuff up. I don't want any of the kids seeing this. Who *brings* these pictures in here, anyway?"

In addition to being uninhibited, David Cone had one of the best senses of humor. He wasn't only a good athlete, he was also smart, down to earth, and considerate. Of course we always thought of him as having the highest sex drive because of his obsession with photographs of the "fair sex," as he used to say. But his little weaknesses didn't stop with drinking and women: he also liked to smoke, and I mean smoke in places he wasn't supposed to smoke. Man, was he a fiend when it came to smoking during games! You'd see him back in the clubhouse by the clothes dryers inhaling from these long cigarettes he used to light up at all hours of the day and night. Or you'd catch him in the middle of the bathroom, or sometimes near the showers, whiffing down Marlboros like there was no tomorrow, and trying to hide from any authorities who might tell him it was off-limits. His best trick, though, was to walk around with a cup of Gatorade in one hand so that he could douse the cigarette if he was approached by a security guard or administrator. He was such a little kid sometimes, it was funny to see him in action.

One day Coney came to work with an oversized bandage on his hand, but he was too embarrassed to tell anyone what had happened. Finally, Joe Torre called him into his office and told him to come clean. The door was open and everyone was listening. Joe knew that this interview was public, but he didn't care. What he cared about was that his star pitcher had a bandage on his throwing hand. That's got to make you worry. We could see Coney walking back and forth, and we could hear him hemming and hawing until Torre demanded the truth. Next thing we know Coney is admitting that he was bitten on the index finger by his mother-in-law's dog! *Oh, for crying out loud!* Torre is saying. *Oh, for the love of Pete!*

While doctors examine the pitcher, he tells what happened in his own unique style. "It's a small little dog, and I had a fight with it, and that little son of a bitch bit me on the hand!" Players are rolling on the floor laughing out loud.

Orlando Hernandez had to be called up from the minors to cover for David, but luckily El Duque turned out to be so good that they kept him in the rotation for the entire 1998 American League Championship Series.

Coney, true to form, used the downtime to flirt with girls in the stadium—then on July 18, 1999, he stopped fooling around long enough to pitch a perfect game against the Montreal Expos. But before we get to *that*, let me introduce a baseball legend.

Yogi Berra walked into the clubhouse with his hands jammed into his jacket pockets, looking more like a general than a retired baseball player. A short, dark guy with big ears, as soon as he entered the room everyone stopped and stared. For a fraction of a second you thought something must have gone wrong, it was so quiet; but no, he was telling jokes even before he reached the lockers. He was in a very good mood. He was chatting with Jeter and Bernie Williams, putting smiles on their faces. The man who's been called the greatest catcher in baseball history had arrived to start the game by catching the first ceremonial pitch of the day. In fact, that day happened to be Yogi Berra Day at Yankee Stadium. He had returned to the ball park after being away for fourteen years . . . fourteen *long* years during which he was feuding with George Steinbrenner. Their disagreement had started because Yogi felt insulted when Steinbrenner canned him as manager. (The same bad blood like when the organization canned Torre in 2007, only worse.) No wonder Yogi was in such a good mood today—the two men had put their differences behind them and were friendly again.

Little did Yogi know it but today was going to make history all over again—just as *he* had made history by catching Don Larsen's perfect game in the 1956 World Series.

Yogi was talking baseball, of course. There was laughter and optimism in the clubhouse. Meanwhile the day's starter, another world-class pitcher, David Cone, was looking relaxed, too. He was cracking jokes with Yogi and other players. Then he was at his locker getting dressed. I thought he looked more at ease than most starting pitchers. They're usually concentrating and focused and sometimes a little isolated because they have to keep their mind crystal clear and alert.

But David Cone was talking with Alfonso Soriano and Scott Brosius, and he even went to breakfast with them before the game in the players' lounge. I happened to pass by as I entered to get some coffee for one of the other guys. Cone was eating a solid meal of eggs and bacon and drinking a tall glass of milk. You need your energy to pitch. I filed that away in my mind because I wanted to learn from the best. After breakfast he disappeared into the trainer's room for a massage. I was getting some laundry squared away and I could hear SLAP! SLAP! SLAP! SLAP! SLAP! SLAP! as the trainer's hands hit the pitcher's back to limber him up. Lucky man, I thought. A pitcher loves having his muscles lengthened and loosened before games. SLAP! SLAP! SLAP! SLAP! SLAP! SLAP! The sound died away as I entered the locker room again. Yogi near the door. Joe Torre nowhere to be seen. (He was in his office, just down the hall.) Bernie Williams tying his shoelaces. General Manager Brian Cashman striding up to Yogi. "Ready, champ?"

Then Yogi marched up through the tunnel and out . . . and it began. And me not knowing that I was going to be part of it. Having no idea.

When Yogi Berra walked up through the tunnel and out onto the field you could hear the roar of the crowd. A few minutes later they roared again when Don Larsen threw out the first ceremonial pitch of the game to him. A strike! *Yaaaaaaaaaaaaaaaaaay!* went the crowd. Of course a strike in this case doesn't mean that a *batter* has a strike against him. At this point there's no batter in the box yet—it's just Yogi squatting behind home plate and Don on the mound. When the zinger came in over the plate the fans were screaming. What do you expect from Don Larsen, anyway? Even after forty-three years he's still right on the money.

No, you don't want to make mistakes before a New York crowd. In 2001, for Game 3 of the World Series, President George W. Bush came to throw out the first pitch. He wasn't going to stand on the mound because it was so far from home plate.

"You better throw it from the mound, otherwise you're gonna get booed," Jeter warned him. "This is Yankee Stadium."

When the president went out, he stood on the mound. He paused for a few seconds before throwing the opening pitch of the day. The crowd cheered. The president smiled like he knew a secret.

New York crowds love ceremony, too. They cheered as Yogi and Don walked off the field. I turned to look at my hero, the starting pitcher. David Cone's face was red as he walked out onto the mound. It wasn't from embarrassment. His face is always red on hot days. And he usually sweats a lot, too. Powerhouse of a player. So finally he was out there and the temperature was ninety-eight degrees and you could feel that July sun and humidity through an overcast sky. I knew it was going to be a tough day for *all* of us, especially David Cone.

Now you have to understand something to see how the magic of that day unfolded. This is something most fans never think about, but when a game begins the starting pitcher isn't expected to stay there for the entire game, instead he's "relieved" when the manager sends in another pitcher. But there's one exception to this general rule, and it's a manager's decision to make that exception. If he thinks it's a good idea to keep the starter on the mound, then he keeps him there. And about the only time a manager does that these days is when there's magic in the air. I remember Joe Torre coming out of his office only a few times that day, but as the innings wore on there was more anticipation building, making every-thing seem a little different. The magic had started to build because nobody was getting a hit off David Cone.

Three innings went by—perfectly—and then it began to rain. It was a light rain but it caused the umpires to call a rain delay.

I was standing in a tunnel under the stadium when Cone came up to me and told me to put on a glove. Keep in mind that I was seventeen, and David Cone was, at the time, one of the best pitch-ers in the world. I had been standing in the tunnel to keep out of the rain. Most of the other players had gone down into the under-ground clubhouse and were waiting out the rain delay. I don't remember why I was standing in the tunnel. I might have gone up there to get a breath of fresh air or maybe to see if the rain was letting up. Whatever the reason, that's where he found me and said, "Get a glove, Luigi." I'll never forget that moment. But that was just the beginning.

I guess I'll never forget it because it's something that happened when I was young, but more than that it's something that came out of the blue and brought me into another world. I had entered the Yankee world by putting on the uniform, of course, but it was the call from one of the best pitchers in the League that thrust me up another step and into another level. The first thing I did was check my mind-set and ask myself whether it was a dream or reality. It was hard to say because the day suddenly had an unreal feeling. There was fog hanging in the air and colors looked gray and dull. On the one hand, I knew he was serious because he addressed me by name and he had a glove on and he wanted my help, but at the same time I had a feeling that things were quickly getting beyond me, that I was jumping into something much bigger than I had ever anticipated when I came to work for the Yankees as a bat boy.

I remember thinking about the rain as I ran to get my glove. I remember thinking that it was the third inning and that the Expos had no runs. I immediately started thinking about things more seriously than I had ever thought before. All of a sudden it was as if I had more at stake in the game. It was like the 41,930 fans there that day were suddenly part of *my* world. It was as if the score were now related *to me*—not just to the Yankees and to Yankee *history*, but to me personally—as if it were suddenly up to *me* to *do* something about it. It occurred to me that I would wake up and it would all be a dream. But the glove on my hand seemed so real, and then I was running back to the tunnel. Brian Cashman, the general manager, had announced that there were twenty minutes to play time. That announcement was echoing in my brain as I ran up before David Cone, thinking, *I'm helping the starting pitcher warm up twenty minutes before the game resumes!* I felt my nerves making me jittery as I stood before him.

I wonder if that's how they all feel, the first time they walk out and begin to play for the Yankees. I wonder if they all have a sense of unreality. Over and above everything were the fans, the crowd that was audible even there in the tunnel where I stood with my glove waiting for David Cone to throw the ball to me. My heart was hammering in my chest. I knew that starting pitchers usually don't talk to anyone: their concentration is absolute. It has to be. They focus on their work, their strategy, their game plan. Never before had a starting pitcher said anything to me on the day of his game. But David Cone *had* spoken to me, there was no question about that, which was why I was standing in the tunnel with a glove on. I felt that anyone could walk by and say, "Hey, kid what are you doing?" But no one would say that, not even the manager or the owner of the team. *No one would interfere with the starting pitcher.*

So I'm standing there and I begin to realize it's actually happening when I face him, this 1994 American League Cy Young Award winner. He's tall and broad-shouldered at six foot one, imposing and full of presence and energy, and his windup is impressive. I knew what he was going to pitch because he gave me a signal beforehand. A Major League pitcher has a vast assortment of different pitches he can fire at a catcher, all intended to do one thing—fool and frustrate the batter. These include fastballs, curveballs, sliders, sinkers, knuckleballs, and more. I was expecting a fastball because that's the signal he gave me: thumb up. I held my glove in front of my chest and hoped for a good catch. I knew the ball would come right at me. David Cone doesn't miss. I also knew well enough that his pitch is hard to hit precisely because he throws fast and hard. What he would be firing at me here would not be play throws, like when you're playing catch with your dad. These would be the killer pitches that make the Expos strike out. They would be *dangerous* pitches, too, and I didn't want to get hurt. I knew where the pitch would hit, which helped me prepare for it. This might be a warm-up session and a warm-up pitch, but he's going to throw with force. I took a deep breath and waited for his windup and then the pitch. It came at me just as I had expected, high and direct. I have good eyes, thank God. I can see a fastball coming at me just as a batter would, but knowing it's going to be a fastball (instead of a curveball, for example) helps you prepare for the catch. As the fastball approached me what happened was that all of my view of the baseball field behind David Cone seemed to telescope into a funnel shape and I could hear the air snap and hum as the ball streaked the last few feet toward my glove and then with a *whuuuuuump* hit it hard. Coney looked up. "The pipes are too low in the tunnel," he said. "Let's go out onto the field."

He turned and walked out of the tunnel onto the playing field near the foul line between home plate and first base. I was supposed to follow him but suddenly all the energy seemed to drain from my body and I was frozen like a statue. Was I actually expected to go out *onto the field* with the starting pitcher and . . . It was so hard to believe and unreal that at first I couldn't react. But the sting of having caught that fastball was real enough. My senses returned one by one and I took a deep breath. *Okay*, I told myself. *You caught the ball and you're warming up the starting pitcher for the New York Yankees. Get control of yourself. Move, man, move!* I trotted out after Cone. When I stepped onto the grassy rain-damp field I had a rush of adrenaline and jittery energy like nothing I had ever experienced before. I had a responsibility to do the job right and the responsibility, above all else, to make David Cone's warm-up a good experience for him. If I screwed this up I would be in bad shape with him—and with the universe. I knew *that* like I knew my name. But inside my head I was thinking, *I'm going to be sick.*

I had so many thoughts going through my mind that I can't begin to tell you what they all were. I stepped forward and raised my hand to throw the ball back to Cone. Behind him on the field the Montreal Expos were warming up, too. At any other time I'd be relaxed when throwing a baseball. I've thrown thousands, probably even tens of thousands, in my work as a pitcher for a team that plays in Central Park. But there were so many mental considerations in my brain that when I let that first throw out of my hand I instantly knew it was going to be bad and I groaned. *This is going to make David mad*, I thought. *He's going to have to jump to catch it. Why did I do that! I'm a jerk! My God, what if I hurt him! What if he leaps up for the catch, and—just to be nice to me—what if he really goes for the ball, a ball that he should just let sail by, and what if he injures his throwing arm in making the catch!* At just that moment I saw him leap to the side and raise his glove and twist his body to catch the ball. *Please, please, please*, I was saying to myself. *Please let him be all right. Dear God*, I was praying, *don't let me hurt him.*

So, star athlete that he is, he made the catch, but I could tell he was pissed. I had thrown like I had the yips. But he came right back at me with a slider. First he gave me the signal, then he let it loose. *Zzzzzzzzzzzzzzap!* It hit my glove and I steadied myself on my feet. Back to him I threw it. And it went like that, back and forth, seven times. Before he threw each pitch he'd give me a signal to let me know what to expect: fastball, slider, sinker. It's a courtesy very good pitchers—guys who can hit a fly on a wall at sixty feet—extend to professionals who are helping them warm up. Typically a pitcher will throw five to seven pitches to warm up in the bullpen before going back onto the field. So I was prepared for it to end. But honestly I had so much adrenaline pumping through me at the time that I wasn't keeping track of the *number* of pitches Coney threw. All I was thinking about was, Make sure you catch 'em, make sure you throw 'em back good. So after he threw the seventh he said, "Okay, Luigi, we're done." What a nice guy, I thought. He let me know we were finished instead of just walking off.

Joe Torre and Don Zimmer were sitting in the dugout, getting ready for the game, and they were laughing their asses off because they saw how nervous I was. I was walking back behind David Cone. Zimmer was covering his mouth, probably saying, "Look at him—he's gonna pee his pants."

Although Coney was my favorite pitcher even before I became a clubbie, after I warmed him up I was even more concerned about that game. Once play resumed I was out on the field again. (The total timeout had been thirty-three minutes.) I looked at David Cone on the mound with admiration and pride. My position: by the right foul line. I was sitting on a stool next to first base, maybe twenty feet from it, waiting for foul balls. My job was to retrieve them and get them off the field. Behind me, of course, was a sea of fans, every seat taken. They were a noisy crowd, but I remained focused, my eyes on the batter. So next inning Ricky Ledee, the Yankee outfielder, came up to bat and hit a rocket down the sidelines. I saw the ball streak through the air overhead and I was off my stool, leaping to my feet. It hit a red advertising sign and bounced off. I quickly got in front of it as it sailed down in a looping curve, and I made the catch. I was happy but also a little nervous because I remembered how on my first day Lou Cucuzza had warned me never to do that. But this ball had come right at me, so I had an excuse. Since it was an out-of-play ball I tossed it up to one of the begging fans, giving it away as a present and a memento that I knew the kid would cherish forever. The action on the field was always being recorded by cameras, and this "play" of mine on the sidelines was no different. My catch was caught on camera and televised to the nation.

The nation also watched as David Cone did something very

unusual. It's almost unheard of for a starting pitcher to come back after a long break like we had during that thirty-three-minute rain delay. This is because his muscles cool down when he's not working and it's very difficult to get back up to speed. My helping him warm up contributed to allowing him to do the impossible. But every time he went down into the clubhouse after each inning no one would talk to him. Before long no one was even *there*. It was like a ghost town—deserted and empty of players, managers, and even bat boys. There's a superstition about talking with a pitcher when he's in the middle of a winning streak with a chance at a perfect game. It's like the superstition of not talking to your wife on the day of a wedding, only it's worse. He's isolated and alone—sometimes when he needs someone to cheer him on more than ever. Even Joe Torre avoided him, sensing that something very special was happening. There was magic in the air. We all felt it. Torre never considered taking him off the mound. In hindsight, of course, we know that Torre made the right decision—let him stay there and chase history.

One man, however, had the guts, or the confidence, to buck tradition. Chili Davis, who played for the Yankees during the 1998–1999 season, was from Jamaica. Maybe that's why he didn't buy into the superstition about not speaking with the pitcher when he's in the middle of a winning streak. Fooling around and acting clownish, Chili put on a catcher's mask and mitt and tried to joke about things and keep Coney smiling. It did cheer him up for a few minutes.

Two other highlights from that game stand out in my memory. One involved Chuck Knoblauch. Keep in mind that Chuck Knoblauch was a 1997 American League Gold Glove Award winner.

That means he rarely made errors. Yet by 1999 the award-winning second baseman couldn't throw to first base. This unusual condition—some would call it a psychological problem—is known in sports as "the yips." There's some speculation that the condition affected Knoblauch because he was having personal problems. Well, in order to pitch a perfect game, you can't allow any batter to reach first base and your team can't make any errors. In the eighth inning a ball was hit up the middle and the whole stadium held its breath. When the ball approached Chuck Knoblauch he backhanded it, catching it with his glove reversed, and then, because he had been thrown slightly off balance, he took a few steps to steady himself. A fraction of a second later he turned toward first base. Would it be another case of the yips? Would he throw wild? Recently he had thrown so erratically that he had even hit a fan in the head! But as if sensing that perfection was demanded of him today, he threw a laser to Tino Martinez at first. When he made the play the whole stadium went crazy. Everybody knew about Knoblauch's history, and the sense of relief when he made the throw was felt by all the fans. It was so close to a perfect game now that *nobody* could afford to make a mistake.

By the ninth inning all the spectators were standing. They knew something amazing was in the works. David Cone threw the first Expo out. Then there was a fly ball hit to Ricky Ledee, who was playing left field, but the sun was in his eyes. In the old stadium the sun would always bother left fielders. Everybody thought he dropped the ball. *He* didn't even know he caught it. "I didn't know I caught it," he said. "It must have been the angels that made me catch that ball. I just stuck my hand out and hoped for the best."

Was it destiny? Or was it pure luck? Or was that day meant to be? Nine out of ten times it's supposed to drop—but it didn't!

The last of the Expos to bat was Orlando Cabrera. David Cone fired his final pitch, the eighty-eighth of the day. Cabrera hit it high into the sinking sun. David Cone whirled to look but couldn't find the ball. He pointed up into the sky toward where the sun was making it invisible, toward where the ball *must* be—as if no one knew where it was! Third baseman Scott Brosius ran under it, squinting to see. *Oh, God*, everyone was thinking, *don't mess this one up!* When it finally dropped into his glove to make the game perfect, the roar of the crowd was deafening.

A perfect game is simple to define for anyone who has even the most basic understanding of baseball. It means that nobody on the opposing team ever got to base. Nine innings and nobody even got to *first* base! This is such a rare accomplishment that, to date, in all of Major League Baseball history, it has happened only twenty times. Let me tell you, everyone was excited. Myself included, of course.

David Cone was so overcome with emotion after Brosius caught that ball that he fell to his knees and raised his hands in joy and triumph. Joe Girardi, who had caught the game, ran out to the mound and dropped to his knees and hugged him. Within seconds all the other players rushed onto the field and lifted Coney high to celebrate. I could have run onto the field to congratulate him— believe me, I wanted to—but I was so choked up with emotion that I hesitated. And then when I saw them cheering and celebrating and lifting Coney up, I restrained myself. Yes, of course I wanted to rush out and join them and I felt a *need* to join them, a need to celebrate along with the team, but I held back out of respect for the players. After all, it was *their* victory, they had done the work, David Cone had done the work. It was above all *his* victory. I wanted to let it be theirs and that's why I stayed on the sidelines. But I knew I had helped. In my small way I had been part of it. And as I stood there watching them, trembling with the surge of excitement that victory always brings, I couldn't stop the emotion from overcoming me. By the time they raised Coney up and carried him away, there were tears blurring my vision.

Afterward I congratulated him in the clubhouse. I had a couple of photographs of the two of us and I waited until things calmed down a bit before asking him to sign them. He stayed in the clubhouse for an hour and a half after the game, wearing a blue T-shirt and his uniform pants, enjoying the personal victory of this accomplishment. He made phone calls to his father and then to David Wells, who had scored a perfect game the year before. He and Wells had become good friends because they were the two powerhouse pitchers for the Yankees. Finally I approached and asked for an autograph. GLAD TO SHARE THIS MOMENT WITH YOU, he signed one of the photos. Then he signed a baseball, gave it to me with a smile, and strolled out of the clubhouse, excited with his win.

As usual, I stayed behind to do the laundry.

There are two postscripts to this story, both of which highlight David Cone's generosity and personal warmth. It's a tradition for pitchers who have a perfect game to give gifts to the members of the team, usually a ring. For example, David Wells gave rings to the Yankees in a small ceremony in the clubhouse in 1998. But David Wells didn't give rings to bat boys.

David Cone was a union guy, and never one to forget the little man. He decided to give a luxury Swiss watch—manufactured by Ebel, costing upward of $3,000—to each player. David Cone came in with his agent carrying a heavy box, and I helped carry in the second big box containing the gifts. Before long, Joe Torre called a general meeting, and David stood up to make a speech and thank everyone. Then he started handing out watches. Nothing was given to the bat boys except for Joe Lee, who had worked with him for years before I arrived. When he was done and people went their separate ways, he saw me and said, "Hey, Squeegee." I looked up, surprised that he had used my nickname instead of calling me kid. "Come over here." I approached, expecting him to ask me to carry out the trash. Instead, he reached into the big box, where he had a few watches left, and handed one to me. "Here, this is for you," he said.

"No, you don't have to do that." I tried handing it back.

"No, no," he said, smiling. "I *want* you to have it."

Only Joe Lee and I got one.

I thought he was simply being generous, but after he left the Yankees and started playing for the Red Sox I got a lesson in how generous he really was, and how much he thought of me. I got a call one day, and it was Coney.

"Can you come down to Shea Stadium and be a bat boy for me while I'm in town tomorrow? I'm pitching against the Mets." Because the Yankees were on the road that day I had nothing else to do, but I hesitated. What if I were seen in a Red Sox uniform?

Would I get in trouble? But in the end I decided to do it. We had been through hell and high water together, and he had taken the time to show me how to throw a fastball. In fact, when I pitch now I regularly break bats with his technique, and I've been approached by minor league scouts. I attribute that to having worked with a professional who often reached out to help me.

So the next day there I was, wearing a *Red Sox* uniform. Talk about a strange turn of events! That sure was one for me. I didn't know any of the other bat boys or players, except by reputation. I felt like a traitor to the Yankees for helping the Red Sox, of course, but David made me feel good by asking me to do this favor for him. Yes, there was an awkward moment when I first walked out in front of everyone in a Red Sox uniform. I thought I was going to get in trouble. Honest to God, I was hoping that nobody noticed that I was a bat boy for the Yankees and might think I was a spy.

But when you make friends in baseball, you'll do the darndest things for them.

8

I Ain't Smilin' . . . Just Take the Freakin' Picture!
Joe Torre

Arthur Richman is a *very* old man. Compared with a fifteen-year-old bat boy . . . well, he's ancient. A patch of white fuzz over his ears surrounds a shiny bald head. Gray eyeglasses sit low on a pointy nose. His square jaw makes him look odd enough to scare a young man away. He's always holding a clear plastic cup filled with vodka, which he sips through a cocktail straw. Sunken at the bottom of his drink is a wedge of lime. The more he drinks, the more he sings his sad refrain. He makes a twitching motion with that square jaw, inviting me into a not-too-cozy corner of Joe Torre's office.

Unfortunately, I can't just walk away from him because he's George Steinbrenner's right-hand man; the Boss's trusted advisor. But what in Heaven's name can Richman want with *me*, after all? . . . Oh, fool that I am! I should have known that it's the same line he's been giving me for years.

"Lemme tell you somethin', kid." His hand is shaking so bad

the vodka spills onto my shoes. "I'm the one who got Joe Torre hizzzz job . . . and I don't get no credit for it! Now, I ask you, is that fair? Come here, kid." I'm standing right next to him, I can't *get* any closer. "I told Steinbrenner to hire him in '96. Did you know that?"

Did I know it! I only heard it a hundred times from him. I'm trying to figure out some way to leave the office . . .

"Nobody fucking knows that I was responsible for getting Torre his job . . ."

Truth is, just about *every*one knows it. Arthur doesn't think he got enough credit, that's all. It happened back in 1996 when Steinbrenner was searching for a manager, and he asked his veteran advisor—former sportswriter Arthur Richman—to make a short list of potential candidates for him. Richman suggested Torre, despite the fact that Joe hadn't much of a record. On a hunch, Steinbrenner went with the suggestion, and the rest, as they say, is history.

But that history has never been described in all its unusual details, as I will reveal in the following pages, for there are secrets that even Joe Torre didn't tell about himself in his own biography, and there are important things about Torre that no reporter ever saw or heard.

To begin with, the new manager looked like a Mafia don. The players called him Godfather because he spoke soft and low and walked in silence, on the balls of his feet, as if he were carrying dynamite. But when he spoke, he'd whack you. If he took a player into his office and closed the wooden door, you knew it was trouble—big trouble. They would come out like they saw a ghost. Everyone, and I mean everyone, respected him. He had earned it.

Mr. T smoked cigars all the time and never smiled, even when people took his picture. In the eight years I knew him I never saw him smile once—even when he was telling a joke. I always thought he was a grumpy guy. He was all business. But that's what worked and that's what made him so good for the team. He was a player's manager—a great manager—because he was all about winning. He would only talk to them if they lost. He started meetings in a quiet voice. He never cursed. But he told them what to do in a voice that *sounded like a curse.* He'd say, "Play hard and have fun. Don't be afraid to make mistakes." Nobody made jokes or said anything during his meetings. They listened. There was a tradition that at the end of every meeting Joe always had to ask Posada, "What do we have to do?" And Posada would make a fist and say, "Grind it!"

One of Torre's signature moves was protecting individual team members from administrators like George Steinbrenner and Brian Cashman. He did this by telling the players, in closed team meetings, what Steinbrenner wanted, and then explaining what *he* felt was a better approach. This usually produced smiles. He also protected the team as a whole, as he did in Boston in 1999 in an ALCS game at Fenway Park, where fans were throwing bottles and cans onto the field. Everyone knows that Torre called his players off the field, but none of the sportswriters was there to see just how Torre accomplished this maneuver, and with what determination he pursued his goal of getting them out of harm's way. I was standing two feet from him when enraged Boston fans began hurling beer cans and bottles. We had seen this kind of behavior before, but never at this intensity. Torre sprang to the top steps of the visiting dugout and tried to hail the home plate umpire. The crowd was noisy and Joe couldn't get the guy to turn around. He raised his voice, shouting at him.

"I want my boys off the field, and I'm gonna call them in now!"

His face was red.

"Did you *hear* me?"

A moment later he stepped onto the field. He had not been heard by the umpire because the roar from the fans was deafening. Now, more concerned than ever, Torre began waving both arms toward his players, yelling at the top of his lungs.

"Get back in here! Come on! Get off the field!"

One by one they turned, noticed him, and then realized what he was saying. Yes, he was right—there was danger! Yes, we better get inside! As the players came in off the field, dodging bottles and beer cans, Torre stepped aside to let them in. Like a mother hen shepherding his players out of harm's way and into the narrow shelter of the dugout, he said reassuring words to them as they passed.

"This is fucking crazy," Knobby said. The players all agreed that Joe had saved them from a dangerous situation.

Joe and Don Zimmer, the bench coach, had their heads together all the time during games. It was as if the manager was listening to the voice of wisdom and to all the things that Zimmer knew about the game. The funny thing was that sometimes they weren't talking about baseball. As you'll see shortly, they were often talking about horses.

Few people know this, but Torre worked out in the team

weight room almost every day. He would show up in a Windbreaker and New York Yankee shorts. He had rather hairy chicken legs, and he always carried the *Daily News* folded under one armpit and a bottle of water in his hand. He would head out of the clubhouse from his office, walking down the hallway to the weight room, which would be empty before players arrived. He loved to get on the treadmill. He didn't go fast, the way A-Rod would; instead, he would prop the newspaper up on the front of the machine and walk for thirty or forty minutes. Then he'd come back into the clubhouse drenched in sweat, a white towel around his neck like he had just finished a boxing match. I got the impression this routine was a much-needed stress reducer.

Part of that stress came from the mismatched group of players Brian Cashman and the front office had saddled him with. Things didn't come together for us the way they had during the late '90s and early 2000s. The mind-set of these new players was brought home to me after the Yankees played the Anaheim Angels in Los Angeles for the 2002 American League Division Series—and lost in the first round of the playoffs. I was at the airport waiting for them to unload the truck so we could get on the plane and go home. Raul Mondesi walked up and sat across from me in his suit. It was especially disappointing to lose because we had made it to the World Series and lost the year before, so I thought Raul would be in the dumps.

"Man, you know, we lost," he said. But he wasn't bummed out the way I expected him to be; in fact, he was enthusiastic and upbeat, which surprised the hell out of me. He even smiled, for cripe's sake, and said, "Don't worry, there's always next year."

Always next year! I couldn't believe my ears. You would *never* hear Jeet, Paul O'Neill, Bernie Williams, or any of those guys say anything like *that*. Because for *them* it was winning that counted, not just playing the game well or upping your stats. But these were the attitudes that some of these new players brought with them. I guess it was because these guys were always on losing teams before so they were *accustomed* to going home early.

Torre had to deal with this new mentality, and it started to wear him down. You could see the effect of the strain on him. Little by little I'm convinced it did funny things to his thinking. True, he still acted like a manager and did and said the things a manager does and says in public, but in private he seemed to be suffering from unusual fears. He began acting as if he thought people were out to get him, that they were spying on him, listening in on his private conversations. There was one security guard in particular who he feared. He didn't just fear him, he hated this guy. Now, you have to understand that this guy was a pleasant enough fellow, but even I could see that there were two sides to him. And he always seemed to be hanging around at the wrong time. We found out later that he was George Steinbrenner's spy, so Joe *was* correct in mistrusting him. But it got to the point where it was like that comic strip *Spy vs. Spy*, and you would see Joe creeping around to his office, looking over his shoulder when this guy was in the clubhouse. And then you would see the guy talking to a couple of players and laughing it up with them, and then leaving. And Joe started to have this closed-up frightened look about him which spread to other players. After George's spy walked out one day, Ruben approached me and put his finger to his lips.

"Don't talk to that guy. Don't tell him what we do. You know . . . we can't trust that guy."

At least the stress didn't cause Mr. T to become superstitious—like some of the other players—but maybe it *did* contribute to his insistence on one little routine that had to be followed without deviation or he would get annoyed. It involved my delivering water to him and Don Zimmer before games. Seconds before game time, I would dash into the coach's room and open the refrigerator. Inside would be five bottles of cold water that I would remove. Then I'd run up to the dugout, holding one bottle in my right hand and four in my left. First I would give the single bottle to Zimmer, who was always sitting on the bench. "Here you go, Chief," I'd say. (He called *me* Chief, too.) I would then turn and face Torre, holding the remaining four bottles in front of him. He would close his eyes, think for a few seconds, and then select one of the bottles.

"I hope this'll be the winning one for today," he would say. Then in a joking way he would yell, "Now get out of here!"

If we didn't win he'd claim that I gave him the wrong bottle. But one day I was so busy with other chores that I forgot our little tradition. When Torre spotted me in the dugout before the game, he gave me a dark look.

"Squeegee, where's my water?"

"Right now, Skip!" I always called him Skip.

Fast as lightning I ran to get the bottles and bring them up to him. When the routine was over and the two men had received their water, Torre pointed a finger at me.

"Don't let that happen again!" He took a sip, then added, "This better be the *winning* bottle!"

I prayed that things would go well for us that game. To my great relief, we won.

On July 27, 2003, Torre surprised us by pulling Raul Mondesi out of a key game against the Red Sox. Mondesi was a nineteen-year veteran. Claiming he was in a slump, Torre sent in Ruben Sierra to pinch-hit for him. Mondesi was pissed.

"What the hell do I need these fucks for?" he said. "I'm going."

He stormed into the clubhouse and threw four bats at his locker. We were in Fenway Park and I guess he didn't care if he broke something. He started cursing in Spanish, threatening to walk out.

"You can't!" I told him. "There's a rule against leaving during games."

But he wouldn't listen to reason.

"Are you coming with me?" he asked.

Since I was so cool with Robbie, I would do some work for the team on the road—even though the Yankees didn't pay me—so naturally Robbie wanted me to stay. But it was actually Mondesi who was paying for my hotel room in the Ritz-Carlton, the same hotel Torre was staying at. So I felt pressured to leave. He was sitting on the couch, fuming. Then, as if he had made a decision, he jumped to his feet.

"Grab your bags, we're leaving."

"For God's sake! You could be fined."

"I'm going. Are you with *me* or them?"

I turned to Robbie.

"I have to go," I said. "Can you call us a limo?"

Mondesi and I started walking out, and all the fans were looking at us. They usually don't see players up close during games. This was at the top of the eighth, and here we were walking out of the stadium! We stopped at the hotel to collect our luggage.

"I need a bottle of Jack Daniels," Mondesi said. During the three-hour limo drive home we were drinking together from that bottle, and he was on the phone to his agent, saying, "Get me out of the Yankees!" I was the first one who knew that he wanted to be with another team; in fact, I knew it before Joe Torre.

"Come to Arizona with me," he said.

"I can't do that."

"I understand. But this is a piece of shit organization you're staying with."

Mondesi was traded to the Arizona Diamondbacks two days later.

When the Yankees got back in town a few days later, everybody in the clubhouse was telling me I was in trouble. Zimmer walked in to have breakfast and said, "Oh, boy, Skip wants to see you." Little did I know they were playing a joke on me. Practical jokes had always been part of the team's way of relaxing, but now they were getting meaner. Torre arrived in full street attire, pointed at me, and said, "Come to my office." I was shaking. He closed that wooden door and I knew that meant trouble . . . this time for *me*. With him were Brian Cashman, Don Zimmer, and hitting coach Rick Down. The clubhouse staff were at the door listening. Torre pointed at the chair.

"Sit down."

I sat. He glared at me.

"What did Mondesi say about me?"

I didn't have the guts to tell him how Mondesi had cursed him to high heaven for three hours. Plus I thought I was in big trouble. So my brain was working fast to try to figure out what to say, and I finally hit on it. This would save me!

"Joe, he fucked *me*, too!"

Torre's eyes twinkled, the closest I've ever seen him come to a smile.

"Get the fuck out of here!"

Everybody burst out laughing and I got up to exit.

"Look at him," Torre said. "He probably pissed his pants."

On October 16, 2003, before Game 7 of the American League Championship Series, Torre got a surprise at the end of the team meeting when he said, "Does anyone else have anything to say?" Enrique Wilson raised his hand. A utility player for the Yankees, Wilson usually kept silent. Torre's eyebrows went up.

"Yes, Enrique?"

Enrique stood. He was in his underwear. He walked to the front of the room. He looked like Gumby, with a bald head and dark complexion.

"Guys," he began, struggling to speak his best English, "I got something to tell you."

It was so quiet you could hear the wall clock ticking. Posada was sitting on the floor, other guys on chairs, all eyes on Wilson.

"I was coming off the field today and Manny Ramirez [a Red Sox slugger who happened to be Enrique's friend] was coming in from BP and he said to me, 'Pack your shit early, baby. You're going home to the Dominican Republic for a vacation.' He was trying to tell me that *they're* going to win."

This got the room pumped up.

"Hell no, they're not!"

"We'll show 'em!"

"Fuck them!"

Enrique's remark had the intended effect, getting the guys worked up so that they wanted to put the Sox in their place. As a result, Torre was pretty happy with the mood of the team going into that important game. Later in the day, he selected Aaron Boone, the Yankees' third baseman, as a pinch hitter. Between innings, I was peeing in the men's room when Boone walked in and started relieving himself in the stall next to me.

"Nervous?" he said.

Truth be told, we were *all* a little nervous because it looked like we were going to lose the Series.

"Yeah," I said.

"Hell, you shouldn't be." He chuckled. "You've been through this before."

Later in the game, Boone went out to pinch-hit. First pitch from Tim Wakefield of the Red Sox was a knuckleball, just a junk pitch, which was all the guy could throw. Boone hit it hard into left field where it landed in the stands. His walk-off home run sent the Yanks to the 2003 World Series. We were all high on the excitement. After the game everyone was laughing and celebrating. Enrique was strumming a broomstick in the clubhouse. Looking forward to facing the Florida Marlins, the song we were playing was Will Smith's "Miami" and we were singing along with the chorus: "I'm go-ing to Mi-a-mi."

Unfortunately, we lost the World Series that year. Let me tell you . . . You *don't* want to be around the Yankees when they lose a

World Series. Torre doesn't talk to anybody. Jeter doesn't joke with you. Everybody minds their own business like they're at a wake.

The Skipper was getting more distracted by the antics of his new star players. These guys who came into the club after 2002 were fine athletes, but the way they focused on their own performance to the exclusion of team cohesion caused problems. Which brings to mind the story of Kevin Brown . . .

On September 3, 2004, I was in the clubhouse hanging clothes during the sixth inning of a game against the Baltimore Orioles. It's a boring task, but one that has to be done. The only good thing about it is that it lets you get a chance to see what players keep in their personal area, such as good-luck charms, men's magazines, or even what pills and supplements they're using. I had to keep turning around to pick up Miguel Cairo's stuff, and while I was doing that Mel Stottlemyre happened to walk by behind me. I didn't think anything about that since I saw him in the clubhouse every day.

All of a sudden I heard a thunderous BANG! It was so loud that I jumped. I thought a picture had fallen off the wall. I looked around and, to my surprise, saw Mel Stottlemyre and Kevin Brown, the starting pitcher, standing in the hallway between Torre's and Robbie's offices. It wasn't unusual to see players and coaches there, but what *was* odd was the way that Kevin was standing, with both hands together in front of his body, rocking his torso up and down. In front of him was a jagged hole in the cement pillar in the clubhouse. Little pieces of plaster were dangling from it, and a stream of crumbled plaster was sifting out.

Mel strode away from Kevin and disappeared up the tunnel leading to the dugout. I wondered what the hell was going on. Kevin was still standing in the hallway, and what he did next made me rub my eyes to make sure I was seeing right. He was bending over at the waist and appeared to be throwing up. Then he started marching back and forth in the little space between the office doors, turning on his heels so he could go faster, but moving in a jerking manner like a string-puppet. A minute later Joe Torre came in from the dugout, wearing his Yankees jacket. This surprised the hell out of me because the team was going up to bat and the manager never leaves the dugout at a time like that.

Torre started screaming at Brown. You fucking this! You fucking that! I was afraid to go near them. All you heard were F-bombs!

I was so frightened I ran to the end of the clubhouse to try to find someone to tell what was going on. I ran into Mitch, the clubbie who prepares the food, and I started jabbering incoherently, saying, "Mitch, my God! Something happened . . . I mean . . . Kevin Brown's in the hall . . . Joe Torre's cursing him out . . . I don't know what . . . He's yelling at him like the guy committed murder."

The two of us crept back into the clubhouse to see what we could see. From the way Torre was yelling and what he was saying, we soon put two and two together: Kevin had punched the cement pillar! It took us a while to get over our shock because Kevin was the starting pitcher and he was supposed to be pitching in a few minutes. Yet here he was, clutching his nonpitching hand in agony. Torre was still upset, and so was Mel.

"This is not good," Mel said.

Torre couldn't stop yelling at Kevin, berating him for injuring himself, and for doing it right in the middle of a game. Then Torre left to get back up to the field. He had to use somebody from his bullpen to take over for the injured starter.

Next day, left hand in a cast, Kevin was ordered by Torre to apologize to all the players during the team meeting. This was one meeting I didn't want to miss. As usual, Posada was sitting on the floor, and all the other players were sitting in a semicircle, listening to Torre speak. Then Brown got his opportunity. He made a speech that was short and to the point, but there was no conviction in it. He stood in front of them, his arm in a cast, and spoke as if reciting words from memory. "I'm sorry I lost my temper and punched the wall. I broke my hand and was not able to pitch. I made a mistake."

When he exited the room, presumably to visit the team doctor, there was a hubbub of talk. No one believed him! No one thought his apology was sincere!

"That fucking asshole!" Posada said.

"He should hang himself from the George Washington Bridge!" Ruben said.

Naturally, Robbie charged Brown for the cost of repairing the cement.

Even during the rockiest and most difficult years of his being manager, Joe Torre was usually focused and kept his nose to the grindstone. There was only one thing that distracted him from work, however, and it wasn't women—it was horses.

I found out about this quirk of his during a late-season game. Torre called me over in the dugout, and from the dark look on his face I thought it was something serious. He waited until I was close and then lowered his voice. "Go down to my office," he said. "I want you to check the score on the Off-Track Betting channel and see who won." I was stunned. It was during a game! I had never before been asked to leave my post.

"Make sure you find out the exact track and horse," he added.

The exact track and horse? What the hell was he talking about? You need to know that during a game it is most unusual for a bat boy to be sent on *any* errand, except one that relates directly to the game. Not only was I puzzled that I was being asked to do something relating to horses . . . but I was shocked that the request had come from the manager during game time.

I ran down into the clubhouse and found Joe Lee.

"Joe, Mr. T just asked me to find out something about which horses won," I said. "What's he talking about?"

Lee was chewing gum and looked unimpressed about the whole thing, as if he had experienced it many times before.

"Yeah," he said. "Don't you know why he's got that TV in his office?"

"No."

"It's usually just tuned to one channel."

"What's that, the YES Network?"

"No, the OTB station."

Lee led me into Torre's office and showed me how to decipher the race results, which were flashing across the bottom of the screen. He wrote out the horses and track numbers on a piece of paper.

"This is what he wants to know," Lee said, pointing to the list. "These are the winning horses." Then he handed it to me.

I jogged up to the dugout and gave the race results to Torre, who grabbed the paper and studied it like his life depended on it. Here was the man considered the greatest contemporary baseball manager with his nose in a bunch of horse results! When he had discovered the information he wanted, he turned to Zimmer and showed it to him. The older man's eyes lit up, and before I left they were talking excitedly not about the next batter but about the OTB results!

As time went on, Torre's insecurities blossomed into a strange state of mind where he started to become offended if a player *looked* at him the wrong way. This was most evident with Red Sox power hitter Manny Ramirez. When he came to the plate, Ramirez always looked over at the Yankee dugout. Torre started having the idea that he was looking at *him*. I guess he forgot that every player has a few favorite things they always do when it comes to preparing to hit. For example, A-Rod holds the bat out with one hand like a samurai sword. Kevin Youkilis makes circles overhead. Well, Ramirez would go through his routine at the plate where he would lean backward and forward, take off his helmet, and stare at the Yankee dugout. It was probably an unconscious action that had no meaning, but Torre and Willie Randolph took it personally.

"What the hell is he staring at?" Torre would say.

Suspicion tends to spread, especially when a group of men are working together. So it's not surprising that Torre's anger rippled over to others.

"That's horseshit," Zimmer would say.

Posada would jump in with some comment. Jeter would run to

the railing to see what was going on. And to make matters worse, when Manny walked, he would stroll right by the Yankees' dugout and give that famous stare. It seemed to drive Torre crazy.

And yet this is exactly what endeared him to us. He was so much a Yankee guy—so devoted to winning—that he even got annoyed at the way opposing players *looked* at him. You've got to love a guy like that.

Even if it *was* eccentric.

On the evening of October 19, 2004, I happened to overhear Torre make a mistake that would cost us the American League Championship Series. We had just lost Game 6, and Torre closed the door so no media was around. There was no team meeting. It was quiet and tense inside the clubhouse. The next day the Yankees would be going into the seventh and deciding game against the Red Sox and Torre didn't know who to select for his starting pitcher.

Unfortunately, his three best choices—Mike Mussina, Jon Lieber, and El Duque—had pitched recently and were out of the running. It was either Javier Vazquez or Kevin Brown. Not an easy decision, especially since Brown was, at best, an uneven postseason starter. Torre was pacing in the clubhouse, trying to think. At one point he sat down next to Kevin Brown and had a few words with him. No reporters saw this, but I was there when Torre, in full uniform, walked into the players' lounge a few minutes later with Mel Stottlemyre. Brown, who had broken his nonpitching hand a month and a half before, was standing at the buffet table with Ruben Sierra. Torre went up to Brown.

"Can you pitch tomorrow?"

Brown put down his sandwich. For a while I thought he had been surprised speechless.

"Give me the ball," he said. "I'll do my best."

"You're on."

Later, Ruben told me that he had almost died when he overheard that exchange.

"Why?"

"Are you kidding me? You don't want a guy who says he'll do his best. You want a guy who says, I'll rip their heads off! You want someone with con-fi-dence."

As it turned out, maybe Brown *didn't* have confidence that night. Because we lost Game 7 by a score of 10–3 and Brown lasted only two innings before Torre realized he had made an error and replaced him.

No matter what happened, though, Torre always had his same calm personality, even as team spirit was falling apart after 2004. In hindsight it's easy to spot, but even then I could see the signs. There was almost a strain or a contest going on in the clubhouse. Players didn't slap each other on the back as much. They stood apart when they were in the locker room. It was like they tried to avoid one another. It was not the same team that had welcomed me into a family atmosphere in 1998. Bernie Williams still played the guitar, but something was different. There was less of a party atmosphere. He wasn't applauded as much, there was less laughter, there was more of a business attitude. Players got dressed together and still talked and joked, but there was none of the buddying up that I remember from the 1990s.

The Skipper was always an easygoing guy, though, approachable and humble. He had an awe-inspiring sense about how to encourage people to work as a team. That ability, combined with his baseball know-how, helped him lead the Yankees to the postseason every year he was with them. In addition, the Godfather was at the helm as the Yankees won four World Series. It was indeed an honor to work with him, even as he struggled with a new group of difficult-to-manage players. I felt sorry when team chemistry broke down after 2001 and he was faced with guys who didn't have the team spirit that *he* always had.

I felt even sorrier when I learned that the Yankees had let Torre go.

9

The Absent-Minded Professor
Bernie Williams

The idea that he might win a batting award wasn't on the top of Bernie Williams's mind on the last day of the 1998 season. To tell you the truth, he had forgotten about it. By the time the seventh inning rolled around he was singing in the shower, unaware of the drama unfolding in Boston and New York that would propel him, within the next few minutes, into the national spotlight.

Joe Torre had taken him out of the game to protect him for the playoffs. Then Torre sat in the dugout to manage the remainder of the contest between the Yankees and the Devil Rays. I was working as a bat boy in the dugout when the wall-mounted telephone rang at 3:02 P.M. Steve Donohue picked up the bulky black metal handset and started yabbering into the line. A trainer with the Yankees, Steve is a relaxed kind of guy who always seems to be trying to lose a few pounds. I thought nothing of the fact that he had answered the phone until I noticed him standing upright, as if he had received a shock.

"Yeah, yeah," he was saying. "Give it a me again . . . Okay, I got 'em right here and I'll pass it along." Talking fast and acting like he was on the phone with the president.

He turned to Torre and told him something I couldn't hear over the noise of the crowd.

"Squeeg," Torre snapped.

That tone of voice!

"Skip?"

"Get Bernie Williams up to the dugout."

"Right away."

He didn't have to tell me to run. His tone of voice said it. *This is fucking important, kid!* I shot down the runway to the clubhouse, but Bernie wasn't there. Which is when I heard singing, a high-pitched voice—unmistakably Bernie's. I turned the corner and entered the shower room.

"Yo, Bernie."

"What's up?"

"Mr. T wants to see you in the dugout."

The shower cut off. A dripping face materialized out of the steam. Brows raised high, Bernie's dark eyes gleamed. He looked at me hard, his jaw dropped, and he said, "Joe wants me? Serious?"

"Yeah."

He wiped water out of his eyes and stepped, naked, up to a locker and grabbed a bath towel. He was drying himself as I followed him into the clubhouse. With every step he was moving faster, as if he had realized that this wasn't an ordinary summons.

Bernie is fast, in fact one of the fastest runners I ever saw round the bases, but in the cramped quarters of the clubhouse he was like a bull in a china shop, stampeding toward his locker.

Something had happened in Boston that neither of us knew about. Minutes earlier in Fenway Park, Red Sox slugger Mo Vaughn had finished up his last at bat for the day, but had *failed* to best Bernie's batting score. Which meant that Bernie Williams was the winner of the 1998 batting award. As soon as the Yankees' front office got word, they telephoned the dugout . . . and Steve Donohue relayed the message to Joe Torre . . . and Torre, without telling me why, sent me to get Bernie.

But Bernie sensed that something was up, something important. *Why else would Torre call him back to the dugout!* Neither of us knew it, but they had already flashed the news on the big Titan-Tron screen in Yankee Stadium:

BERNIE WILLIAMS WINS
1998 BATTING CHAMPIONSHIP

The fans went crazy and began chanting, "Ber-NEE! . . . Ber-NEE!" But he wasn't in uniform! He was stark naked now, in the clubhouse, looking for something in his locker to wear.

Bernie stuck his right foot into a yellow flip-flop with his number 51 on it. They were rubber and he was fumbling and falling off balance as he struggled into the second one, his feet still wet. He could hear the fans chanting his name, and there was no time for his trousers and belt, or for prettying himself up in front of the mirror. He pulled on a pair of Yankee shorts and threw on a T-shirt and a Yankee jacket and tore off through the runway up to the dugout, where the roar of the crowd rose to embrace him.

Torre clapped him on the back and said, "You're the . . ." but the rest of the greeting was lost in the noise from the fans.

"What?"

"You're the *batting champion!*"

Torre made him understand the news, clapped him on the back again, and turned him toward the cheering fans. Bernie stepped out in front of the dugout, before a crowd of more than fifty thousand—in flip-flops and shorts.

Everyone on the team was crying tears of laughter. Yup, another Bernie moment, as they had come to be known. It was a historical moment for his career, and he was dripping wet and standing in front of the world like he was on the beach.

You've probably seen photos of Bernie, or maybe you've seen him play on television, but nothing prepares you for meeting him in person. Taller than he looks in the media, more brutal and muscular, he's actually a quiet, sincere man, almost prayerful. Born in Puerto Rico, he radiates the warmth and friendliness of a native of that outgoing, welcoming commonwealth. One of the most intelligent players I ever met, acquainted with music, art, politics, and science, he still speaks with an excessive number of pauses, as if he were sizing up his audience and trying to see if you were really taking in everything he said. For example, one day he wanted me to put a box in his car. Bat boys and clubbies do favors like this for players all the time, and we don't mind doing them, either. But instead of coming right out and telling me what he wanted, he called me over and then stood there in uniform, key ring in hand, muttering.

"Um . . . listen, um . . ." Then he would click his tongue. *Schlurrrrrrrrp!* "Squeeg, um . . . can you do me a big favor, and . . . um . . ." Sucking in his tongue. *Schlirrrrrrrp!*

Just spit it out, Bernie! For crying out loud, just say what's on your mind. It takes him two minutes to make what should be a thirty-second request.

Other times he would ask me for help on the field: "Um . . . Do me a favor and . . . um . . . play catch with me," he would say on many occasions, as if my doing it were a special service for him. He liked playing catch with me because even though I was fifteen years old, I had a strong arm and sharp eyes and could give him a good workout. It was an honor for me to be there in the outfield with Bernie Williams. Compared with other Major League outfielders—not with *me*—he had a weak arm, so he always liked to work on his throwing. We would be out there during batting practice for fifteen minutes before a game, doing maybe thirty throws. Bernie liked practicing the long toss, where he would throw high to me, rehearsing the same kind of throw that he'd have to make in a game—from the outfield all the way to center field.

"Um . . . Say, can you . . . um . . . go back a little more," he'd tell me.

I used to throw directly to him, but he would often one-bounce it to me. Not because he couldn't reach me—he could do that easily enough—but because an outfielder needs to be able to have the option of throwing a one-bounce so that other players can intercept it if a play at home plate looks iffy. Often, too, a bounce will arrive faster than a ball lobbed high.

One thing I'll say about Bernie is that he sure could haul real estate. He could cover left to center field and make it look effortless. He could also track a ball well. Nowhere was this better demonstrated than during his memorable catch to end the 2000 World Series. I was in the dugout and biting my nails with the rest of the lineup in the bottom of the ninth as the Mets sent Mike Piazza to bat against Mariano Rivera. There were two outs, the score was 4–2 Yankees, but Piazza was aiming to tie the game. Mariano delivered the pitch—his unhittable cutter—but there was a dreaded loud *SMACKKKKKKK!* as Piazza blasted it toward the outfield. The sound of that hit was like a knife to the heart of every one of us in the Yankee dugout. We leaped up and ran to the railing, looking skyward, expecting the worst. It was a deep, high fly ball and we were afraid it would sail out of the park. For some unknown reason Bernie Williams was relaxed, backtracking like the old Yankee Clipper. He raised his glove over his head and the ball plopped right into it. Done deal! The crowd at Shea Stadium was stunned into silence. Bernie went down on one knee, as if thanking an unseen heavenly power, and he took off his cap and saluted the baseball gods. But the only cheering was coming from us in the dugout since Bernie's catch had won the World Series for us in the Mets' home court.

When he wasn't winning a World Series for you, Bernie was usually napping. It got to be a standard joke around the clubhouse when he'd wake up from one of his siestas.

"Hey, Bernie," Jeet would say. "You ready to work?"

"Look at this!" Posada would chime in. "Bernie woke up!"

I knew more about his napping patterns than anyone since I was the guy responsible for waking him. In those days, when games started at 7:30 P.M., he would tell me, "Wake me up twenty minutes before the game." I was his human alarm clock. He would stretch out in the players' lounge, which was off-limits to visitors and media. There were a couple of TVs in there, three coffee tables, and two couches. He'd lay down in full uniform with his bat beside him. Once he closed his eyes he would be snoozing within minutes.

One day Tim Raines started clowning around, telling Jeter that Bernie was a sleepyhead, and teasing Bernie about his naps. Bernie didn't let it faze him; he just rolled over and turned a deaf ear. I wish that just once George Steinbrenner had caught him! That would have been fun. You weren't supposed to sleep during work time. If there had been an issue with his performance, of course, it might have been another matter, but Bernie could perform along with the best of them; in fact, the naps energized him. He'd go to sleep an hour before a game and get a good solid snooze in before he had to play. Well, on this occasion, Tim Raines caught me waking Bernie, who was sprawled on the couch. I tapped Bernie on the shoulder, which was my usual method of awakening him. Bernie blinked open his eyes, sat up, and looked at the wall clock.

"Bernie, come on, man!" Tim cried.

Raines couldn't believe that a star like Bernie was so casual that he was napping before a game. But this ribbing didn't faze Bernie in the least. He got up and smiled and went about his business. A few minutes later he would go out and play like a superstar. When we had batting practice, the team had to be on the field by 4:15 P.M., but Bernie was in Group B, so technically he didn't have to be there until 4:35 P.M. He would always cut it close, napping from 3:45 P.M. to 4:20 P.M. During night games, he would nap from 6:35 P.M. to 7:10 P.M., and hustle to get out for the 7:30 P.M. start. The only time he wouldn't nap was if we had a day game.

One afternoon I was running an errand for another player and I had to leave the stadium to go to the player's parking lot. I couldn't make it back in time to wake Bernie. As a result he was late for batting practice. He didn't let it bother him, and he never reprimanded me for my error. If only more people could be like him the world would, I'm sure, be a more peaceful place.

Despite Bernie's wide-ranging interests and his ability to talk about any topic under the sun, he was often forgetful about little things and would zone out at the most inconvenient times, which is why we used to think of him as the absent-minded professor. ("A lot of times, Bernie doesn't know where he is," Derek Jeter would say.) One day we were at a party at Ramiro Mendoza's house after he left the Yankees to play for the Red Sox. A number of Yankee players were in attendance because they were still friends despite the fact that Mendoza was now with our biggest rival. Many players were very religious, and on this occasion we were gathered for an informal prayer meeting. Mariano Rivera was standing in the middle of the living room, trying to get Bernie's attention. But good old Bernie, who was sitting on the couch with me, was lost in his own world, playing a video game.

"Come on, Bernabé," Mariano was saying. "We're ready to pray."

I got to my feet and started laughing to myself to see Bernie so absorbed in a kid's game.

"Yeah, this is cool," he was saying.

In his own reality.

Another time he forgot his son at Yankee Stadium. This is a classic Bernie moment and one that we still talk about whenever I get together with players who knew him. After games Torre would let children come into the clubhouse to see their dads and fool around in the players' lounge, which we had set up with ice cream and games to entertain kids. Wives weren't allowed, just children. On this occasion Bernie was in the shower, and his son, who was about seven, was playing a video game. Bernie came out, got dressed, did an interview, and then grabbed his keys and got into his car and started driving home. He was halfway there when it dawned on him that he was alone in the car. Whoops! He looked in the rearview mirror. He turned his head to glance behind him. Nope, not in the backseat either . . . Where *is* that son of mine? Finally he flipped on his cell phone and called the clubhouse.

Joe Lee got the call. He was talking on one of those old-fashioned wall phones, and I happened to see him break into a grin and put his hand over his mouth to prevent himself from laughing. He left the phone dangling and started walking out of the room.

"What is it?" I said.

"Bernie. 'Check to see if my son is at the stadium,' he said. Can you believe it! He left without him."

We both started laughing.

"Where is he?" Joe asked.

"He's probably in the lounge."

Robbie overheard us and started laughing, too. We went to look in the first place we knew the boy would be: in front of the television. Sure enough, he was having fun, the stick control of a video game in his hands, eyes glued to the screen. Joe Lee went back to tell Bernie to come and collect his son. Meanwhile, I broke the news to the boy, explaining that his dad had accidentally gone home without him but would be returning in half an hour. A chip off the old block, the boy was as nonchalant as his dad. He shrugged and kept playing.

Bernie chuckled when he came in. We all nodded to ourselves. Another one for the books. A Bernie moment for sure—like the time he forgot his wife, Waleska Williams, at the stadium and had to come back and get *her*.

Despite his problem with short-term memory, Bernie had a fine long-term memory, as I can prove from an incident that happened recently. I got word that there was to be a book signing and that the public could meet Bernie at a local bookstore on the Grand Concourse in the Bronx. He would be signing autographs for two hours. Tina Lewis, who had helped me get the bat boy job, called me and we went together to say hello to our old friend. She and many of the Bleacher Creatures knew him personally, and I was eager to catch up, not having seen him for five years. The store manager didn't believe we knew Bernie, and he refused to let us in. We had to wait on line with hundreds of fans since they were only letting in five people at a time. But as soon as our turn came and we got inside, Bernie jumped up and came over and gave me a hug. We started talking about the good old days. When the media saw Bernie hugging me, they knew they had a story. FAMILY REUNION was the headline the next day in the *Bronx Times*.

———

Probably my favorite Bernie Williams memory, though, comes from the many times he would sneak into Yankee Stadium on his motorcycle. Players weren't supposed to take unreasonable risks since the Yankees needed them to be in good shape in order to get back their investment. This is why Steinbrenner frowned on Jeter partying late. But Bernie's love of motorcycles overcame his fear of being called on the carpet for a violation of his contract. He used to drive in through the loading dock to avoid detection, hiding his bike in the batting cage. He would remove his helmet and flame-retardant jumpsuit, stash them on top of the bike, then cover everything with a tarpaulin so that he wouldn't get into trouble for coming to work like a Hell's Angel.

Sometimes we would be in the clubhouse and would hear the roar of his motorcycle. I would open the door and there would go Bernie . . . in a trail of dust.

The thing he feared most was being seen with a motorcycle helmet. As anyone with a motorcycle can tell you, when you're away from your bike, the biggest giveaway that you're a motorcyclist isn't the jeans, boots, or even the leather jacket. It's the helmet that marks you as one of *them*. The problem was that sometimes his absent-mindedness would cause him to forget and he'd have his helmet with him and his motorcycle suit on in the clubhouse. One day I saw him sneaking out, walking on tiptoe through the back hallway.

"Bernie?"

"Hey, Luigi."

"What're you up to?"

"Listen, I'm trying to get out."

"Out?"

"Yeah. Is there another way out of here?"

I thought for a minute. Because of my job, I was familiar with all the hallways and exits.

"Yeah, I know a way."

"Show me, will ya?"

"Follow me, then."

I led him to a wooden door. Inside was a built-in closet criss-crossed by steel wire spiral ventilation tubes through which lint and hot air from the laundry room vented. The room was like an old cellar from a horror movie, everything covered with scary-looking dust and fuzz. In some places it was caked so thick it looked like gray pudding.

I didn't go into the room, I just opened the door and pointed the way. Then I watched a most unusual sight: Bernie began inching sideways through the narrow space, trying not to get lint on his black motorcycle uniform. He moved on tiptoe, peering ahead into darkness. A dim paleness at the far end marked the exit. Toward this weak light Bernie moved, silent and careful, until he disappeared into a gray cloud of dust.

I closed the door.

Yep. Another Bernie moment.

10

Who Says I'm Upset?
Jorge Posada

"You see that stuff?"

"Yeah, Sado."

"This is important."

"What's up?"

He glanced left and right and lowered his voice. "Make sure that no one touches my helmet." He nodded for emphasis. "And don't *ever* wash it."

I stood dumbfounded in front of Jorge Posada. Who in the name of heaven is going to *want* to touch that filthy helmet, anyway? I was thinking. And the word *filthy* is no exaggeration: He had such an aversion to washing it that the inside of the thing had become encrusted with pine tar and grease. Since I was the only one he trusted to bring his equipment up to the dugout, I saw the decrepit state that his helmet was in every day. As the years rolled by it got worse, until I felt astonished that he could fit his head into the thing, it was so caked and plastered with gunk.

Because he was a switch-hitter, he actually had two helmets, and they were *both* in the same condition.

It never occurred to me until after I left the Yankees that some of the players I was working with were eccentric. I was so wrapped up in my job responsibilities that it wasn't until years later that I had time to reflect and see them objectively. Take Posada, for example. Superstitious. Like a man afraid to step on a crack. I can't account for his behavior in any other way than to call him the most superstitious man on the team. But we're not talking fear of black cats or the number thirteen. Instead, his worries all centered around his catcher's equipment—the face mask, shin guard, throat guard, knee guards, and chest protector.

A catcher is the most covered-up guy on a team, wearing the kind of protective gear that makes him resemble a knight in armor. In many ways, a catcher is the most removed from reality, too, behind all that tech foam and high-strength aluminum. Maybe that's why Posada felt unreasonable fears about anyone touching his stuff, to the point where he would say to me, "Make sure that nobody even goes *near* it except me." I would have to follow his directions to the letter and bring his collection of equipment to the bench in the dugout and have it waiting for him. He'd walk out with only a glove, then dress himself for battle. Warrior that he was, his superstition only made his little quirks stand out all the more, in sharp contrast with his otherwise perfect sense of duty and obligation.

But you had to see him with Derek Jeter to get a true sense of the man. They always entered the clubhouse together. When the door opened and Jeter came in, Posada was always at his side. And Jeter was always on the right, Posada on the left. I can't account for how that happened, but that's how they entered together.

"What's up, biatches?"

"What's up, mother-uckers?"

It was the same routine every time: the first line Jeter's, the second Posada's. They hung around together and were pals, and in many ways they were similar. Sometimes I thought Posada might have made an even better team captain because Jeter was silent and quiet so often, almost like an observer rather than a participant. In contrast, Posada was quick to let you know what he thought; in fact, he was often *unable* to keep his thoughts to himself, especially when strong emotions got involved or if it was a matter of team pride and winning. Naturally, Jeet wanted to win, too; it was just that he approached winning in a more restrained and silent manner, often with a look or body language—even a simple frown or a shake of his head—to indicate approval or disapproval of a player's actions. Posada, on the other hand, would come right out and say, "You're no good! You're not playing to win! You don't care!" His enthusiasm and energy were what the Yankees needed to push slacking players into action. Posada would have made a good captain . . . except for one thing, which I'll get to in a moment.

To look at Posada is to see opposites put together: Built like a rock, with arms cut and muscular, a thick neck, and quadriceps like a football player, he nevertheless had a girl's butt and a softness in his eyes that didn't seem to fit with his athletic abilities. You could see sensitivity in his expression, a real love of the game, and a deep liking for the competitive environment in which he thrived.

He was organized, too, which is a trait you want in a leader. Jeter was organized in a different way, gifted with a keen awareness of what had to be done and when. But Jeter's locker wasn't neat the way Posada's was. In fact, Jorge and Matsui were probably the biggest neat freaks in the clubhouse. I never had to pick up socks or shoes in front of their lockers, never had to throw any wastepaper or unused newspapers away from their area. Posada also had a let's-get-the-job-done attitude that would have served him well in the army.

But like an ugly scratch on a new car, there was one very visible flaw in the character of the great catcher: No one on the team could take the title of hothead from him. Even Paul O'Neill, the cooler basher, didn't have Jorge's temper, which would flare up like road rage if anyone on the team—or even on *other* teams—did any-thing to annoy him. And he got annoyed at very specific things. It wasn't bad manners or sloppiness that ticked him off; instead, it was what he perceived to be not playing up to your capacity. Strangely enough, this sharp sense of what a player *could* do was what might have made him a great team captain, but he got so an-noyed that he wouldn't simply take a player aside and coach him quietly, the way Torre would, or the way Mel Stottlemyre would. Instead, Jorge would blow up at the guy, flinging abuse on his head, and using strong language: "You fucking got no heart! You don't know how to compete! You don't care! You don't *want* to win!" To hear him was to know that he had slipped into one of his tirades, and there was almost no stopping him on these occasions.

Posada's hotheadedness often caused him to storm into the dugout when he struck out and cry "Fuck!" and bang his helmet into the cubbyhole. He was like many players in this regard, unable to contain his frustration. But his temper would often overboil and get the better of him, and there were times when he couldn't put the lid on it and he had to be stopped from do-ing harm to himself and others. Jeter knew his friend well and, in fact, teased him in an attempt to help him let off steam. If a player would say something to Jeter about Posada, even something complimentary, then after Posada arrived on the scene, Jeter would start in with his ribbing.

"Oh, boy, Sado, wait until you hear what Raines was just saying about you."

Posada would look up, worried. "What? What did he say?"

"Man, it was so bad I can't repeat it."

"Are you serious?"

"No, no," Raines would say. "I didn't say nothing."

"Yes, he did. Go on, Tim. Tell Jorge to his face what you said about him."

"It wasn't nothing."

"Tell me," Posada would beg.

Until after a while it would dawn on him, like a fog lifting, that his best friend was pulling his leg.

But you had to let Posada vent or he would blow up. That's why Jeet used to rib him so much: he was doing him a favor. Yet even if he *did* vent he *still* blew up more often than not. There was really no way to prevent it.

Emotional as he was, the veteran catcher usually channeled his feelings in a constructive direction. He would get angry at something that related to the game—something which, if corrected, might have allowed us to win. Like a child, though, he was unable to control his feelings or hide them inside. In a way it was an attractive quality since his feelings were always about making the team better.

For a guy who was so ready to fly off the handle, he was surprisingly controlled when it came to alcohol. You never saw him down large quantities of beer or hard liquor the way Ruben or Coney would. In the eight years I knew him, and through all the late-night drinking binges in hotels, bars, and nightclubs, there was only one time that Posada had too much to drink.

It was in St. Louis after a regular season game, when Ruben, Jeter, and I were in a bar together. Posada had two beers and then a third and a fourth, and he started wobbling. I think it was partly that he couldn't hold his liquor the way some of the other guys could. "Okay, you had enough, man," Ruben said, putting his arm around Posada's shoulder. "Come on, I'll call you a taxi and make sure you get back to the hotel all right." Jeter was sitting in a booth with two girls who looked like kamikaze pilots, and he smiled across the bar at his friend. Ruben paid for the cab and made sure Posada got in okay and gave the driver instructions where to take him. But for a baseball player on a team that liked to celebrate into the wee hours, Posada was the most straitlaced guy I knew. That one episode was the exception, not the rule.

I was there for the historic transition when Posada was being groomed to be the next starting catcher by Joe Girardi. I used to see them talking together and hear Joe making suggestions. Posada was a good listener. He treated Girardi like a mentor, attending to his suggestions as if they had the potential to transform his life. Before you knew it, a slight transformation started taking place. Posada began walking and moving more like Girardi every day. He took to wearing his chest protector and carrying around his shin guards and face mask, wandering through the clubhouse with all this gear.

After Posada took over as starting catcher in 1999, he began to amass a record not only as a terrific catcher but also as a batter, so much so that he's often compared with Ivan Rodriguez, the greatest hitting catcher of the contemporary era.

Posada used to sit in the dugout like he was frozen solid, eyes staring forward. I thought something was wrong. I would see him doing this every day. At first I thought he was spacing out, because his eyes never wavered left or right. But after a few weeks I figured out what he was doing. He was focusing on what was happening on the field. I'm convinced that part of the reason he became such a good hitter is that he would sit in the dugout and study pitchers. Other players might consult coaches, look at videos, or read stat books, but Posada used to sit there for hours, eyes burning out toward the pitcher's mound as if he had supervision and could see the way the pitcher was holding the seams of the baseball. You didn't want to break his concentration when he was studying a pitcher.

All his studying paid off in 2003 when he tied Yogi Berra's record for the most home runs hit by a Yankee catcher in one season. He had a total of thirty home runs to his credit. But despite his success as a catcher and slugger, Posada was under a great deal of stress at home, and often it would erupt into conflict with another player, especially guys who were a lot like him. In some strange way, it was almost as if he wanted to pick a fight with . . . himself.

One Friday in 2000 before a home game I was going down the runway to put bats and equipment in the on-deck circle, and coming toward me I could hear the sound of two guys arguing. I was carrying so many bats that it was difficult for me to look up without dropping them, but when I managed to do it, I saw an amazing sight.

Posada and El Duque were walking side by side in the narrow hallway, coming toward me, heading to the clubhouse after an inning, speaking in heated tones in Spanish, and they were at each other's throats.

"Cut your shit out," Posada was saying. His eyes were watery. That was the strangest part. Even though he was arguing with the new pitcher, yelling at the top of his voice, he looked like he was about to cry.

"You can't talk to me like that," El Duque said. And *he* was on the point of crying, too.

"You don't know what the fuck I'm going through. My son's medical condition is on my mind day and night. I can't sleep. I can't think. I can't concentrate."

In a bizarre twist of fate for one so talented and physically skilled, Posada's son had been diagnosed shortly after birth with a rare medical condition that required numerous surgeries. The psychological pressure on Posada was immense. I saw how it affected him emotionally in the clubhouse. After you take off the uniform there's life beyond baseball, and Posada is still very much a family man. Whether we won or lost a game, he had the condition of his son weighing heavily on his mind.

But El Duque, who was a rookie at the time, was also under pressure. Having escaped from Cuba in a small boat on Christmas Day in 1997, he was weighed down by nightmares of his sea voyage. He had come through shark-infested waters from the Communist island, and there were times when he had flashbacks to the incidents surrounding his misadventures.

"You don't know what the fuck *I've* been through," El Duque insisted. They didn't even look at me as they passed, they were so involved in their argument.

Theirs was a complex love/hate relationship. We used to joke that they were like the Odd Couple. They were happiest when they were actually on the field pitching and catching together. They also got along well on days when they *weren't* working as a pitching-catching pair, and on these nonworking days they were like a dating couple: talking, laughing, even giggling together like girls. But off the field *on game days*, when Posada had to catch El Duque . . . Oh, boy, you didn't want to be around! They would fight like cats and dogs all the time. Nobody could explain why.

No one saw or heard their argument in the runway that afternoon except me. I remember wondering why they were so noisy as they approached, and then why they were fine and working like clockwork on the diamond during the next inning. The fans watching them pitch and catch had no idea. Nobody but me knew that there was a pressure cooker boiling in the background, waiting to explode.

Sure enough, next day the explosion occurred. It was a Saturday morning game, and El Duque was working out in the clubhouse with dumbbells. Meanwhile, Posada was talking with a group of people by his locker. There was media inside the clubhouse, too. I was at my locker, and despite there being four concrete pillars in the middle of the room, I could see everything. El Duque walked toward Posada with two light weights in one hand. Posada was sitting with his back to El Duque, a creatine shake in hand. All of a sudden there was a terrific *Whummmmmmmmp-Clank!* It was the unforgettable sound of El Duque, in a fit of resentment, hitting Posada's back with the dumbbells! *Incredible!*

Posada sprang to his feet. The two men squared off and started scuffling and cursing: "Fuck you!" . . . "Fuck you!" . . . "Fuck you!"

Joe Torre hurried out of his office and tried to calm them down, but it was too much for him. Paul O'Neill and Tino Martinez were grabbing the guys, attempting to break it up. One of the clubhouse kids, Mitch, accidentally got in the middle and caught a black eye. Shakes were thrown, dumbbells went flying, picture frames fell from the walls. They went at it like two kids in a schoolyard and had to be separated by a gang of other players.

The clubhouse was in shock, and Joe Torre kicked out the media. Because you don't expect that from Posada, or from El Duque, for that matter. Although he yells a lot and has a quick temper, Posada's not a guy who gets into fistfights as a general rule, and neither is El Duque. But somehow these two rubbed each other the wrong way. Posada is a fierce competitor but not an antagonistic guy if you don't do anything to annoy him. It had to be because his son's problems were taking a toll on him. And then you had El Duque, whose temper could easily get the better of him.

After the guys pulled them apart, Paul O'Neill stood between the two with his arms outstretched, looking from one to the other. Every time Sado or El Duque would try to make for the other guy, Paul would call them off.

"Hey! Leave him alone! Back off! Back off!"

El Duque tilted his head down like a matador, pointing at Sado.

"This ain't over," he said in Spanish. "You embarrassed me in front of everybody, and you know it—talking shit about me. That's why I swung at you. If I get fired or traded, you're not going to see the end of me."

He wanted to fight him after the game!

"Meet me in the parking lot after the last inning, and we'll finish this."

Mike Borzello, the bullpen catcher, walked into the room after the quarrel. When he saw the tail end of the commotion, he was confused and he was asking, "What in hell are these guys saying?"

Everybody was asking me the same thing. They wanted to know what the fight was about since I was one of the only people there at the time who could translate what was being said. Posada was speaking English, or I should say *cursing* in English—there were a lot of fuck-you's going around—so the question people kept raising was, "What did El Duque say?"

"It's not good," I told them. "You don't want to know. They're at each other's throats." I explained to Mike Borzello, who happened to be Joe Torre's godson, that I had seen them arguing when coming up the ramp the day before. That bad feeling had apparently simmered below the surface all night, only to erupt into the mess we saw before us.

Thankfully cooler heads prevailed. But you'd think Posada would learn a lesson and take steps to curb his temper, wouldn't you? Well, it wasn't long before he got into another conflict, this time with Pedro Martinez, the Red Sox pitcher.

It began at a game in New York in which Martinez wasn't pitching. Because it was his day off he had a lot of free time on his hands, and when it came to Pedro Martinez *that* meant trouble. He was in the visiting team dugout making fun of Posada's ears. Willie Randolph, the Yankee bench coach, tapped me on the shoulder and nodded his head toward the Boston dugout. "Take a look at this, Luigi. Can you believe it!" I was directly across the field in the Yankee dugout, and I had a ringside view. I was stunned to see Pedro Martinez, in full Red Sox uniform, pushing his ears out and then pointing at his backside, as if to say Posada had big ears and a big butt. Posada was warming up and did his best to ignore the jokester. But Pedro knew how to push buttons and he kept at it, standing on the top step, out of view of the fans but in direct line of sight to Posada.

Posada knew better than to look at him and lose focus. He was already on the field, the starting catcher of the game. But Pedro did this every time the Yankees faced the Red Sox, and it annoyed Posada. He's only human and, of course, it used to get to him.

"Sado," Martinez started yelling. "Woo, woo, woo, woo." Shouting like a monkey, he kept pushing his ears out and pointing at his bum.

"What a fucking jerk," Willie said. He looked at Martinez and frowned. "He's a fucking clown."

Pedro was laughing so much that we could see his front teeth bared in an aggressive smile as he taunted Posada and tried to get him off his game.

This guy was always on Posada, and you knew one day our big-hearted catcher would snap. That day came in Game 3 of the 2003 American League Championship Series.

I was in Boston for the game despite not having to work. I was such a baseball aficionado that I followed the team from New York to Boston and went to Fenway Park. Pedro Martinez used to throw baseballs close to the Yankees' batters, and it was no surprise when he tried this tactic. In the top of the fourth he hit Karim Garcia in the back.

Posada bounded out of the dugout and began screaming at Martinez, pointing at him. He had put up with enough of Martinez's taunting and he yelled across the field at the man, "Do that shit to *me!*"

Martinez turned to him and pointed at his (Martinez's) head and then at Posada, as if to say, "You're next, Little Man! You're asking for it now. Next opportunity I get I'm going to bean *you*." Martinez later denied this interpretation, explaining why he had pointed at his own head: "When I pointed to the head it wasn't precisely to tell him that I wanted to *hit* him in the head. Nah. He's a human being, he has a family, and I'm a professional. It was because he cursed my mom. I was telling him, 'I'll *remember* that.'"

Although Martinez claims that Posada cursed his mother, Posada's not that type of guy. He was just warning Pedro not to pitch so close that he hit Yankee batters. Besides, it was only natural for him to yell at Martinez because the guy was always picking on him and mocking him.

In all fairness, Posada wasn't the only hothead on the team. The highlight of the game occurred when Yankee bench coach Don Zimmer got so worked up that he went after Martinez. He hated Martinez and thought it was a disgrace to the game the way he acted like a clown. He was just waiting for a chance to explode, and it came in the bottom of the fourth inning when Roger Clemens fired a high inside fastball at Manny Ramirez. Incensed, Ramirez charged the mound, which brought both dugouts onto the field. During the ensuing melee, Zimmer rushed out and tried to throw a punch at Martinez, who knocked the seventy-two-year-old Zimmer to the ground. Later Zimmer went to the hospital for X-rays, but he wasn't hurt. He eventually apologized to Pedro for trying to take a swing at him, and Pedro apologized for knocking him down. But the civility of apologies never seemed to cool the rivalry between Posada and Pedro, or between the Yankees and the Red Sox.

Later that year I was promoted to clubhouse attendant, and ever since I've been troubled by a question that baseball fans must consider if they love the Yankees the way I do. Why is it, I have asked myself, that Posada lashed out at David Wells, one of the best-performing pitchers he ever worked with?

This question is especially appropriate when you think about how vital Wells was to the Yankees in 2003, when he had a 15–7 record. It was in this year, too, that Wells racked up his 200th career win. The man was on a roll, and yet despite this stellar performance, Posada freaked out one day and attacked him.

On this particular afternoon, Wells was pitching, and it was going badly for him. Such an occurrence, statistically speaking, was unusual. But you can't be perfect every time, it's just not possible. Apparently Posada didn't think that way. He's very competitive, and for him winning is an obsession. The only problem was that Posada often took his desire to win to extravagant lengths, as in the case with Wells that day. Wells was coming off the field into the clubhouse, intending to refresh himself in the middle of the game. He had a towel around his neck. He was red as a lobster from his inning of pitching, and he was trying to control his feelings of humiliation and failure at having not lived up to his own expectations during that dismal game. Posada was walking behind him. I happened to be in the clubhouse, carrying a stack of clean towels to put in Joe Torre's office. All of a sudden, Posada started yelling at Wells. Posada is an inch shorter at six foot two, but he looked taller at that moment because he was furious.

"You're fucking giving up! I read your body language. You're not even trying."

Wells spun on his heels. "Get out of my face!"

"You're not putting yourself into it."

Wells turned even redder. He took the towel off his shoulders and squared off, facing Posada.

Posada inched closer.

"You don't give a *damn* about this team!"

"Okay," Wells said. "Let's settle this between you and me. Let's fucking *do* this!" His hands were balled into fists.

I got dry in the throat I was so nervous. Alone with these two, I was thinking, Who can I call? They're going to start fighting! I'm trying to scream for Robbie, but no sounds are coming out of my mouth. It's a ghost town in the clubhouse and there's no one who would hear me even if I *could* get a word out, which I couldn't. I felt like I was in a nightmare, unable to stop a catastrophe. They were just about to start throwing punches.

"You wanna do this?" Wells said. His face was blotched red.

Posada put his nose right up to Wells's and it looked like a fight was about to start.

Suddenly Jeter materialized, moving swiftly between them, saying, "Cut this shit out, fellas."

Posada and Wells were beginning to shove one another. Jeter

had to put his hands out to keep them from coming to blows. Sweat was running down Posada's face into his eyes, which were blazing at Wells. The standoff continued until finally Jeter steered them toward their respective lockers. Next inning, they went out to pitch and catch and actually seemed to be functioning okay together. Wells later apologized to Posada for suggesting that they should fight. Yet Posada had started the conflict by criticizing his teammate when Wells was down.

It was as if Posada felt the weight and responsibility for winning so personally that he needed to tell any player what to do if that guy wasn't, in his opinion, contributing enough toward the win. When he thought Wells was slacking off, he couldn't keep it to himself. If only Posada had been able to control his temper a little more, he might actually have been a more effective team captain, in my opinion, than Jeter. Because some of these players *needed* someone to bark at them now and then.

11

The Stuntman of Yankee Stadium
Paul O'Neill

Tall and rugged, with a long step and broad shoulders, the man heading back to the dugout is riled up. Well aware that things could get dangerous in the next few seconds, I move away from the entrance. When he strikes out—or in some other way doesn't live up to his own high expectations—Paul O'Neill is liable to start throwing things.

Little do fans realize but those who work with him can actually read him like a book, even to the point where we can predict when he's going to explode into a rage. That's the advantage of having worked side by side with this complex right fielder. Now, as I watch him approach from home plate, where he just struck out, humiliating himself in front of more than 50,000 fans, I can see the telltale signs that he's going to launch into one of his famous cooler-busting outrages. He always gives bat boys fair warning—but it's all in gestures, and it begins with his helmet. When he's halfway to the dugout he takes it off and holds it by the peak. This is the first sign. I brace myself, waiting for the second. When he's five yards away, it comes: He throws his helmet to the floor of the dugout, all the way at the end, so that the bat boys can retrieve it. Now I know what's coming next—the cooler.

Sure enough, as if he's playing a part in a dramatic production that has been carefully choreographed, he steps into the dugout and everyone clears to make room for him. At six foot four he's tall enough to touch the ceiling, and he reaches out with both arms to embrace the water cooler as if it were an old friend. Then, lugging the heavy box up over the railing, he hurls it onto the field, where it smashes open, spilling ice cubes and drinks onto the grass. No one says anything to him, but we bat boys know what's next. Without a word, he picks up a stack of plastic cups and flings them onto the floor. Don Zimmer used to laugh at it. But not us. Because we'll have clean-up work to do during the game, and that's never fun.

The big misunderstanding in the media was that Paul O'Neill was a hot-tempered player, and that was pretty much the size of it. The truth is that the quirky right fielder had a dual personality, part of which included emotional outbursts and cooler throwing, which confused the clubhouse and amused fans. His fiery behavior, however, was only half of the story. In fact, O'Neill was very pleasant and talkative with teammates when things went well. He only got depressed when the Yankees lost or when he didn't live up to his own high expectations. For O'Neill baseball wasn't a game, it was a life-or-death contest. And it was this obsession with winning that led him to act like a man possessed.

Unlike Posada, who curses at others, O'Neill curses at *himself* in the clubhouse. He walks around in a haze, muttering, "You fucking suck!" One time he went 0 for 4 and in his last at bat he struck out, something he hates to do. He ran to the dugout. I glanced at Paulie as he passed by. (That was his nickname.) I'm ten feet from him and I can see the expression on his face that is invisible to the cameras and the crowd, and I can hear what he's saying to himself. There's a knot between his brows, and despite the fact that he has his glove up to cover his mouth, I can read that expression of frustration and disappointment. "Fuck!" he yells into the glove. He passes me at a run. "Fuck. Fuck. You're horseshit." An umpire hears him and his eyebrows go up. His own worst critic, he tongue-lashes himself until he reaches right field.

But it doesn't end there. He can't cool off, can't let it go. He's got to hang on to it and work it off physically. Unfortunately for me, he singles *me* out to be his catching partner. I'm sixteen years old and much shorter, but it's part of my job to do what Major League Baseball players request during a game, and I jog out onto the field with him. Who can speak truthfully about the difficulties of playing catch with a professional baseball player who is in a fury with himself and working out his distress with unseen demons? If only I could explain it to you so that you could feel it the way I did. Paulie begins throwing lasers to me, fastballs that POP! into my glove with the force of a tackling lineman, throwing me off balance. I have my back to home plate, and O'Neill is facing me, zinging them faster and faster until my hand feels like it's starting to blister. Then he hurls a high throw that I know I'm going to miss, even though I give it my all and jump to try to snag it. Sure enough, it goes whizzing by, heading toward home plate—where Posada is warming up, catching—nearly beaning the pitcher. Now O'Neill is cursing *me* for flubbing his misthrow. I'm in a panic, I can't keep up with this guy: not with his emotional ups and downs, and not with his furious warm-ups where he tries to vent his feelings with wild throws.

As I head back to the dugout, John Hirschbeck, the first-base umpire, says, "Is Paul O'Neill always like that?" He recognized that the guy was wailing on me, a short little kid doing my best to help him.

"Yeah," I said. "Well, you know how he is."

The umpire nodded and said, "Don't worry. I'll talk to him for you."

I guess he really *did* talk with him and make him aware that he was ten times stronger than me and that I wasn't built to jump for those high throws or withstand the fury of repeated fastballs, especially ones fired off to try to let him vent his anger and frustration. In my mind I can hear the soothing voice of Mr. Hirschbeck dropping words of wisdom into Paulie's ear. And good old Paulie, who's really got a heart of gold and is a terrific sensitive soul underneath all his erratic behavior, I can imagine him listening and accepting the advice of this veteran umpire. "You've got to be aware that this is just a kid, Paulie. You know he can't keep up with you." Then I imagine the look of recognition appearing in Paulie's eyes. Hell, yeah! Sheesh! Of course! What the heck was I *thinking* anyway? And, to my great relief, after that Paul O'Neill became nicer to me.

But he was no less harsh on himself. Indeed, he might have become even harsher on himself since he couldn't take out his frustrations with me and my fellow clubbies anymore. One day in St. Louis he didn't do well, and on top of that the Yankees lost the game. Later, overhearing an announcer saying, ". . . and O'Neill went 0 for 4" he glares up at the TV in the players' lounge and shouts, "You gotta be fucking *kidding* me!"

As luck would have it, it became my responsibility to warn other players about Paulie's quirks. El Duque joined the team in 1998 and we were out at batting practice one afternoon before a home game. He and Paulie were in the field and I had to tell El Duque, "Listen, when you're in right field shagging fly balls, give plenty of room to O'Neill." El Duque turned his sun-bronzed face to me.

"Why's that?"

"Because . . . well, it's like this . . ." How the heck to explain it to him? "It's because he always wants to catch when he's out here since this is his spot of turf during a game. Right field. And everything that goes along with being a right fielder. Just trust me. You gotta let *him* catch anything that comes out this way."

A light went on in El Duque's brown eyes, and he nodded. Oh, yeah, he got it. *The guy's a complete hog for fly balls and you gotta cut him slack.* The cool thing about El Duque was how savvy he could be about other players. I mean, he got along with everyone, with the exception of Posada. I only had to tell him once about Paulie and he gave him space and let him do his thing. But I had to laugh to myself because here I was, a sixteen-year-old kid, giving fielding advice to MLB players. I admit I really loved my life.

Sometimes I thought of Paul O'Neill as a guy who lived in his own private world. When he cursed into his glove, or battered the ice cooler, or flung plastic cups, or had to be the only guy to catch those fly balls in right field during BP, Paulie was doing his own thing and doing it his own way. He wasn't intentionally trying to hurt anyone, as demonstrated by his calmer behavior toward me after the ump talked with him, but he *was* lost to some extent in his own world where the rules were written by him and no one else. I saw him going about his business every day with the professionalism of an athlete on a Major League team, yet somehow existing in another dimension where he was marching to the beat of a different drummer. Demons seemed to hound him, demons and angels, and he had his head in the clouds as he tried to outrun the first and fly high with the second. Driven toward his own brand of perfection, he had the most amazing way of separating himself from reality and from other players so that he could live in a world where things revolved around him and his desire to do good on the field.

There is no better example of this separate world that Paulie lived in than the way he would take practice swings when playing right field. I'm working the right foul line, sitting on a stool not more than a few yards from him, and the first time I saw him do this I thought I was imagining it. Because a right fielder has a responsibility to patrol the space out beyond first base and to make sure that his eye is on the batter so that if a fly ball comes his way he can catch it. But instead of focusing on the action of the game, Paul O'Neill would often do something so unusual and weird that it surprised fans and coaches alike. Just as the pitcher would be winding up for a throw, Paulie would go into this elaborate silent physical action, lifting his right leg, bringing his glove and his other hand together, and then following through with a swing! As if he were batting in the outfield! No one had ever seen anything like this. It drove coaches nuts and made them laugh at the same time. They were always trying to get his attention. And it frightened *me* because he would even do this as pitchers were unleashing a pitch. I mean, the guy was supposed to be planning out in his mind what he would do if a ball was hit in his direction, but he was focused instead on practicing his swing! I was afraid he wouldn't see the ball even if it was hit directly toward him. Most amazing of all was that he was taking these practice swings without a bat and right in the middle of a game. It was the action of a man living in his own private world.

Paulie was dedicated to the team, though, no one can take that from him. Unfortunately, he learned that his father had died just before Game 4 of the 1999 World Series. Of course he could have gone home immediately to take care of family matters, but he showed heart and stayed to play. We won the game—and the series—though the emotional toll was evident when he came back to the dugout after the win in tears. I knew how he felt because my dad was on his deathbed. Paul hugged everyone in the dugout and then went up the runway to the clubhouse, holding his glove up over his eyes. I knew that he was crying not because we had won the series, but because his dad—who he would later write about as a major influence on his taking up a career in baseball—had not lived to see this special day. Paulie had decided to play in that game because he felt that's what his father would have wanted him to do. It was touching to see this emotional side to the man.

Another emotional highpoint of his career came during Game 5 of the 2001 World Series. It was hard emotionally because he had made it known that he would be going into retirement after the series was over. During the last inning the entire stadium began chanting his name. He raised his hat in acknowledgment of their love, and when he came back to the dugout his eyes were watery. I had a chance to see these emotional sides to a passionate and dedicated player, an athlete that George Steinbrenner nicknamed the Warrior because of his undying devotion to the game.

Yes, there was a lighter side to the man, too, and I had the opportunity to catch a glimpse of it that no one else ever saw. One day I was in the clubhouse and a call came in for Bernie Williams. I went to find him, and learned he was with Paulie in the electrical room, where we stored wires, microphones, and lights. I opened the door to a sight I'll never forget. Paulie was sitting behind a drum set, playing a riff on the snare drum, his tongue hanging out of the side of his mouth, his face relaxed and smiling in an expression of pure joy. Bernie Williams was playing electric guitar.

Paulie stopped when he saw me.

"What's up, Squeeg?"

"I have a message for Bernie. It's your wife, on the phone."

"Tell her I'll call her back later."

I nodded and closed the door behind me. The sound of drums and guitar started up again.

But playing drums wasn't O'Neill's only secret. The Warrior had another side to him that no one else knew about. I saw it because I was in the clubhouse when he got dressed. During playoffs he was suffering from some ailment that made him walk around like a zombie. When he stripped off his undershirt and pants, I was startled at the appearance of his body. Wrapped from shoulders to groin in gauze bandages, like the Mummy, he refused to sit out these important games.

O'Neill's split personality included a touching dishonesty. Like a kid telling a white lie, he played a good number of games with aching ribs without ever telling anyone about his deteriorating physical condition. In contrast with players like El Duque—who would complain about a toenail—Paulie willingly inflicted punishment upon his body, as if pain were the price of glory. Upset at himself for not being perfect, he was actually terrified of going on the disabled list.

When I think back on the eight years I spent with the Yankees, I have to say that it was players like O'Neill who made me proud of having worked with the team. Having an opportunity to work alongside someone with his dedication was an inspiration and a thrill. And to see his dual personality was a lesson in human behavior that taught me something about greatness: There is a *human* side to every tower of power. I'm forever thankful that I got to meet the real Paul O'Neill.

Both of them.

12

The Man Who Walked Through Walls
Ramiro Mendoza

Twenty-seven-year-old Ramiro Mendoza walked into a mess on October 18, 1999. The son of a Panamanian fisherman, the young pitcher had been prepared for difficulties in life, but this was ten times more challenging than anything he had ever encountered.

The Red Sox had the bases loaded, there was only one out, and two of Boston's best hitters were coming to bat. Making matters worse, it was Game 5 of the American League Championship Series and Boston was desperate to break the Curse of the Bambino, having failed to get to the World Series for the past eighty-one years. The Yankee relief pitcher also happened to be in Fenway Park, where fans were known to have unfriendly impulses toward his team. That was the mess facing Mendoza when Joe Torre said, "Go get 'em, kid." The thin young man went out to the mound and into the glare of 33,589 Boston fans, almost every one of whom wanted him to fail.

But Mendoza is a man who walks through walls, as I have

come to think of him. The challenge of that inning was what pitchers refer to as a setup for failure, yet he began by firing fast-balls at pinch hitter Scott Hatteberg until he struck him out swinging. The crowd let out a groan of despair and disappointment. But then the fans got revved up again as Trot Nixon prepared to do battle. A tall, dark-eyed bruiser, he stepped up to the plate with a sneer on his face. "It's not just me," he seemed to be saying. "It's me and three runners on base facing you. More than that, it's 33,589 fans and eighty-one years of waiting for this moment facing you, so you cannot . . . you *will not* prevail!"

Everything is focused on these two men, one holding a bat that could make history with a single well-timed swing, the other preparing to throw a baseball that needs to be placed within a fraction of an inch over sixty feet if it is to save the Yankees from crushing humiliation.

With each pitch Mendoza unleashes, the crowd leans forward as if to take pleasure in the devastating blow that a Nixon homer would deliver. But Mendoza is almost arrogant as he repeatedly fires the baseball at his opponent, until Nixon finally pops out to Scott Brosius at third base. Mendoza did so well that Joe Torre let him close the game, one of the few times after 1996 that Mariano was not called upon for this task. The manager and the media had nothing but praise for Mendoza's pitching. "He was awesome," Derek Jeter said. In fact, Mendoza's success allowed the Yankees to clinch the American League pennant that year, and, what's more, to go on to the 1999 World Series, which they would win.

The way Mendoza reacted to the win, though, surprised me. It was as if it were all in a day's work. His modesty probably comes from growing up under difficult circumstances. The first big challenge he had overcome as a young man was the one between poverty and professional baseball. True, other players had broken through that barrier, but not exactly the way Mendoza did. A wild young man, the last of many brothers and sisters, he was found by scouts throwing rocks in Panama and secretly brought to the Yankees' farm system, where he excelled. But despite his winning ways with the Yankees, including sending them to the 1999 World Series, and then participating in the winning team for 1999, he didn't follow the lead of many other players who went out to celebrate in high-class Manhattan nightclubs after their triumphs. Instead, Mendoza preferred to stay close to his new home, Yankee Stadium. Before long he would regularly come to visit me and my family in our two-bedroom apartment on 152nd Street in the Bronx.

My friend Steven Garcia, a tall skinny kid from the neighborhood, recalls those visits: "One day, Luis told me that Ramiro Mendoza was coming over. Yeah, right, I said. Like *that* could ever happen! I thought he was having daydreams or something. Then the bell rings, and in walks Ramiro Mendoza. Man, was I floored! But once I got used to the fact that it was true, that a Major League pitcher was in the room, I started wondering, Geez, what *else* is gonna happen here? And the crazy thing is that before long *lots* of other players were visiting Luis. It was like his apartment had become a Yankee hangout."

Ramiro loved to play pool with us. I guess it helped him wind down and relax from the pressures of pitching. We would go to a billiard hall around the corner from where I lived and he would put a hundred dollars on the table and challenge anyone to beat him. There were always locals willing to try but never anyone who could shoot pool the way *he* did. What amazed us was that the more he drank the *better* he played.

One night Randy Choate, a pitcher the Yankees had acquired in 1997, was drinking at the stadium and he waited for me to finish my chores and then he accompanied me to my house. We bought a six-pack and the two of us sat in front of the television and got hammered. Then Choate, Steve, and I started rolling dice on the floor. Roman Rodriguez (the bullpen catcher for the Yankees) happened to be living at my place at the time. I had done him a big favor by letting him stay with me, but when word got out that he hadn't paid any rent for *three years*, players found the situation hysterical, and they would invariably get a laugh out of it. He peeked into the living room and shook his head. As the night progressed the stakes got higher, and as luck would have it, we won $700 from Randy. What a sport! He handed over a bundle of cash that would pay our rent for a month.

After a while we decided to go clubbing and we piled into Roman's tiny rented car and wound up at República, a Latin nightclub frequented by baseball players. Randy was screaming out the window when we got there because he saw Erick Almonte and thought he could get in for free. When we finally entered the club, we met up with Raul Mondesi, Enrique Wilson, and Alfonso Soriano. Mondesi bought drinks for everyone in our party. We were in the VIP area, but Randy must have felt out of place with everyone talking Spanish and playing Latin music. He took Steven by the arm and raised his voice over the music.

"Would you mind being my bodyguard tonight?"

There was a pause while Steve looked blankly at him.

"Hunh?"

"Just drink water and watch out for me."

Once he understood what he was being asked to do, Steven put down his beer and for the rest of the night he followed Randy around, even standing inches from him while the pitcher gyrated on the dance floor with a girl in a white dress. Those were the kinds of nights—where players hung around with each other and had fun—that helped bring us together as a team.

A few weeks later I got a call from Ramiro at 4:30 in the morning. Now, you have to understand that I'm not exactly an early riser. Unless it was a school day I typically got up around 2:00 in the afternoon.

"Where *are* you, Luigi?"

I was still half asleep.

"Who's this?"

Turns out I had agreed to go fishing with him and had forgotten all about it. I had no idea we were supposed to leave before sunrise or I never would have agreed to such an off-the-wall idea. But I got dressed, grabbed a pack of cigarettes and a nylon jacket, and tumbled out the door into the cold night air. Ramiro was waiting at the curb in his silver-blue Toyota Sequoia. Before I could get a sip of coffee we were rolling down the New England Thruway to Connecticut. Ramiro was wearing some crazy getup, too: green vulcanized wading boots and a fishing vest full of hooks, tape, and knives. I was thinking, Is *this* the guy who throws 95-m.p.h. fastballs for the New York Yankees? I lit up a cigarette. Ramiro jammed on the brakes and nearly swerved off the road. "Put that out," he said. "You know it can kill you." Don't you love friends like that? I told him I'd stop smoking when *he* stopped dipping—that is, chewing tobacco. But to this day he hasn't. It's a dirty little habit shared by a lot of players. They put it between their bottom lip and cheek to sharpen their reflexes. The Yankees organization doesn't want players using it because, for one thing, it killed Babe Ruth. For another, it looks terrible when you spit.

I must have dozed off for a while, but when I blinked open my eyes we were stopped on a stone beach at some godforsaken lake. We got out and started putting bait on the lines. I was disgusted by the whole procedure. "What the hell are you doin' with that worm!" Ramiro said. "That's no way to hook it!" This was the only time he ever raised his voice at me. I burst out laughing. But he was dead serious about fishing; it was therapy for him. He showed me how to bait the line. Then he waded into the dark water and began casting his line out in the lake. I shook my head, thinking, No way in hell is he ever going to catch anything *here*. In the end, though, he did catch some trout, and what amazed me was that he seemed more proud of this accomplishment than he had been about winning the World Series. The day wasn't a total loss for me, either, since he drove us home and cooked his catch with white rice and a spicy sauce.

Ramiro and I became even chummier later that year when he invited me to travel to Panama with him and his family. Now *this* sounded like an exciting prospect. Wow, I thought, an all-expenses-paid luxury vacation, compliments of my millionaire Major League Baseball player friend! Little did I know what was in store for me this time.

I soon found out that Ramiro lives in a modest—and I mean *very* modest—little ranch-style cottage with his mom and siblings in a run-down village in the middle of nowhere. This isolated house is where we stayed. No electric lights on the streets. I felt like I was back in the Stone Age. I didn't even see the Panama Canal. I slept in the same bedroom he used to sleep in as a kid, but my sleeping got to be a problem since Ramiro liked to get up at 5:00 A.M. and guzzle coffee to start his day, whereas I used to snooze through the middle of the afternoon. "C'mon, man!" he would complain. "Get your butt out of bed. Damn, you sleep too much! We have things to do and sights to see."

One day after he had dragged me out of bed for a walk, he stopped under a banana tree and pointed up into dense leaves. "Look at that beauty," he said. Sitting on a high branch was a green lizard. Before I could tell him how ugly it was, he picked up a rock, fit it into a slingshot, and took aim. I'm not kidding—he carried a slingshot with him! Ace pitcher that he is, one well-placed missile knocked the monster dead. It dropped to my feet with a menacing *splaaaaaaat!* I stepped back, nauseous at the sight. But my friend picked it up by the tail and said, "We have dinner!" He must be kidding, I thought. A few hours later I had forgotten all about it. We were sitting on the front porch, smoking cigars and talking baseball with his dad. His mother, an attractive woman with dark eyes, came into the room in an apron and called us to dinner. It smelled like fried chicken, and I sat down with a big appetite. I was wondering why everyone was looking at me as I dug in for my first bite. "Oh, boy, it's good," I said. Everyone burst out laughing, especially Ramiro. His mother leaned across the table and broke the news to me: "It's the iguana." My stomach did flip-flops. I thought I was going to be sick, but hunger and the mouthwatering taste overcame my fear. There were plenty of chuckles throughout that meal as I gobbled it down.

A few months later during spring training in Tampa, I went

to a sports bar with Mendoza and his friend D'Angelo Jiménez, one of the hottest prospects in baseball. (Unfortunately D'Angelo would get into a car crash in his hometown in the Dominican Republic in 2000, which would put a momentary damper on that promising career.) After I entered the club, the bartender approached our table and apologized, explaining that he wouldn't be able to serve me since I was underage. D'Angelo and Ramiro stopped playing pool but they couldn't talk him out of his position, so when he went back behind the bar, D'Angelo lowered his voice and told us what he *thought* was a bright idea, but which turned out to be a big mistake for everyone involved, especially me.

"Go to my car," he said. "I have some liquor in it. You can drink in the car and no one will bother you, and then when you're done you can come back and join us."

D'Angelo handed me his keys and I went out to the parking lot and opened the glove compartment. Inside were six little bottles of Jack Daniels. Thinking they were miniature beers, I opened the first one and drank it. My mouth began to burn and there was fire in my stomach. Within ten minutes I had consumed all six, coming to the conclusion that this brand of beer was too harsh. I then returned to the club. Ramiro put down his pool cue and turned to me.

"What did you drink?"

"Six Jack Daniels."

My friend turned pale, which frightened me. "You drank *six*? Oh, man, good luck, little brother." He put his hands on my shoulders and looked into my eyes.

Before long Ramiro went home, but D'Angelo and I started clubbing. We drove downtown and went into a nightclub and that's when it hit me. My head went down on the bar and I fell into a daze. Seeing my condition, D'Angelo walked me out to the curb. I must have passed out because the next thing I remember is sitting on the sidewalk at night, crying. D'Angelo's arm was around my shoulders, propping me up, his other hand holding a phone. He was speaking to Ramiro: "Come pick up Luigi. He's had enough." That's all I remember before I passed out again.

The next time I woke up, I was on Ramiro's couch in his Tampa home. He and his wife, Cynthia, were standing over me. Cynthia placed a damp towel on my forehead. I opened my mouth to speak but no words came out. Faces swirled before my eyes and the room spun. I was sick for twelve hours. Ramiro and his wife nursed me back to health as if I were their kid brother. I recovered with a great excuse for not going to work that day. In fact, Ramiro called Rob Cucuzza and explained that I wasn't feeling well. Usually when I'd call in with an excuse, my supervisor would bite my head off, but because the call came from Ramiro there was no problem.

Luckily for me, our friendship persists to this day. Ramiro will come to my house and sign autographs for neighborhood kids. When my father was sick with cancer, Ramiro visited and signed a baseball for him with the inscription, "Keep up the fight." This act of kindness inspired my dad through his last days. And when I was having trouble with my rent, Ramiro sent Cynthia with a blank check to meet me in the parking lot of Yankee stadium.

"How much do you need?" she asked. I was embarrassed, but she took out her pen and insisted I tell her: "Whatever it is, just let me know."

When I admitted how much I needed, she signed a check for $2,000.

In 2004, Mendoza faced another challenge when the Yankees let him become a free agent. I was devastated. My best friend on the team, a guy who had become a big brother to me, started receiving offers from other teams. By chance I met him in the stadium garage one night. He was getting ready to leave and had a valise in one hand and a suit jacket in the other. I came right out and pleaded with him to stay.

"I was shocked when I heard you were considering an offer from the Red Sox. How could that be! Please, Ramiro, think about what you're doing. Please, don't go . . . to the enemy."

He looked down at his hands, then up into my eyes.

"I have my wife and kids to think of."

The next thing I know, we're facing the Red Sox in the 2004 American League Championship Series . . . and who's in a Red Sox uniform? None other than good old Ramiro. It was hard for me to get used to that. I guess in some ways it was difficult for him, too. In order to reconnect and show our friendship, before the play-offs we made a bet. I said I would wash his car every day for a month if the Sox won the series. If the Yankees won, he would buy me a case of beer.

We shook hands on it.

After the Yankees won the first three games, I was feeling pretty confident about winning that beer. It looked like a sure thing to the sportswriters, too. Nobody could imagine anything but a Yankee victory with such odds. But when I ran into Ramiro after Game 3, he said, "We're going to *sweep* you."

Sweep us! He had to be kidding. That was just boldness talking. Still, he had a look of determination on his face. I later learned that he and the Red Sox were literally down on their knees *praying* as a group in their clubhouse for deliverance from this potential major defeat. Meanwhile I—and the entire sports world—was convinced that it was impossible for the Sox to win, especially since they were down *three games*. I was smacking my lips and dreaming about how good it was going to feel to drink those beers.

But then the Red Sox won Game 4. Now the score was three to one. Then the Sox won Game 5, and the score was three to two. When we came home, the Sox won Game 6 to even the score, three to three. From almost sure victory to being on the brink of defeat! Everyone in the Yankees organization was on edge. Then the final game at Yankee Stadium. How can I describe it? The sense of loss was overwhelming after the Red Sox won. Actually, the crowd was silent. But Ramiro's prediction had come true. They won by a reverse-sweep! The Sox would go on to defeat the St. Louis Cardinals and win the 2004 World Series. Along the way, Ramiro Mendoza would become the first player since Babe Ruth to win World Series rings with both the Yankees and the Red Sox.

After the final game, while all the Yankees were feeling bad because of the defeat, I ran down to the Red Sox dugout, where everyone was cheering, and right in front of the photographers and television cameras I congratulated Mendoza. The media saw a bat boy in a Yankee uniform hugging a pitcher in a Red Sox uniform. They must have wondered why. Well, the explanation is simple. It wasn't just because he was a fantastic pitcher who had won a big series against us. It was because this guy had walked through walls and into my life in a way no other player had.

I still haven't washed his car, though. And he still gets on me to this day because of it.

13

King of the Dancing Horses
Ruben Sierra

His thighs and arms are massive, his neck so fat with muscles that he might be a power lifter instead of a DH for the Yankees. Now if you can imagine this wall of strength with a friendly personality, you've put together a good image of Ruben Sierra. Yet there's one final trait that makes up the full picture of Ruben, one which no journalist has ever written about since no one ever got as close to him as I did during the years that we were friends: He's so confident it's almost laughable.

You don't meet confidence like this in the real world, and it's even rare in the unreal world of professional athletes. Ruben doesn't have to go onto the field during games, like Jeter or A-Rod. Instead, as the designated hitter, he sits on the sidelines, or paces back and forth in the dugout, or walks to the clubhouse for a drink of juice and a sandwich . . . waiting, always waiting—and hoping for the call to action. But Ruben is a DH unlike others since he never used to sit quietly and wait, the way Matsui would. Instead, you would see him pacing, eating to kill time, biting his fingernails, chomping at the bit, and building up this tremendous anticipation and yearning to be let out of the gate to do his thing. And in the process of waiting, Ruben also began to boil like a pressure cooker, determined to do his job. This goes a long way toward explaining why Ruben was always angry at Joe Torre. Because on days when Ruben wasn't the DH but was available to pinch-hit, Torre was the gatekeeper, the man who could, with a simple word or a nod of his head, unleash this dynamo of pent-up energy and hitting power. And Torre was a master of judging just how hot and anxious to let Ruben become *before* unleashing him. Torre would wait for *just the right moment*, letting his prize DH build up all the unstoppable fury needed for a big hit . . . and then let his boy go, confident that he had tormented him to the point of DELIVERING THE GOODS just when the Yankees needed him most.

Ruben reserved his anger for Torre, never taking it out on teammates or me, the kid who had became his closest friend on the team. I used to see Ruben walking back and forth, fretting mad, building up all this tension, and yet he would gently lean over to me and say, "Kid, they're gonna need me in this game. You just wait and see. Torre is gonna call me when the situation is desperate for the Yankees, and I'm gonna *produce* for them." Nodding soberly to me, his dark face serious and focused. I would stifle my laughter at his boasting and confidence.

But this guy *would* deliver on that promise! Time after time. With amazing precision . . . and confidence like no one I ever met before or since.

I'll never forget Game 5 of the 2003 World Series, when the Yankees were down in the count and the bases were loaded. He told me, "They're gonna need me now and I'm gonna produce." Produce was his favorite word. I don't know how many times I heard him boast, "I'm gonna *produce* for them!" but it must have been close to a hundred. Sure enough, Torre gave the signal, and Ruben—who had *not* warmed up, and who had not once been on the field with an opportunity to get his brain and body revved up the way other players had—strolls out toward home plate, takes his position in the batter's box, and, as he usually does, lets the first pitch whiz by him without even thinking about swinging, his eyes two tiny points of blackness, sizing up the pitcher and the situation that calls for his special brand of power hitting. Next pitch, sure enough, he slaps one right down the right-field line and ties up the game.

He comes waltzing back into the dugout.

"Jew see that, kid?" He beams at me, stripping off his batting gloves. "That guy got *nothing*. I *told* you, didn't I? Believe in Indio." Referring to himself by his nickname, Indio—Spanish for "Indian." A nickname given to the native of Puerto Rico, as he explains, "in honor of our island's Indian heritage." He's got that Indian determination and tough confidence to prove it.

I could not believe this guy. Most players get out of shape and out of the mind-set of the game if they have to sit around all day doing nothing. But Ruben was like a jukebox. You put in your quarter and it plays your song. No matter how many times you hit D5 it always plays "Like a Rolling Stone." No matter how many hours or games would go by with inactivity, when he *was* called to action, Ruben would always delivered the goods, and, making it even more amazing, he would do this without warming up or taking a single practice swing.

I knew Ruben from the clubhouse, of course, and from seeing

him on the field and in the dugout, but I first met him socially one
night in 2004 when I went to República, a bar in my neighborhood
where a lot of the players hung out. I had gone that night with
Raul Mondesi, and when we got there Ruben was standing at the
end of the bar by himself. He was a loner and didn't socialize with
other players. Raul introduced me and we chatted for a while. He
must have taken a liking to me because before long he invited me
to go clubbing with him. On these occasions he would sometimes
sing on stage, even arranging for a band to back him up, usually
Salsa tunes. When he wasn't singing he would try to do dance
steps, but he was no Fred Astaire. I had to stifle a smile. One night
we were in a crowded bar together and he told me, "Luigi, I needa
take Salsa classes to perfect this." I happened to know a dance instructor, and I hooked Ruben up with him. The teacher would
go to Ruben's apartment in New Jersey and Ruben would pay for
Cha-cha and Salsa lessons. Next time I'd go out with him, he'd tell
me to watch how much he had improved. There's no question in
my mind that he learned to dance to impress the ladies.

Ruben did a lot of things, and bought a lot of toys, to impress
people, but always in a friendly way, never lording it over anyone. It
must have made him feel good to be able to flash a little wealth
after having risen from a penniless boyhood. He bragged about his
collection of automobiles and motorcycles. In New York and
Miami he drove me around town in a white Bentley and a black
Audi. He also tooled around the Bronx and Miami in a new
Hummer, a truck which would eventually play a role in my getting
fired from the Yankees.

One winter he invited me to his farm in Miami for a week
during the off season. He lived close to South Beach, Florida.

I was delighted to get away from the snow in New York and eager to enjoy the warmth of Florida. He had many acres of land and a ranch where he kept forty Paso Finos, dancing horses that are trained—believe it or not—to *tap dance*. He crowed about owning sixty of these dancing horses, two of which were in Puerto Rico and worth more money than most men make in a lifetime. When we arrived at the farm, he parked his Bentley on the shoulder of a dirt access road and made me walk to the top of a small hill overlooking his estate. "I want to show you this side of the world," he said. We strolled down to the corral where his horses were exercising and sunning themselves. Ruben mounted a brown and white Paso Fino and asked if I would like to ride one, too. I backed away, afraid that he would try to talk me into it. Laughing, Ruben rode across his rancho, circling inside a split-rail fence and eventually stopping beside me. He smiled and said, "I have two horses worth a million dollars each. They're in San Juan, and I would like to show them to you someday."

Later that night we were sitting out under the stars and Ruben noticed that I was quiet. "What's wrong, little brother?" he said. "You're not talkative like when we go clubbing. Is it because you're not used to this country lifestyle?" I told him that he was right, but that I was fine. Having grown up in the Bronx, where there wasn't anything like this, I was soaking it all up, adjusting to a way of living that I had never experienced.

Like a big brother, Ruben took me under his wing for three years. Strangely, he never went out with teammates. I've often wondered why Sierra and numerous other middle-aged players were so concerned about a young man's welfare. They hung around with me, took me on vacations, paid for my hotel rooms on the road, and bought me food and expensive gifts, including watches, rings, and necklaces. Some people might think it's homosexual interest; but I saw no evidence of that. In fact, the same players often ran around with women and even provided women for me. It's more likely that their actions were a form of friendship between older and younger men, kind of a mentoring relationship. At the bottom of Sierra's friendliness, I'm convinced, was also a desire to be young again, and a wish to associate with a young man who was in his teens and early twenties when he was nearing his forties and approaching the end of his professional career.

It's funny how some of these players took me so completely into their lives and virtually adopted me as if I were a ward. Their willingness to let me tag along with them, and their generosity in paying for my hotel rooms on the road and inviting me to vacation with them, gave me extraordinary access to their private lives in a way that no reporter ever had. In addition, the fact that I was bilingual allowed me to see and hear things that no English-speaking journalist ever witnessed. Of all the players I became closest to, probably the most amusing was Ruben. A mixture of boldness and machismo, with a halting speech pattern that sounded like a computer when he spoke English, he both amused and befriended me in a way that no other player did.

An accomplished mimic, Sierra's favorite person to imitate was the team manager. He would walk like him in the clubhouse and make gestures with a cigar that made the other guys laugh. But Torre never caught on until October 3, 2004. As luck would have it, that was the day Torre appointed Sierra honorary manager. Every year at the end of the regular season, Torre chooses one player to do *his* job for one day. Once he had been selected,

Ruben came up to me and lowered his voice. "Hey, kid," he said, looking sideways to make sure no one could overhear. "Watch what I'm gonna do." And then Ruben goes out and mocks him! Pants hiked up above his belly button, hat tilted back like Torre, walking to the mound like an elderly patient, Sierra cracked the dugout up by doing the Joe Torre walk.

Ruben liked to talk with me when we traveled on the team plane. One day he saw me sitting up front with another bat boy. He tapped me on the shoulder. "Hey, kid," he said. "Come on back and sit with me." Rob Cucuzza, who was sitting across the aisle, said, "He's okay." But Ruben nodded his head to call me to join him. I got up and followed him to the rear of the plane where Alex Rodriguez was sitting by himself. We sat in the row ahead of Alex. Ruben produced a DVD player and two high-fidelity stereo headsets, handing one to me. We started watching an action movie. Right in the middle of it, A-Rod's head came forward between our chairs. I lifted my headphones off to hear him say, "What are you looking at?" Ruben held up the DVD player and said, "You wanna watch?" It was hysterical because there were no more headphone jacks. A-Rod smiled and settled back in his seat, leaving Ruben and me to watch the conclusion of the movie.

One afternoon when Ruben was in a slump, Reggie Jackson, in plain clothes, came up to him in the dugout and squatted down in front of him. The Hall of Famer was known for being a terrific hitter and everyone respected him. He had come to give Ruben some advice. Reggie put one arm on my knee to steady himself, and said to Ruben, "You gotta hit like this, see?" He swung his arm to show what he meant, giving what he thought was a world's worth of good advice. When he walked away, Ruben turned to me and said, "You gotta be kidding." I stifled a laugh. Yes, Ruben was confident, and even in a slump he wasn't going to listen to *anybody's* advice, no matter if it *was* Reggie's.

He had peculiar hobbies, too. In addition to collecting cars and horses, his strangest hobby was probably buying jewelry. The most extravagant Yankee, he flashed rings, necklaces, and bracelets under your nose. One day he drove me to East 57th Street, where we entered a store that had as much security as Fort Knox. After we had passed through a series of thick steel doors, we were ushered into a studio where we were wined and dined and eventually we met Jacob the Jeweler. Jacob was a bulldog-jawed Arabic-looking businessman who invited us to look at diamond-studded wrist-watches. The price tags on these beauts were in the neighborhood of $100,000. "Yeah, I want this one," Ruben said. He didn't even haggle over the price.

A few weeks later we were near Fordham University and we stopped in a jewelry store. Ruben saw me looking at a $1,000 necklace and he said, "You like that, kid?" I told him I did, and he said he'd get it for me. "No, no," I said. "You don't have to do that." He smiled and told me to go out and have a cigarette. When we got back in his Bentley, he handed me a box. "Here, kid," he said. "I want you to have this." It was the necklace.

One time in St. Louis, I accompanied Ruben to a restaurant where we had dinner with Derek Jeter, Jorge Posada, and Mariano Rivera. Posada joked that I looked like a mini-Ruben. We were wearing identical watches and necklaces: his gifts to me. Meanwhile Ruben was gulping down bread and appetizers. He probably had the biggest appetite on the team. During the meal he stuffed himself with the equivalent of the average man's breakfast, lunch, and dinner. As if this wasn't enough, while he was eating dessert he looked up and said, "Where are we going to eat later?"

Despite being one of my best friends on the team—or maybe because of our close relationship—Ruben was the indirect cause of my being fired.

My troubles began on the night of July 7, 2005 when I got into a mix-up with Matsui's car. The Japanese DH was out of town, and his translator gave Chris, a clubbie, the keys and twenty bucks to get the car washed; Chris, in turn, gave the keys and money to me. I had a friend who owned a car wash in the Bronx, and he used to give me a break on the price, charging only $10–$15. After I got Matsui's car washed I drove to New Jersey to see a friend. As I entered the toll booth to come home the custodian of the booth exited, leaving me stranded with a long line of cars honking behind me. So I drove through the toll booth. Little did I know that a camera had snapped a picture of Matsui's license plate, and the ticket was relayed to the Yankee Stadium front office for payment.

Trouble deepened a few weeks later since the ticket was my fault and everyone in the Yankees organization knew that I had been driving Matsui's car. You also have to remember that Rob Cucuzza knew that when I went to get players' cars washed I would be driving without a license. Sonny Hight told Robbie about the ticket in July, and I got called on the carpet. Sonny Hight and Robbie wanted to know how I got the ticket. I tried explaining, as best I could, but my supervisor's face was long when he heard the story.

Then things got even worse. Before I left for the day on August 2, Ruben Sierra told me he wanted to go clubbing with me that night. Players always get out before bat boys since we have a lot of cleaning up to do, so he sat waiting for me in the coach's room, chatting on his cell phone while I took a shower. When I exited from the shower, Ruben told me to hurry up. I got dressed as fast as I could, and Robbie saw us leaving together.

"Where are you guys going?"

Ruben looked at his watch.

"Just clubbing."

"You want to come?" I said.

"No," Robbie said. "Have fun."

Ruben and I left the stadium together. We entered a place on University Heights that used to be Jimmy's Bronx Café but which had opened under new management as X Bar, a third-rate almost strip joint. While we were at the bar a guy got into an argument with his girlfriend and tried to throw a drink at her, but the drink hit Ruben and me in the face. Under ordinary circumstances we would have laughed off something like that. But without warning the guy began wailing on Ruben. When I saw my friend getting hit, I jumped in and punched the guy who was attacking him. Then four or five of the guy's friends started punching us, and kicking me. Before long we were all bleeding, and one of the guys from the other party had been knocked senseless and was lying in a groggy state on the floor.

Ruben went downstairs and talked with the manager. I came

down and started yelling at the manager, demanding to know why his security was so lazy that a star player would get hurt in his club. They gave Ruben an ice pack for his lip, which was bleeding all over the place.

"We have to go to the hospital," Ruben said. "I gotta get stitched up." Then he took me aside. "This never happened," he said. "I can get in trouble with the front office if they find out I was in a fight. You understand?"

He drove to the hospital and went into the emergency room, while I waited in the Hummer. I had a black eye and a busted lip but I didn't want stitches so I didn't go in with him. While he was being stitched up and medicated, the hospital must have contacted a Yankee team security official and told him that Ruben Sierra was being treated for a broken lip. When you're a Yankee nothing you do goes unreported and unseen. Ruben came back to the car and took one look at me.

"You can't go to work tomorrow."

"Why not?"

"Because they'll see *me* with my stitched lip, and if they see *you* with a black eye, they'll put two and two together. Remember, Robbie saw us leaving together, and if they see us both banged up they'll know that we were in a fight, and the whole thing will get me in big trouble."

"But how can I stay home?"

He thought for a few seconds.

"Make up some excuse."

Roman Rodriguez, the bullpen catcher who was staying at my house, told me that the next day, August 3, Ruben showed up at work with a face torn up and stitched back together. He said that he was going shopping at two in the morning and accidentally opened his Hummer door and hit himself in the face. Everyone looked at him when he said that, and you could hear their minds working overtime. *You hit yourself with the Hummer door? Come on, Ruben. Can't you do better than that?*

Of course, nobody believed him.

In fact, it was one of the lamest excuses I ever heard. I mean, a sixth grader could have come up with something better. But that was his story, and once he told it, he had to stick to it. Meanwhile, Robbie was getting suspicious when I didn't show up for work. He knew that the two of us had gone out together. Here was one of his star players with a busted lip, and his pal—bat boy Luis Castillo—was claiming his grandmother died. Could there possibly be a connection between the fact that Luis was staying home and the fact that Ruben was busted up? Robbie wanted to get to the bottom of it, and he had five other people call me to try to convince me to come to work. Added to this was the fact that I had gotten a ticket a few weeks before with Matsui's car, so there were already two strikes against me.

Robbie called a couple of times before he had other people call me.

"Get in here."

"I can't, Robbie."

"You better come in."

"My grandmother died."

"You have to apologize about Matsui's ticket."

"I can't."

On and on this went, through numerous other phone calls from his associates. Finally he called back a third time.

"I'm sorry," he said. "I love you like a little brother. But I have to let you go. It's not my decision. It's the front office."

And that was how I lost my job.

It was because I had stayed loyal to Ruben and lied for him. If I had gone to work with that black eye and busted lip, they would have been all over me, grilling me about it, and about the fact that I was with Ruben that evening when he got stitches at the hospital at 2:30 in the morning. They would have forced the truth out of me, for sure. And Ruben would have gotten into deep trouble because a baseball player has an obligation to take care of himself physically: he has a curfew, and he's not supposed to get into fights.

A few weeks later Ruben came to my home and apologized to my mother because I lost my job. "Matsui didn't want you to lose your job either," he assured me. I knew that. But in the end it happened the way it happened, and I was let go. I don't know to this day who made the final decision, but I assume it was Brian Cashman, the general manager; Randy Levine, the president of the Yankees organization; or Lonn Trost, the chief operating officer. It doesn't really matter. The bottom line is I was out.

It didn't sit right with me, though. And it sure didn't seem fair. But the unfairness didn't stop there. I did a lot for the team over the years, working plenty of hours without pay, doing odd jobs when they needed me. For example, I worked during the 1998, 1999, and 2000 World Series, and Rob Cucuzza would tell me after every celebration that I was their good-luck charm, saying, "Way to go, kid!" But my pride was injured when I never got a World Series ring. Seeing other clubhouse attendants with rings when I never got one added insult to injury. I did the same work and maybe even worked harder.

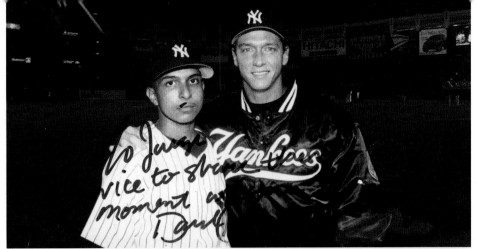

TOP: David Cone and me in old Yankee Stadium, July 19, 1999, the day after the perfect game. Twenty-four hours earlier I had been standing out here with David in front of 41,930 fans as I warmed him up during the 33-minute rain delay. The TitanTron screen in the background says "NY YANKEES 'TEAM OF THE CENTURY.'"

MIDDLE: Orlando "El Duque" Hernandez and me after the Yankees won the 1999 World Series. El Duque was already in street clothes, getting ready to go out and paint the town red, when I caught him for this photo, which he signed (in Spanish) "To Luis, the best bat boy of the Yankees." He's smiling now, but this is the jokester who used to hit me with grapes in the players' lounge and clubhouse and then frown and deny that he had anything to do with it.

RIGHT: Tina Lewis, Queen of the Bleachers, and me in 1997, shortly after I sent in my letter to the Yankees about wanting to be a bat boy. She has her arm around me because we became good friends after my buddy cursed her out and insulted her a few weeks earlier. I have Tina to thank for launching my career with the Yankees. It's funny how a chance meeting can send your life in an entirely new direction.

TOP: *Left to right*: David Cone, me, and bat boy Matt "Spider" McGough (who went on to become a lawyer and a screenwriter). We're celebrating in the Yankees' clubhouse after the 1999 World Series win. David has a cigar in his right hand and we're drenched in champagne. David signed this one for me: "To Luigi— Glad to call you a friend." He usually called me Luigi, including on the day of his perfect game when he surprised me by asking me to warm him up during the rain delay. Later, he would teach me how to throw fastballs with such power that they broke bats.

LEFT: David Wells and me at a Derek Jeter charity function. With a great sense of humor, he used to call me "La Squeegee." He had tattoos of beloved family members on his back. Before going out to pitch he would listen to heavy metal, which would fire him up with energy. Although I never saw him in the gym, I learned a lot just by watching him fire fastballs from the mound.

RIGHT: Here I am with Bernie Williams. He was a spectacular outfielder, but his memory would fail him at the oddest moments. I once had to help him find a back way out of Yankee stadium because he didn't want any of the higher-ups to see him in his motorcycle outfit. Another team rule he broke was the one against sleeping on the job: He took naps before most games, and it was my responsibility to wake him up and make sure he didn't miss batting practice. *(Courtesy of* The Bronx Times*)*.

TOP LEFT: David Cone and me at Shea Stadium. This was after he had left the Yankees for our rival, the Red Sox. When the Sox came to New York, he called and asked if I would be a bat boy for him for one day. So I snuck over to Shea and put on the enemy's uniform to help him out. The things I would do to help friends! I thought David looked better in a Yankee uniform, but no matter where he played he always pitched like a winner.

TOP RIGHT: The tall guy is John Olerud, first baseman for the Seattle Mariners. He wanted to meet me because we had both suffered head injuries. I wore a metal plate in my head, and he wore a batting helmet in the field. We're standing in front of the visiting clubhouse in old Yankee Stadium. I don't look like a squeegee man in my uniform, do I?

BOTTOM: Ticker-tape parade down the "Canyon of Heroes" from Broadway to City Hall after beating the Atlanta Braves in the 1999 World Series. *Back row, left to right*: Derek Jeter (facing left), Chuck Knoblauch (facing front), me (facing left), and Scott Brosius (holding up a tomahawk, the Braves symbol). The night before, I was in a bar until the wee hours with the players, which is why they're wearing sunglasses.

TOP: Bill Clinton, Ryan (clubbie), me, Chris Manzione (reaching out to shake hands), Mitch, the new team massage therapist (in the background), and bat boy Shawn Iodice. Minutes before, Jeter had said, "Keeping out of trouble?" to Clinton.

LEFT: Bleacher Creatures, Section 39. Tina Lewis, Queen of the Bleachers, to whom this book is dedicated, standing in approximately row four from the front. The most loyal fans sit in this section, and this is where I first met Tina.

RIGHT: This is me, at a game, before I became a bat boy, with Tina Lewis, Larry (with the cutoff sleeves), and other fans. I loved sitting in this section because everyone was friendly and passionate about the Yankees, and you had a terrific view of all the action on the field.

TOP: Pitcher Hideki Irabu, who Steinbrenner once called a toad, and me in the players' lounge celebrating the Yanks winning the 1998 ALCS. The very popular coffee machine is to the right, behind me. I'm soaked with champagne. Irabu has a cup in his hand. Good times like these were highlights of our lives as Yankees.

MIDDLE: Mayor Rudy Giuliani, a federal secret service bodyguard for the mayor, and George Steinbrenner. I'm in front of the Boss, wearing a baseball cap. This was the day that a pipe broke in Yankee Stadium, so we were forced to borrow Shea Stadium for a home game! It was a historic event, and the mayor helped make it possible. We even had to wear our home jersey at Shea.

LEFT: Tino Martinez and me at Jeter's Turn 2 Foundation party. Tino was signing autographs at the table. Jeter was walking around, chatting with everyone. Tino, one of the greatest first basemen, was filling the legendary Don Mattingly's shoes. Wherever he went, fans chanted "Teen-OH! Teen-OH!" He was very friendly with the New York media and was loved by New York fans.

TOP LEFT: Lucho (a friend from the Bronx), Ruben Sierra (on his cell phone, wearing his Jacob the Jeweler $100,000 watch and an expensive platinum chain, muscles bursting out of his shirt, and keeping a hat on his head since he was bald), and Ramiro Mendoza (holding dominos at extreme right). Drinking and playing dominos in front of my mom's house in the Bronx was a favorite pastime of these guys.

TOP RIGHT: Ramiro Mendoza signing autographs for kids in my neighborhood before a game. He used to pick me up at my house at 9:00 A.M. and I'd take him to my barber for a haircut. When people saw him sitting in the chair they would crowd around to say hello and ask for autographs. Then we'd drive to the stadium together for the 3:00 P.M. game.

BOTTOM: Darryl Strawberry and me at the new City Field in 2010. This photo was taken at a game Soriano gave me tickets to attend. Straw was getting a ceremonial award from the Mets. He told the security guard to hold me there so we could get a chance to talk. Very religious now, he said, "God bless" before we parted.

TOP: On June 13, 2003, Roger Clemens recorded his 300th win and 4,000th strikeout. He took this photo with me and other clubbies, bat boys, and Rob Cucuzza, who's standing between Roger and me.

LEFT: First baseman Tino Martinez at one of Derek Jeter's Turn 2 Foundation functions. Tino had been signing autographs earlier in the day, and I had been handing him baseballs. During Pitchers' Fielding Practice he and Andy Pettitte worked on Andy's pickoff move and prevented me from getting on base. Joe Girardi is sitting in the background, partly visible over the woman's shoulder.

RIGHT: Don Mattingly and me on Old-Timers' Day at Yankee Stadium. He wasn't a coach yet, but he was Tina Lewis's favorite player. In 2004 I hung out with him in a bar and in my hotel room in Boston, where I introduced him to Corona beer.

TOP LEFT: Here I am in the Yankees' dugout with Chuck Mangione's flugelhorn. I was always doing odd jobs for the team, one of which was holding the great musician's hat on the field while he played the National Anthem. *Courtesy of Steve Crandall.*

TOP RIGHT: Ramiro Mendoza, Ruben Sierra, and backup catcher Wil Nieves at my mom's house in the Bronx in 2005. We had been playing dominos and were getting ready to go clubbing. My apartment was a regular hangout for many Yankee players.

MIDDLE: Arthur Richman and me at Chase Field during the 2001 World Series against the Arizona Diamondbacks. After 9/11 we wore NYPD and FDNY hats during batting practice. The late great Arthur never tired of telling me—and everyone else—how he "got Joe Torre his job."

BOTTOM: My buddy Ramiro Mendoza (far right) signed with the Newark Bears in July 2009 after he left major league baseball. This photo was taken that same year, when he was playing in their independent league. Ramiro and I were in the lounge of a New Jersey hotel with another Bears player. It's funny how I can remember almost every bar I ever went to with this guy.

I wasn't the only one who saw the unfairness. One day Ramiro Mendoza took off his World Series ring and offered it to me.

"You should have gotten one," he said. "Take mine."

Of course I told him no. Getting it from him wasn't the same as getting it from the team. Instead of a ring, what I got from the Yankees organization was a slap in the face—and worse.

A couple of months after I got fired I saw Robbie at a club one night in Boston. I was taking a pee. He came into the men's room and started peeing in an adjacent urinal. He was very splashy, and I was trying to lean away from him, hoping none of it sprayed onto me. While I was leaning to the side, he turned to me and said, "I'm sorry you were let go. I'm going to try to get you your job back."

I really didn't care at that point. And it wasn't just because I had a few drinks in me. It was because I was moving on with my life, pitching in a competitive league in Central Park, and working on other projects, including my own fashion line. I got out of that bathroom as fast as I could, wiping my suit with a paper towel. Yeah, I thought, the Yankees sure pissed on me . . . The bottom line is, they treated me like dirt.

That's the way they operated with a lot of players over the years, so why should I have expected them to treat one of their clubhouse assistants any different? Even one, like me, who had served them over and above the call of duty for eight years, going out of my way to help players and administrators with all sorts of errands that you wouldn't believe, and that were never part of my job responsibilities. I held my head high as I exited from that men's room, though . . . I only looked down long enough to wipe off the Yankee front-office piss.

14

The Biggest Error in Baseball History
Chuck Knoblauch

The biggest error in baseball history occurred on October 7, 1998, in Game 2 of the American League Championship Series. At least that's the way it appeared to Chuck Knoblauch.

I was standing on the field watching the action, at my usual post in foul territory, about twenty feet from first base. It was the top of the twelfth, and Jeff Nelson was pitching for the Yankees. Enrique Wilson, a pinch runner for the Cleveland Indians—who would later play with the Yankees—was on first. Travis Fryman stepped up to the plate and made a sacrifice bunt to try to send Wilson to second. As the ball skidded into the field, Fryman began running for first. Tino Martinez, the Yankee first baseman, sprang forward and fielded the ball, scooping it up in fair territory, then whirling for the throw toward Knobby, who had dashed over to cover first. By this time, Fryman had almost reached first, but he wasn't in the three-foot-wide running lane; instead he was inside the baseline as he ran the last few feet toward the base.

The throw by Martinez accidentally smacked into the back of Travis Fryman, hitting him between the shoulder blades as he stepped on first. The baseball bounced off his back and rolled twenty feet away, still in fair territory and still in play. But Knobby didn't pick it up. Instead, he started talking with the first-base umpire.

Meanwhile, Enrique Wilson was running like mad for second, and everyone in the crowd started screaming.

At the point when he started arguing with first-base umpire Ted Hendry about the call, Knobby made a fatal error.

Jeter was yelling, "Get the ball!"

Tino was yelling the same thing.

With Wilson rounding second and heading for third, the Yankee dugout came to their feet. Torre was screaming, "Pick up the ball! Argue the call later!"

Paul O'Neill was waving his arms like a crossing guard—as if Knoblauch could see him—screaming, "Knobby! Knobby! What the devil are you doing?"

My eyes almost bugged out when I saw Chuck Knoblauch, one of my favorite players, standing calm as ice, hands at his sides, blowing a pink bubble with his gum. He was trying to convince the first-base umpire that Travis Fryman should have been called out. The rules of baseball are clear on this point: a batter-runner going from home to first must run *inside* a three-foot running lane after he gets halfway to first. But Fryman had not been in that running lane; instead, he had been running inside the baseline—that is, to the *left* of the line connecting home and first (See diagram on page 186).

The rules require that a runner who is outside the three-foot-wide running lane, and who unintentionally causes interference, is out. This pretty much described what Fryman had done, and

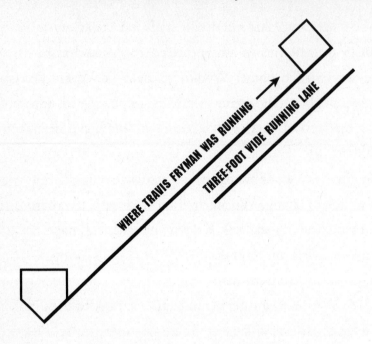

technically Knobby was right: Fryman *should* have been called out by the umpire. But Knobby made the error of arguing with the ump *before finishing the play*. He should have been fielding the ball and trying to stop Wilson. Everyone agreed that he should have waited until the play was over before bringing the matter up with the umpire.

It was driving us all nuts to see Knoblauch let Enrique Wilson advance around the bases. In a few seconds, if this continued, a run would score! It was painful to think that Knobby didn't have the presence of mind to pick up the ball and make the play. The game was tied 1–1 at this point, so if Enrique scored it would give the Indians a devastating psychological advantage. Hardly believing his luck, Enrique gave a look back, as if he couldn't figure out what was going on. All he knew was that *no one was trying to tag him, no one had the ball, and no one appeared to be about to throw him out—even though he had run from first to second and was now rounding third!* In fact, he was so amazed that he stumbled as he came off third and headed home. Would he make it? Would Knoblauch wake up in time? The game seemed to be moving in slow motion. The crowd rose to their feet, screaming at Knobby, "PICK UP THE BALL!"

By the time Knobby realized what was going on, and that he had to keep playing, Wilson was more than halfway from third to home. Knobby belatedly fielded the ball and made the throw home—but too late to prevent Enrique from scoring. Two more runs came in for the Indians in that inning, and since the Yankees couldn't get any runs in the bottom of the twelfth, the Indians went on to win it 4–1.

Poor Knobby! He was booed as he left the field. Later he tried to explain away his actions to reporters. But the next day he saw the play on tape and admitted his error.

"Sometimes as a play occurs on the field you see it a certain way," he told reporters. "That's how it appears in your mind. I did my best trying to describe what I remembered. We flew to Cleveland on the charter that night and I saw the replay. I thought, Oh, my God. It wasn't the same as I described. I barely slept that night."

For Game 3 in Cleveland, all the Yankees were booed as they were introduced—*except* for Chuck, who received an embarrassing standing ovation. Unfortunately, it would be a while before he put this error behind him. In his mind it must have felt like the greatest blunder in baseball history and I know why. I've never seen a player stop playing right in the middle of a game the way he did. Watching helplessly as Enrique Wilson scored from first base is what was so frustrating to all the Yankee fans and players. Add to that the fact that Chuck was blowing bubbles while it happened, and you could see why we were disappointed. Even Bill Buckner's 1986 error at Shea Stadium—when the ball rolled under his legs, leading to the Mets winning the World Series—even *that* didn't rise to this level in our opinion because Bill Buckner's error was a slip of the mind, or a failure of the muscles to move fast enough. Knoblauch's error was the incredible act of standing stock-still with his back to the action while an opposing player ran from first to home.

Not to say that Knobby wasn't the sweetest, kindest, friendliest guy you ever met—and one of the most talented lead-off batters. But baseball can do strange things to even the most talented players, putting the spotlight on them and making them heroes, or, as in this case, nailing the coffin on their reputation forever. And all because of one error.

Jump ahead one year, and thankfully Knoblauch redeemed himself and played well, helping the Yankees clinch the 1999 World Series. And then there was the celebration, which I had the privilege to see. The room was total chaos: horseshoe-shaped booths jammed together at awkward angles, chairs scattered across the cramped floor, partygoers stuck trying to squeeze past one another in excited states of intoxication. Lights were low, Salsa tunes blaring, and Derek Jeter and Chuck Knoblauch were dancing in the VIP section. There was a stage at the far end of the room where four girls in glitter dresses danced to the rhythm of guitarists in black outfits. Jimmy's Bronx Café had been selected as the perfect place to celebrate winning the 1999 World Series.

My friend Carlos and I muscled our way up to Jeter and Knoblauch. A few hours earlier I had been on the field together with them when the win occurred. Now we could hardly get close, there were so many people.

Jimmy Rodriguez, the club owner, was talking in an animated voice with his celebrity guests. Carlos gave me a glass of Moët champagne for Jeter, and I managed to break through a few private conversations to hand him the cup, which he immediately passed to a girl wearing silver sequins. "What, is he too good for my drink?" Carlos said. "This guy's a party animal," Knoblauch said, referring to me. Derek laughed and I told them what a terrific job they had done that afternoon. They were smiling, but I don't think they heard much of my conversation over the crash of the band and the hubbub in the bar.

Even in that crowded room filled with party animals, Knoblauch's short muscular frame was unique. Jeter stood a head taller, but there was a hyper quality about Knobby that carved a space around him. Unlike the more serious players, he acted crazy sometimes. Full of energy, he used to come to work and surprise us with his antics. He wasn't predictable, like Scott Brosius or Jorge Posada. Sometimes he would run up behind you and yell "Gaaaaaaaaaaaa!" Then he'd dance away, giggling. So we were glad to see him in a relaxed frame of mind in the bar, where his off-the-wall behavior wouldn't cause a disturbance.

The last thing I remember about that night is Jeter and Knoblauch checking out the women and gabbing with the owner.

Next day was the ticker-tape parade up Broadway. I managed to get on the float with my drinking buddies from the night before. Jeter and Knoblauch were wearing dark sunglasses, a sure sign that their eyes were red with late-night hangovers. Not that they had much work to do on the float. Now it was all celebration, relaxation, and laughs. Confetti floated down from the skyscrapers as we passed through the Canyon of Heroes. The sidewalks were jammed with well-wishers, some in Yankee uniforms, many with cameras. Those who had no confetti threw toilet paper. When a roll clunked down into my hands, Knobby leaned forward and said, "Throw it back!" But I hesitated. "Give me that," he said. Then taking aim, he hurled it back into the cheering throng. He laughed and giggled. The same Knoblauch I knew from the clubhouse: a party lover, a guy for whom having fun came before almost everything. I was glad he was enjoying himself and feeling free enough to be silly. You wouldn't see Pettitte or Mariano doing something like that—but Knobby, well, he was in a class all his own, and everyone enjoyed his laid-back company.

The baby of his family, with four older sisters and an older brother, Knobby was a people person if ever I saw one. Never at a loss for words, he was friendly and sociable to all—including teammates, the media, and clubhouse attendants. He loved going out at night, and the famed China Club must have been his favorite hangout. Unfortunately, his father, a gifted baseball coach who had taught Chuck how to play the game, began to show symptoms of Alzheimer's just about the time that his son started getting famous as a second baseman with the Yankees. It was around this time, too, that Knoblauch began to experience a series of puzzling difficulties on the field.

The first problem to surface was his inability to steal. He had been brought to the Yankees because of his intimidating batting skill and his fleet-footed base running. "Whenever we played the Twins our entire focus was on how to get *him* out," George Steinbrenner once said. "He'd ignite every one of their rallies. As Knoblauch went, so went our chances." In New York, Knobby continued hitting well, but his speed was significantly diminished. He used to be a great base stealer, but New York seemed to intimidate him. He still stole, but not as often.

One day Joe Torre approached him in the clubhouse and said, "Listen, there's some guys I need to give the signal to—but *not* you. You're in a class with Jeter and a few others as far as stealing, okay? You're one of the guys who has the green light." Meaning: Don't wait for my okay. Use your own judgment. You're fast enough to go when you see an opportunity. Surprise me. Surprise the other team. *Steal!*

The other problem that surfaced, which was much more troubling, was his inability to make one of the easiest plays in baseball, one that many a fan could make, namely, the throw from second to first. This is a crucial play to get guys out and prevent them from starting a rally. It was one he had been good at when he was with the Twins. But in New York, after 1999, he started to develop what baseball pundits call the yips. Nobody knew what the cause was . . . But we were all wondering . . . WHY? WHY HIM? AND WHY NOW? Those were the questions on everyone's mind. That, and, WHEN WILL HE FIX IT?

While I saw Chuck develop the yips, and saw how hard he worked to try to fix his problem—for example, going in for extra throwing practice—I also saw that the problem was *not* going away, at least, not anytime soon. If anything, it was getting worse. I tried not to think about it. During this time he was his usually bubbly self, fun, easy to be with, and entertaining. He was closer to my height than most of the other players, who were giants compared to me, so maybe that's an additional reason why I took a liking to him.

One day he came up to me and, knowing I needed a glove, he handed me his. It was a second-base glove—which is smaller than an outfielder's glove to help the quick release of the ball for a throw to first for a double play. This glove was broken in, made of oil-tanned steer hide, and designed with an open back for increased flexibility. I might have paid $185 for a mitt like this, and I was thrilled. Yet for some reason, when he gave it to me, I was in a distracted state of mind and didn't smile.

"Geez," he said, flashing a grin. "You could at *least* look happy!"

A few weeks later I was coming in from the loading dock, a gate toward the back of the old Yankee Stadium near left field. I was carrying some ketchup and sliced bread for the players' lounge. I was surprised to run into Chuck Knoblauch and Nick Johnson since players usually enter from the other end of the park, through the press gate behind home plate. I said hello to them, and Knobby gave me his usual grin.

"Hey, Luigi!"

"What're you doing coming in this way?"

"I came by train."

"Train?"

"Yeah, the number 4."

He had taken the *subway* to work from his Manhattan brownstone! The guy was so thrilled with New York, so excited to be here, that even riding the subway was part of the fun. He didn't need to lounge in the back of a limo like the celebrity he was. Instead, he would ride the train, together with good old Nick Johnson. At the time, people on the train might not have recognized Nick, who was a backup first baseman, but if they were any kind of fan they sure would have recognized Chuck Knoblauch. Imagine getting on the train and seeing one of your Yankee heroes? People got excited seeing him, and he got off on that, too.

Now, one strange thing about the way the yips affected Chuck during these years was that the more time he had to *think* about a throw, the worse he was. This had an effect on the way he reacted in David Cone's 1999 perfect game.

As I described in chapter 7, I was on the field during that entire game. With one out in the eighth, David Cone delivered to José Vidro, who hit a ground ball down the middle. Knoblauch darted to the right, backhanded the ball, and then planted his feet on the soggy grass to steady himself. (There had been a rain delay earlier.) But there was only a fraction of a second hesitation between the catch and the throw, with Knoblauch making a small mental calculation, which had more to do with making sure his feet were planted firmly under him than with the mechanics of the throw itself. As I watched him steady himself and reach into the glove for the ball, my heart skipped a beat. Collectively the crowd held its breath. This, after all, was *Chuck Knoblauch* making the throw. The guy had had the yips for months. What's he going to do? Is the ball going to fly wild? Is he under pressure? Is he nervous? Does he *believe* he can make it? Is his mind settled? Please, please, please . . . DO IT RIGHT!

The hand came out of the glove. For a split second my eyes flicked to David Cone. Turned at the waist on the mound, his lips pressed to a pale line, I swear I could hear him thinking, Don't fuck this up, Knobby! At the same time, Vidro was tearing down the running lane for first. You could hear a sigh from 41,930 spectators. Then Chuck unleashed the throw. The ball seemed to leave a trail of white steam in its path as it struggled through the air toward first . . . MAKE IT! the crowd was praying. MAKE IT RIGHT! And then . . . *Ziiiiiiiinnnnnng!* Yes, yes, yes! Into Tino's glove . . . Into the glove!

Another sigh, this time of relief, from the fans.

Not only from the fans, but from the Yankee dugout, too . . . from the administration . . . from the manager . . . from the owner, watching on closed-circuit TV . . . from Chuck himself. Most of all from David Cone, whose lips returned to a normal color as he turned back to the task of pitching that perfect game.

Things went a little differently on June 17, 2000. Greg Norton hit a ground ball that Knoblauch fielded. Knobby then threw toward first, but the ball sailed wildly high, bouncing off the top of the dugout and picking up reverse spin, and then heading *into the stands*. INTO THE FANS SECTION! A *throw* into the fans! As the ball went wild, Knoblauch twisted to the side, so as not to watch where it was going, knowing full well that he had sent it madly off course. He hung his head so low that all you could see was his sad silhouette and his number.

"Oooooo!" and "Ahhhhh!" the crowd cried.

The ball kept going on its freakish path . . . until it struck an elderly woman right between the eyes. One of the lenses of her glasses popped out. Gasps from onlookers all across the stadium! Medics rushed to the scene. They were surprised to find that the victim of the bad throw was Marie Olbermann, mother of Fox sportscaster Keith Olbermann. Fortunately, Mrs. Olbermann wasn't seriously injured. In later years, after his mother passed away, Keith made a touching video tribute to his mother in which he stated that she didn't hold it against Knoblauch. She claimed she actually enjoyed the attention Knobby had given her. A diehard baseball fan, she attended hundreds of games and became known, ever after, as the woman who had been hit by Chuck Knoblauch.

The runner was awarded second base because of the wild throw. After the game, no one said a word to Knobby, not even Jeter. I felt sorry for him. It was a dark day for Chuck, and I sensed that a change was brewing. We all sensed it, no one more than Chuck himself.

"I'll beat it," he said, acknowledging his problem. "I've got it in me. It's a mental thing."

But he never did get a handle on it. With throwing errors mounting, Torre moved him to left field in 2001. From there he would never return. A talented younger player was brought in to replace him on second: Alfonso Soriano, the subject of another chapter in this memoir. The fact that Soriano had talent for this position and had caught the eye of Joe Torre didn't help Chuck Knoblauch, whose playing in left field would lead, within a matter of months, to his permanent retirement.

Because of his throwing problems, the New York press was unusually harsh on Knobby. They thought it was funny to call him

"Blauchhead" and other derogatory names. "My character was being judged," he said. "That was real tough. The only certain thing you can hold on to is your character." I thought it was interesting that Knoblauch turned out to be one of the most perceptive commentators about the same New York media that dragged him through the mud. He offered sharp comments about their need to spin stories, saying, "I don't know *who's* competing harder in New York, the writers or the Yankees. Here, there are so many eyes and ears . . . They feel the pressure in *their* jobs, too." Leave it to good old Knobby to be sensitive even to guys who were criticizing him!

There were accusations during his most troubled years, beginning in 2001, that he had used human growth hormone (HGH), a nonsteroid performance enhancer. In the Mitchell Report (2007), Brian McNamee, the Yankee assistant strength coach, claimed that he injected Knoblauch seven to nine times with HGH bought from Kirk Radomski, a former Mets bat boy and author of *Bases Loaded* (2009), an exposé about steroids and baseball. Although I saw no direct evidence of illegal drugs while I worked for the team, I did notice that Knoblauch and a few other players occasionally had the quick mood swings and bursts of emotion that have sometimes been linked to performance-enhancing drugs. For what it's worth, Knoblauch's locker was right next to Jason Grimsley's, and they often departed together, joking and laughing. McNamee claims that Knobby paid for HGH through Grimsley, but, again, I don't know if that's true.

After he retired in 2003, Knoblauch wanted to become a private citizen and get away from the public eye. "I don't have any friends from baseball," he said. "Baseball doesn't control my life anymore."

I happened to run into him after his retirement. The year was 2004. He was no longer playing, but he made an appearance at Yankee Stadium as a spectator. I was then a clubhouse attendant, and on this particular day I had to go upstairs to do a favor for one of the players. While I was walking through a crowd of spectators toward the players' parking lot, I found a heavyset square-jawed guy facing me. He was wearing blue jeans and a green dress shirt. There was a bit of stubble on his face. He looked like an ox, but I was in a hurry to get this errand done, and I was surprised when this guy didn't move to let me by.

"Hey," he bellowed.

I looked up into his eyes. Who *was* this guy? He had a fat neck . . .

"Don't you even say hello?"

That crazy voice—*that's* what finally jogged my memory! I recognized him as the man who had been a fun-loving presence on the team for so many years. I wish that I had had more time and wasn't in a rush so I could have chatted with him, but he took a step forward and gave me a friendly bear hug.

"What's up, Squeegee?"

He was with Joe Lee, another clubbie, and they were talking as I hurried away to do my errand.

Here was a class act, and an icon of the Yankee dynasty years. And now, a few short years after his retirement, claiming he's got not a single friend in baseball! Sometimes that's the way it is, though. I moved away, toward the ticket office, wondering whether *I* would have friends from baseball after those glory years.

15

The American Dream
Orlando "El Duque" Hernandez

"Every time we drove up to the north coast of Cuba it was night and the ride was five hours and by the time we got there we were tired and frightened that everybody was watching us to see if we were going to try to escape."

Orlando "El Duque" Hernandez would share his memories whenever he had an opportunity, repeating bits and pieces of the story until I knew it by heart.

"But it wasn't just our imagination," he would say. "They *were* watching us—the moles we called them, the squealers. So we would sit in my friend's car and eat crackers and try to get the smell of fish out of our nostrils and then make the long drive back home. I tried seven times to escape, and seven times took that ride, and seven times felt too afraid to go.

"But on the eighth attempt we set sail in a small fishing boat about the size of a rowboat. Maybe that will give you some idea of how crowded it was with eight men on board. We set off from

Cuba at five in the morning so that we would evade detection by the informers and the military. But by noon the seas had become rough and my companions were all seasick and leaning overboard to throw up. I was afraid that we might capsize, which was a real worry because of the sharks.

"The voyage was difficult for another reason: I was leaving my homeland, my daughters, and my family. Before long we ran ashore on a sand bar between Cuba and the Bahamas. The speedboat that I had arranged to pick us up never came. Stranded on that un-inhabited island for four days, we did our best to survive on a sack of brown sugar and a few cans of Spam. On the last day, shortly after sunrise, the U.S. Coast Guard arrived. I didn't know whether to laugh or cry. No other baseball player ever did anything so idiotic by trying to escape the way I did. They arrested us and threw us into a stinking hole of a jail in Nassau with three hundred refugees."

The best pitcher who ever played in Cuba, when word of El Duque's escape hit the sports world there was a burst of activity, and arrangements were made to bring him to the United States. Through the help of wheeler-dealer agents and politicians, he was eventually signed by the Yankees for $6.6 million and sent to the minor leagues. Then we had the ridiculous disaster of David Cone being bitten on the hand by a dog in 1998, which led to El Duque being brought up to the Majors.

He lifts his leg so high his kneecap reaches the top of his head. *The balance!* Then he fires with his right hand, dealing fastballs, cutters, off speed balls, the works. Not skinny like Mike Mussina,

El Duque is V-shaped and muscular, with especially thick thighs. He wows the New York crowd from his first appearance.

I liked working with him because he was a mystery. There was always something going on behind those dark brown eyes. In fact, there were things about his great escape that he never talked about, horrors he never described. He liked working with me, too, because I understood what he needed.

One of the things he needed most was mud—Lena Blackburne Baseball Rubbing Mud, to be precise. Baseballs fresh from the factory are too slippery for professional pitchers, which is why they're rubbed with this special mud. Despite the fact that the rules require umpires to rub baseballs with mud before each game, the dirty work is usually done by a kid designated to do just this job, and in our club his name was Petey.

"Petey's leaving too much mud on them," El Duque used to tell me. "I want you to lighten 'em up for me."

So when he was pitching I would rub off three balls at a time and run them out to the umpire. It happened that one day Fox News set up a camera in the dugout to show viewers what happens during a typical baseball game. Keep in mind that what I was doing was technically illegal. If other teams had seen me, they wouldn't be too happy since, for all they knew, I might be adding rosin to give our pitchers an unfair advantage. But I didn't consider what I was doing wrong since I wasn't adding anything illegal. At the request of El Duque, I was simply removing some of the rubbing mud, which has the consistency of chocolate pudding. While I was doing this, Joe Torre happened to see me and he came over and leaned close so that the newscasters wouldn't pick up his words.

"You see that camera?"

"Yeah, Skip."

"Well, then the camera can see *you*, too."

"Okay."

"It's *not* okay! If you get caught doing that it could mean trouble—*big* trouble!"

I stopped what I was doing that day. But when the cameras were gone I went right back to doing it to help El Duque. That was all part of the home field advantage: You got to do neat things like that to help your team. Of course, Joe Torre knew it was considered cheating. Nothing got by him . . . Oh, wait a minute—there *was* one thing that Orlando did that got by him, and it was also illegal.

He used to put pine tar in his glove. According to the rules, pitchers are allowed to use rosin to steady their grip, provided they apply it directly to their hand and not to the baseball itself. In fact, a rosin bag is available for their use at the pitcher's mound, placed there by the umpire before the game starts. But pine tar—which is even stickier and provides an even better grip, in the opinion of many pitchers—is prohibited by section 8.02 of the MLB rules. Despite what it said in the rulebook, before he went out to pitch, El Duque used to corner me in the tunnel when I was alone and ask me for a favor.

"Get me the pine tar rag."

I would grab the pine tar rag, and he would walk back and forth to make sure no one was coming. The rest of the team would be on the field so we had some privacy. Then he would take the rag and transfer pine tar to the tip of his glove. Since his glove was black it was impossible to see. I guess he felt that since he was using only a dab it was okay. But he used to yell at me if I wasn't doing it right.

I've worked with guys who were calm, like Andy Pettitte and Scott Brosius, and guys who were emotional, like Jorge Posada and Raul Mondesi. But no one was as worked up as El Duque. I'm not talking about being hotheaded. He didn't fly off the handle and have uncontrolled fits of anger. Instead, he felt things deeply and expressed himself without holding back his feelings the way most men do. If he made a bad pitch he would scream and shout and hit his forehead with his pitching hand. You would see him do this on the mound and in the clubhouse. Once when he felt frustrated I even saw him break down and cry during a game. But none of the fans saw how he reacted emotionally inside the clubhouse. If he was having a bad inning, he would storm in and bang things around and make noise. You didn't want to be near him.

"Coño!" he would yell—a mild Spanish obscenity.

Once he came into the dugout after giving up two runs and he went ballistic. He banged his steel cleats on the wall to get the dirt out. Then he stood in front of the metal telephone box, which housed the land phone; it had a hinged metal door that could be locked with a key. He was staring at it. Steve Donohue, the trainer, touched me on the arm to get my attention. I turned just in time to see El Duque pound his head against the box. *His head!* He was screaming and cursing in English and Spanish, a bad sign.

"Loco!" Steve said.

He even got emotional if his *toe* hurt! Admittedly, he had

bunions, but he would scream about them like a baby. "Why did God give me this problem?" he would cry. Sometimes the pain caused him to give up a few runs and he would get even more worked up because of his apparent personal failure. But he seemed to talk about that pain so much I felt he was attached to it; he might even have *needed* it to fire him up.

Which is when it started to get weird. It dawned on me that El Duque wasn't like other players. He was able to tolerate an extraordinary degree of pain. But not only *tolerate* it: on many occasions I actually saw him *seek out* physical punishment, as if doing so would make him stronger. For example, he used to smoke the harshest cigars, holding smoke in his mouth for a long time until he coughed. One night in Boston outside the hotel lobby he stood smoking his cigar like a madman while other players hung around inside drinking and talking. I went outside with my friend Victor Martinez to say hello. A swarm of Red Sox fans wearing T-shirts had gathered around El Duque, begging for autographs.

"No," barked El Duque. "Not now."

"Please," they were begging him. "Please."

"No! Not now . . . I sign tomorrow in ball park."

Then, as the fans began to walk away, he went into a coughing fit.

In addition to relishing his own pain, he also liked to inflict pain on others. One day I was delivering a tray of salad to the players' lounge when something hit me in the back of the head. I couldn't imagine what it could be until I looked down and saw a black grape—the same kind that was heaped onto platters on the buffet table. Behind the cement pillar stood El Duque. I went up to him for an explanation.

"Did you hit me with that grape?"

He had a serious face on, like someone had pissed him off. I never knew whether he was serious or playing around. His tone of voice and facial expression were hard to read.

"What are you talking about?"

"I got hit by a grape."

"Come on, Luigi, I have things to do."

Then he would look angry, as if I had interrupted something important. That was the strange thing about him. He could be emotional but he could also clam up and be cold as stone. When I asked him about the grapes he would never admit anything. It got aggravating because if it's a joke I expect a player to own up to his behavior. But his denials were so serious and he acted so annoyed, I sometimes doubted my sanity. Could the grape have flown off the plate by itself? There wasn't anyone else in the room. It *had* to have been him. A few days later I was walking by the players' lounge again when another grape struck me in the neck. I turned to see Orlando hiding again behind a concrete pillar in the clubhouse. When I approached, he had the same bitter expression on his face. As if I had hit *him*! The guy refused to admit what he had done.

"El Duque, was that you?"

"Hunh?"

"A grape hit me."

"Come on, man."

And he would just walk away.

The problem was that he was a professional pitcher and he had such good aim that he could hit me from thirty feet. The speed of those grapes has never been clocked, but they used to hit me right in my back and they stung. I wouldn't be surprised if I had red welts from some of them.

Another time there was a rain delay and he flung a rosin bag at me! Then he stepped behind a column in the clubhouse. I almost passed out. You may have seen rosin bags being used by a pitcher on the mound, and sometimes white powder is visible. You might expect it to be soft, like baby powder. But you also have to remember that rosin is composed of hard thumb-sized crystals. We put them into a sock and break them up with five-pound weights from the gym. That's what produces the fine powdery consistency. But there are always good-sized crystals remaining inside the bag even after they're crushed. This was a lot more painful than a grape. But again he denied doing it and acted like I was crazy.

Many players can't deal with the New York pressure—from fans, from the media, and from themselves trying to live up to expectations in the Big Apple. But El Duque was the perfect player for New York. He never let pressure get to him; instead, the more pressure there was, the happier he became.

"Pitching in New York is no pressure for me," he would tell me. "Try getting on a boat and navigating through shark-infested waters to the States. That's pressure. Here, no one's going to kill me if I make a mistake. This is a game."

In the 2000 World Series I was bat boying with George Brown and we would sit right outside the dugout in Shea Stadium with two stools. We were blown away by El Duque's pitching. Some say Andy Pettitte was the best contemporary pitcher for the Yankees. Not in my opinion. In the first eight starts of his Major

League career, El Duque was 8–0 in the postseason. He was unbeatable. The Yankees loved it. And the postseason is where you have to produce because the whole world is watching, not just Yankee fans. He finished with a 9–3 record. The day he pitched against the Mets in the 2000 World Series he struck out twelve guys. He was on pinpoint control. He would come into the dugout huffing and puffing, and when it was time to get back to work he would *run* to the mound, welcoming the physical demands the game made on him. He struck out Mike Piazza, a terrific hitter who used to give Clemens headaches. El Duque holds the record for the most strikeouts in the World Series by a Yankee. For some reason as the stakes got higher, his performance became better.

The more I learned about El Duque, the more convinced I became that he enjoyed pain. For one thing, he was a physical therapist in Cuba, so when he came to the Yankees he didn't need anyone telling him how to punish his body in the gym. He was his own best taskmaster. Clemens and Pettitte may have needed Brian McNamee and Jeff Mangold to push them, but El Duque didn't. He knew how to inflict punishment on himself. Before games he used to soak his hat in ice water and plaster the freezing cap onto his head until his eyes almost popped from their sockets. You would see him in the outfield before a game, practicing that high leg kick until sweat poured off his face like tears.

Of all the pitchers I worked with, he was the most self-contained and needed the least amount of coaching and hand-holding. Unlike Pettitte, who seemed to receive psychotherapy from Mel Stottlemyre, and Clemens, who relied on Torre's assistance to fit in with the team, Orlando was his own boss and maintained a sense of independence that reminded me of nothing so much as a boxer. Between innings he would charge into the dugout and grab a seat on the bench with his towel around his neck, as if waiting for the cornermen to work on him. He would keep his jacket on to keep his pitching arm warm. I would make sure he had two bottles of water by his spot on the bench.

"Go out there and do the right thing," he would say, talking to himself. "Don't let them distract you. Focus on what you have to do."

The thing that convinced me he liked pain was the way he acted in the massage room. Rohan Baichu, a short stocky ex-boxer, had been hired as team masseur, and everyone respected his knowledge. Not Orlando. He would pick on Rohan. He would go in and tell Rohan that everything he was doing was wrong: the way he ate, the way he chewed, even the way he massaged! It amazed me how the rough and tough Rohan—who had muscles that stood out like a bodybuilder's—acted like a little brother to Orlando. In fact, unless you acted that way with El Duque, he wasn't happy. And he liked it best when Rohan would apply so much pressure that it hurt. During games Orlando would enjoy staying in that massage room so much he seemed to live in there. He would lie on the massage table as if it were his bed, chin resting on his arms, looking up at a tiny television the size of a cell phone. The three of us would watch TV in there, and during commercials Orlando would criticize Rohan for being too mild.

"I don't feel it . . . Press! Use more pressure!"

"Like this?"

"No, like *this*."

El Duque would turn and show the guy.

"Run your thumbs deep into the biceps to separate the muscle," he would say. "I want it to burn."

Rohan would apply more pressure to Orlando until he made the man cry out.

El Duque treated his body like a temple: no french fries, no fast food like Mariano, no soda. You would see him come in early to check out the fruit in the buffet. He would scoop up one or two bananas before other players arrived. Then he'd load up on oranges, apples, grapes, salads; whatever was fresh.

He had this leadership quality to him, too, but it was edgy and critical, laced with sarcasm. When Jeter went to bat, for example, El Duque organized a little game in the dugout to poke fun at the captain's song, which happened to be Black Rob's "Whoa!" El Duque would sit on the bench in the dugout, and every time the chorus said "Whoa!" he would lift his hands and legs. Before you knew it, Enrique Wilson was doing the same thing. Then Luis Sojo joined the party. One day Orlando motioned me over.

"Quick, sit down."

"Why?"

"Come on, hurry."

Then the music would start and you'd see El Duque, Wilson, Sojo, and a whole line of Latino players raising their legs and arms. You couldn't resist joining them. It built team chemistry, too. But always El Duque was in charge of it.

He used to love to ride Rob Cucuzza and tease him. If El Duque asked for a sock or a hat and Robbie didn't give it to him right away, he would yell at the guy. One afternoon he asked me to relay a message to Robbie, telling him that El Duque needed a hat. But when the hat didn't show up, he came to me.

"Did you tell Robbie to get my hat?"

"Yeah, an hour ago."

"Okay, come with me."

"Where?"

"To his office."

He would stride into Robbie's office and light into the poor guy.

"Robbie, where's my fucking hat?"

Mr. Cucuzza would start stammering out some lame-brained excuse. El Duque would hold up his fist.

"Get it now or I'll kick your ass."

Despite his sometimes stern nature, I felt a special connection with El Duque since we were both rookies at the same time. I started as a bat boy only a few months before he came up from the minors. When he arrived I helped him get accustomed to New York. I also warned him about Paul O'Neill needing to catch outfield fly balls during batting practice. I translated for him. And I taught him to sing.

There was a song by Angie Martinez that he loved, and he asked me to find it and teach him the lyrics. While he was trying to sing it, he would stop in the middle and ask me, "How's the song go?" Which is how he learned the words. I also helped him organize his fan mail, opening and sorting it so that it would be easier for him to reply.

In 1999 after we beat the Atlanta Braves in the World Series, El Duque was ready to go out and celebrate. He was the first one into his street clothes. I'll never forget how happy he looked, standing by the clubhouse door, smoking a cigar. David Cone was still in uniform. Some guys were drinking champagne. They were all emotional, but especially El Duque. He gave me a hug and signed a picture: TO LUIS / THE BEST BAT BOY ON THE YANKEES / FROM ORLANDO HERNANDEZ / EL DUQUE.

Then he started coughing on that cigar smoke.

16

The Secret Life of a Designated Hitter
Hideki Matsui

Two hundred years from now a baseball statistician in a Brooks Brothers suit will be sitting in his office studying a stack of dusty baseball statistics when a fact sheet about Game 7 of the 2003 American League Championship Series will catch his eye.

"Mother of God!" he'll cry. "What have we here? Who's this old-time Yankee player who caused this spike in the numbers in the bottom of the eighth? Can't make out his name . . . Mat-something. Where's that magnifying glass? . . . Ah, here we go: Mat-su-i . . . Hideki Matsui. Gotta look *him* up."

Of course they'll be looking him up hundreds of years from now, especially to find out about *that* game. The Red Sox had a two-run lead going into the eighth, and the win probability chart of the contest looks like nothing so much as the Rock of Gibraltar. There's a big curve up, like a mountain, a 94 percent likelihood of the Sox winning. Then in the eighth inning a steep drop as the chances of the Sox winning fall straight down to sea level. The man who caused that drop, knocking the Sox back down to reality: Hideki Matsui.

After Jeter and Bernie got on base in the eighth, Red Sox manager Grady Little walked to the mound and asked his pitcher if he had it in him. With 115 pitches thrown, Cy Young Award winner Pedro Martinez decided to stay in the game. The crowd was roaring and wild as Little returned to the dugout, leaving his tired pitcher on the mound. Pedro was always less effective in later innings after he had hurled more than 100 pitches, so maybe Little should have sent in his reliever.

Matsui took a few deep breaths before he left the dugout. I remember the way he walked across the field, his thick black hair blowing in the breeze behind his helmet in the warm October air. Although he was facing an award-winning pitcher, he was unemotional and calm. He walked to the plate holding the bat by the sweet spot. In the batter's box he yanked up his pants, pulled out his jersey to get some ventilation, and raised his bat. On the very first pitch from Martinez, he swung hard and smashed a line drive, a ground-rule double to right field. With that hit he increased the chances of the Yankees winning from 18 to 35 percent and carved a place for himself in baseball history, creating what I like to think of as the Matsui Effect. He contributed to a rally that would culminate, a few innings later, in Aaron Boone's walk-off home run, which sent the Yankees to the World Series.

Matsui excelled under pressure: it seemed to increase his ability. Born in Japan, yet much taller than most Asians at six foot two, he brought a feeling of Eastern calm with him to New York, joining the team in 2003 as a designated hitter and left fielder.

"Hello," he would say to me, and to everyone. He was the most polite player I ever met. I'm sorry that he couldn't speak English better because I'm sure he would have been a terrific conversationalist; despite his unemotional facial expression, he has an extremely friendly disposition. Every time he entered the clubhouse he was sure to greet you. And he stayed around and left the stadium after every other player, too, always saying good night to me and other clubbies and staff.

Like Elvis, everywhere he went he was followed by an entourage of reporters. But unlike most players, he was swarmed by not one, but *two* media camps: the New York press and the Japanese. After every game he would give interviews first to one group, then the other. He was always accompanied by his translator, Roger Kahlon, a clean-cut young man. After batting practice when he walked out it was like a million cameras popping. Jeter used to kid him all the time, saying, "You're a superstar." Truth is, he was. Especially in Japan, where he was worshiped.

The nickname "Godzilla" was first used as a negative comment on his rugged complexion, but now it's complimentary, referring to his devastating hitting power. When he went to bat, we would play a video clip of Godzilla on the TitanTron screen in Yankee Stadium. Matsui also wore the largest helmet of any player, a size 8, because he had a larger head than anyone else. It was topped by long black hair, which he shampooed and blow-dried after every game. When he put on street clothes, however, he often looked out of place, wearing Oriental slacks and unusual shirts.

"My older brother was jealous of me," he told me. "When I was in Japan I was a good hitter and my brother, who was on the same team, wanted me to stop hitting right-handed. That's why I shifted over to hitting lefty. I got used to it very easily, and within weeks I was hitting better than ever as a left-handed hitter. There was nothing they could do about that."

His hitting power was demonstrated in his first game as a Yankee. The Yanks faced the Minnesota Twins. In the fifth inning, they had a 3–1 lead. Nick Johnson hit a single and waited on first. Jason Giambi hit a single, and Johnson reached third. Bernie Williams was intentionally walked, loading the bases. Matsui took his time and worked the count full so that pitcher Joe Mays had to throw the ball over the plate. I remember how Matsui stood waiting for that ball to come in, how fans were cheering "MAT-SOO-EE! MAT-SOO-EE!" and how he put his full upper body into the swing, sending a line drive into the right-field bleachers and a crowd of 33,109 roaring fans. Johnson, Giambi, and Williams scored. Matsui rounded the bases slowly. At first his face had a blank look, but the emotional importance of the moment overcame him. The first Yankee to hit a grand slam *in his first game at Yankee Stadium!* As he walked to meet his teammates, a rare smile lit his face. He entered the dugout. But fans kept cheering. Joe Torre sent him out for a curtain call. Matsui stepped onto the field and raised his hat to salute the fans. The roar of appreciation was deafening: WELCOME TO THE NEW YORK YANKEES!

"I never dreamed of it," Matsui said through his translator. "Certainly I feel a little relief."

When he wasn't hitting grand slams, Matsui was busy backstage in the clubhouse and its surrounding area, entertaining another group of fans: his teammates. For the truth is that on a typical day you'd come in and see a group of Latino players in one corner having a chat in Spanish, a bunch of other players talking in English, and Matsui all by himself. But he was a sociable guy and he made efforts to break through the language barrier and come out of his shell. When he was in the clubhouse, he wanted to try to communicate without his translator. So he would go up to a coach or a player and try to talk to the guy himself. The usual response was: "Hunh? *What* did he say?" Then Mr. Kahlon would join the discussion and do a little translating. But the players all loved Matsui because he was never mean, made no demands on anyone (the way A-Rod did), and wasn't quick to anger (the way Posada and O'Neill were). He was relaxed and brought a calming influence to the team.

As far as I was concerned, he was one of the easiest players to work with, mostly because I never had to clean his locker or the area around it. He and Posada were the neatest players, and of the two Matsui was the winner. Everything was organized in his locker, even his food. This was a big issue for him, too, since he never got used to New York food. He avoided the meals that were prepared and set out in the players' lounge. Instead, he had his own food shipped in from Japan. It would arrive in black boxes to be stored in his locker. This included rice, canned food, and spices. One day I saw him eating a small triangle-shaped food made out of rice. I asked him what it was. "Sushi," he said, glad to speak English with me. He offered me some, and I tried it. "Good, right?" he said. I nodded, and his translator explained that I had just eaten seaweed.

Not only was Matsui neat with his locker, he also had the most unique way of treating his clothes. Most players leave uniforms and underwear on the floor or on their chairs. Not Matsui. He folded his soiled clothes and wrapped a thick rubber band around them so that they would get washed as a bundle. Total class act. Matsui was so well liked in the clubhouse it's no wonder he was liked by fans, too. They liked him so much that when he left the team in 2010 he still got cheered by New York fans even when he hit home runs *against* us!

One day shortly after joining the team, Matsui hit a home run and came back into the dugout, where he sat down on the bench to relax. I happened to be sitting beside him, and I noticed that, unlike A-Rod or Ruben Sierra—who usually bragged about what they had done—Matsui didn't say anything. I thought it was odd, too, that his face didn't register any emotion. Usually a player will come back to the dugout excited about his performance. Not Hideki. He was the same whether he won or lost. He sat there and actually put his head down instead of holding it up. He ran his fingers through his long black hair. Robin Ventura came by and congratulated him, and only then did Hideki look up and say, "Ja, Ja," acknowledging his teammate's praise. There was no bragging, no boasting. Never before or since have I encountered a player who was so much in control of his emotions.

The only time I saw him express his emotions was also unique because unlike American or Latin players he didn't express anger or joy. Instead, it was depression that clouded his features. It was after we lost Game 6 of the 2003 World Series. He was sitting in the clubhouse with ice packs on his knee and shoulder. Joe Torre held a meeting after we lost that game to the Florida Marlins. No media. Closed door. It was like a funeral in the Yankee clubhouse. Everyone was depressed. Making it worse, we could hear the Marlins celebrating outside in our own stadium. Matsui must have been wondering, What would it have been like if I helped win a World Series in my first year with the Yankees?

"You have nothing to be ashamed of," Torre told them. "You made your best effort."

But even those reassuring words could not bring Matsui out of his depression.

The funniest thing he ever did occurred the next year during a team meeting. I never knew he had such a good sense of humor. It was before Game 7 of the American League Championship Series, a game which we would lose. The series was tied 3–3 at that point, and it was particularly disheartening since we had won the first three games. But, unknown to us, Boston's comeback was not to be stopped. At any rate, at the end of the meeting it was traditional for Torre to ask Posada what we were going to do. He would reply, "Grind it!" This time—I guess to make Matsui feel more a part of the team—Torre turned to *him* at the end of the meeting.

"What are we going to do?"

Hideki paused for just a second before replying.

"Kick ass. Pop champagne. And get some ho's."

For a man who could barely complete a simple English sentence to fire off that reply stunned the entire room and left them helpless with laughter. Posada couldn't contain himself, he was laughing so hard. Jeter, Giambi, and even A-Rod were all laughing themselves silly.

Matsui told me once that he loves his fans because "it's the duty of a baseball player to do that." In this, too, he was unique. He was the only player who never refused to sign autographs. Ask him to sign a dozen baseballs, he sits there and signs them all for you. Fans prized these autographs, too, because he signed first in English and then, underneath, in Japanese.

A tireless player with the strength of an Ironman, Matsui had a streak of 1,768 consecutive games in his professional career (518 in the Majors in the States, the rest in Japan). Only two other players, Cal Ripkin, Jr., and Lou Gehrig, played more consecutive games. I think he was able to get a record like that because he paced himself and kept his emotions in check.

Sometimes I used to like to follow Matsui around just to get a look at the pretty Japanese reporters who interviewed him. I tried to strike up a conversation with one of them one day, but was met with confused looks. Apparently she didn't speak English. Next chance I got, I asked Matsui for help.

"How do I get a girl's number?"

"What number?"

"Her phone number. How do I ask her for it in the Japanese language?"

He laughed. Then he got serious. He told me how to say it. Even his translator got into the act. They coached me for a week. Over and over I would repeat the phrase, until it sounded right to them. But an hour later it would slip from my mind and I'd mangle it. I realized, then, how hard it must be for Hideki to master English when I couldn't even get a simple phrase like "Can I have your number?" right.

"I want you to try it," Matsui said to me one day. "The pretty girl will be here this afternoon."

After the game I went out to the field, prepared to try my new language skills. Just before going up to the girl, I whispered the Japanese sentence to Matsui. His face turned red.

"What's the matter?"

"You said wrong thing."

"What did I say?"

His translator was laughing.

"You said, 'Can I have your car?'"

I looked over at the girl, who was holding a microphone, ready to interview Godzilla. I just shook my head. Matsui smiled and said, "Maybe next time you get pronunciation right." Then he walked over to do his interview.

No wonder he has a translator.

17

*The Monster in Pinstripes
Alfonso Soriano*

Tall and wiry, the man at the plate is taking his sweet time, and the New York crowd is eating it up like cake and candy. Alfonso Soriano watches yet *another* pitch go by . . . but doesn't swing. Spectators are smiling in the stands, leaning forward in the bleachers, talking excitedly in the front rows. *Hey, hey, hey, look at this!*

Oakland Athletics pitcher Barry Zito looks puzzled.

Soriano is the guy who used to swing at *everything*. Known as a free swinger, he was liable to lean over the plate and try to clip balls that came in outside the strike zone or on the edge of it. He would dip to hit a slider. He would lean back to slam inside balls. He was fast and furious, but most of all he was a hacker. *He had never walked in his entire professional career with the Yankees.* Everyone knew this. It was either hit with a sound like a rifle shot (often a home run), or strike out. There was no in-between with this guy.

Now it's another story. He's not taking the bait on anything! What the devil has gotten into him?

Ball three . . . and the windup . . . and the pitch.

The crowd of 32,888 leans forward as if it's a single spectator, anticipating what Soriano will do, where the pitch will go, what will happen next.

BALL FOUR!

Big wide smile on Soriano's face, he walks—yes, walks, for the first time in his career with the Yanks—to first base. The crowd is cheering, applauding, and making itself heard loud and clear: WAY TO GO, ALFONSO!

In the Yankee dugout we're all laughing and feeling loose. Our man on first has matured at last. He's learned that perhaps it's not a good idea to swing at *every* piece of junk a pitcher throws at you. Even if you do have long arms and quick hands—two of Alfonso's strengths—sometimes it's better for your team if you wait out those pitches and take a walk. I was in the dugout when he got his first walk, and I could see him beaming with happiness on first base as if he had achieved another milestone in his career. And he had! Shane Spencer leaned toward me and grinned. "Tough crowd!" he said, laughing along with the rest of his teammates. Yes, even the fans knew that Alfonso had made a giant leap forward in his playing strategy. We were all waiting to see what he would do next.

Born and raised in the Dominican Republic, where baseball is even more popular than in the States, Alfonso grew up the youngest child in his family, with an older sister and two older brothers, both of whom would play baseball in the minors. Before long the skinny, dark-skinned Alfonso was drafted to play on a Japanese team. Quick to learn new customs and traditions, he soon picked up enough Japanese to get by without a translator. What he didn't learn, however, was how to get used to the grind of Japanese baseball drills in Hiroshima. He never liked regimentation, and that was the Japanese style, just like their strict management style. *Rise and shine at daybreak, do your sit-ups, follow orders.* This ain't the life for me, he was thinking. In fact, as soon as possible he made a break.

By the time he returned to the States and I met him in a Yankee uniform, he had gone up and down from the minors to the Majors so many times he was getting dizzy. The Yankees kept pulling switches on him, too. First he was called upon to replace Jeter when the captain was on the disabled list. Unfortunately, Soriano didn't do too well as shortstop and he made some bad throws to Tino, causing the veteran first baseman to make errors. Later, Soriano would be called upon to replace Chuck Knoblauch when Knobby got the yips, but even at second base Alfonso was having some trouble adapting to the quick footwork and precision throwing needed for a double play. Yes, he was strong in the arm, but he needed work on technique. To his credit, he buckled down to try to perfect every new assignment the Yankees threw at him— shortstop, outfield, second base, and various utility positions. Torre and Cashman watched him carefully, convinced he had potential; the only issue was where to put this crackerjack all-around player.

After a while Alfonso's head was spinning and he felt a little dispirited since he couldn't find his spot with the team, but maybe his biggest strength was his adaptability and his I-can-do-it attitude. Nothing got him down for long. When you saw him smiling, that big wide grin, you knew he had heart. In fact, he used to take off his shirt in the clubhouse and hold up his arms like Popeye and ask me, "Which way to the gym? Hehehe!" The guy was a jokester, full of life and funny energy. Truth be told, he was the kind of guy who never got into arguments or fights with other players. He had a smooth, friendly personality. Skinny as a devil, he was cut and muscular, too, especially in the arms and chest.

"I'm *El Monstro*," he used to say, Spanish for "the monster." His voice was soft and high-pitched and when he wanted to make you laugh, he would add, "You know, you know, baby, that's me."

He was the only one on the team who could talk to Matsui in Japanese. I used to see them having conversations, the two of them gabbing away like old friends so that Matsui's translator, who was never far from the DH, would be amazed that someone else could speak the language.

Sometimes when I was working on the foul line between first and home plate, I would see Soriano looking not at the man hitting the baseball—which is where a fielder's eyes *should* be—but instead up at the fans cheering and yelling in the stands. *The man was looking at the fans!* Usually it's the other way around, but Soriano was such an easily distracted guy, he was different from all the other professional baseball players I've worked with. It was a little funny to see him lose focus during a game like that. At least it was funny to me. But Joe Torre and the Yankee management didn't find it funny.

One day—and I have to tell you that I laugh whenever I remember this—Soriano wasn't paying attention to the signals the coaches were trying to give him. When certain batters get ready to hit, you're supposed to move to the right of second base since these hitters are known to send balls into that area. Experienced fielders will make the adjustment and get set for a ball driven up between second and third. Statistically that's where it's going to go, so you might as well get ready for it. *Wellll,* not Alfonso. He's spacing out, just standing there on top of second. Man, were the coaches getting wild! They're jumping up and down. Joe Torre is waving his arms. Willie Randolph, the bench coach, is turning blue in the face, whistling, and making hand signals to this guy, but no dice, he doesn't see them. Finally Torre whistles to Tino, the first baseman (which is unheard of during a game!) to tell him: "Hey, tell that guy to move over!"

I don't know what it was with Soriano. He was such a nice guy, but his mind wasn't always where you thought it should be.

Like the time I saw him running back into the clubhouse during an inning. *Where the heck is he going so fast?* Then I get inside and I see him click open his cell phone. Now, you have to understand that this is strictly against team rules. You're not supposed to be on your phone during a game. All the veterans know that. They're focused as hell. You never see Mariano Rivera or Paul O'Neill on a telephone of any kind during a game. To them, nothing's more important than the contest going on at the moment between their flagship team and whoever they're fighting.

Then I see Soriano push the button to connect his call and— get this, you're not going to believe it—he bends over in front of his locker and sticks his head into the space between his clothes and the partition. He's in there, with his ass sticking out over the chair, his head buried inside the locker, talking on the damn phone to some girl who's God knows where, sweet talking her. It was so ludicrous I damn near peed my pants.

"Honey," he was cooing. "Baby, where we gonna meet to-night? . . . Yeah, the game's still on. No, don't bother turning on the television now, honey, sweetie pie, I ain't there right now on the bases, I'm in the locker room on the phone. I'm telling you, you won't see me if you turn it on . . . What? . . . You want me to do what? . . . Okay, baby doll, okay, no problemo . . . When I see you I'm gonna bring you a present, too."

Next thing I know, Mike Mussina walks by and spots Soriano with his ass in the air and his head in the locker. Mussina is a dark-haired guy with a pointy jaw who looks like a college kid who's stayed up for an all-nighter. His eyes bug out when he hears Soriano chatting on the phone.

"What the hell are you doing?"

Soriano peeks out just long enough to make sure it isn't George Steinbrenner, flashing Mussina his signature white grin.

Mussina shakes his head and storms out.

"Yeah, baby, yeah, baby," Soriano croons, getting right back into it.

Nothing could stop the guy from having fun. Even if the game was going well, he would have to have *more* fun and *more* laughs. For most guys just being on the Yankees was enough. They would devote every speck of their energy to the task at hand, and even between innings when taking a leak they would be thinking about what they would be doing next. Not good old Sori, as we called him. Not the Monster. This guy needed constant excitement.

I'm not sure if it was his distractible nature or his lack of experience on the field, but he started making more errors after 2001. One day Torre got fed up. I was in the dugout when the manager reached out his hand as Sori was walking by and grabbed the second baseman by the elbow, drawing him close and talking to him like a father scolding his son. "Don't you do that again," he said. The error he was talking about involved a double play and a slipup by Sori that stood out like a sore thumb. Alfonso was criticized on national television. Torre never did this kind of thing, usually waiting for the privacy of his team meetings. But his message got through to Sori, who took it in good humor and who apologized. I distinctly heard him say "I'm sorry." It takes a big man to admit an error in public, and after that day I had renewed respect for the most relaxed man on the team.

Sori liked to party and was seen with girls on numerous occasions when we went out to bars and restaurants. One day Soriano, El Duque, Mondesi, Rob Cucuzza, and Mendoza and his wife threw a birthday party for me, and I was having a blast, drinking and dancing with a girl. But this party turned out to be a nightmare for me, and only Soriano had the wisdom to see the problem coming and warn me about it—bless his heart! I'll never forget his advice, either, although I was too dumb to take it at the time.

We were in Jimmy's Bronx Café, and everybody kept telling me that Mondesi was coming but that he would be late and that he had a surprise for me. We were eating dinner in the VIP section, and then we left and went into the club after our meal. Soriano started dancing with a dark-haired girl who was wearing a silver dress. Finally Mondesi arrived with what looked like a truckload of women. He had seven girls with him, and they were wearing outfits that revealed more than they concealed. These girls were tall and thin and catching the eye of all who saw them, including your unfortunate narrator.

The girl who was my date for the evening was sitting on my lap with her arms around me. I was hammered, having consumed three glasses of Dom Pérignon. Mondesi was wearing a wide-brimmed straw hat, a white shirt, cream pants, and bright diamond earrings. Swaggering and smiling, he looked like a pimp as he led the seven women over to me. Out of the corner of my eye I noticed Soriano making a motion with his hand. So the guy had finally learned how to use signals, I thought, laughing to myself. He had one hand raised and was waving his index finger back and forth in a gesture that might have meant, "No, no" or "Don't, don't." I was wondering what he was talking about but my brain was too numbed to understand.

Mondesi was standing before me, smiling his head off.

"Go ahead, Luigi," he said. "Pick the girl you want."

The seven beauties gathered round in a semicircle, and my eyes widened. Meanwhile, Soriano was waving his finger faster than ever, as if to say, "No, no, don't you do it." I know now what he was trying to tell me, but at the time I had no power to resist. Still trying to save me from my own folly, Soriano sprang forward and grabbed Mondesi by the ear.

"Leave the kid alone!" he was saying.

But Mondesi laughed and pushed Sori away and turned to me again, waiting for my response. The perfume from one of the brunettes filled my lungs as she got closer, and I sealed my fate when I smiled at her and nodded. Before long we were dancing close. Mondesi slapped me on the back and said, "Happy Birthday!" In a haze I hardly noticed that the girl I had come to the party with had turned bright red and was backing away with a frown.

Oh, how right you were, Sori! How I should have listened! If only I had paid attention to your signals. A man who knew women, he had predicted that I would be in trouble, and, like a good friend, had tried his best to protect me.

Mondesi, on the other hand, who I thought was doing me a favor, caused me to break up with my significant other, although he probably wound up with two or three of those little darlings himself. The truth is that girls were almost always around when we went out. Another time in Detroit in 2005, I was in a motel with one of the relief pitchers who had asked me to accompany him to a casino to try to pick up girls. But nothing was happening at the bar, so we went back to his room where he decided to order an escort from the yellow pages. He found a photo of a girl he liked and asked me to place the call. "My God," he was saying. "This girl is hot. Look at her! I can't wait to meet her." Then he got into bed in his Speedo briefs to await the arrival of this doll. When the doorbell rang his jaw dropped. "That's not her!" he cried. "You're not the girl in the picture," he told her. "I don't want you." She demanded payment, and we wound up giving her thirty bucks and then ordering pizza for ourselves.

Girls, bars, and restaurants—those were the favorite ways for players to bond and have fun when they had time off. In fact, after that party with the seven girls, Sori and I got along better than ever. One day I went to work early and he approached me at my locker.

"Hey, kid, how you get waves in your hair?"

In those days it was trendy to have a wavy hairstyle. He and I had similar haircuts, which is what prompted him to ask for advice. I told him my secret, which was a product called Sporting Waves. "I'll get you some," I said. Next day I brought the little blue and yellow box in as a gift, and I explained how to use it. You had to rub it on your hair and then cover it with a do-rag until the chemicals seeped into the hair to make the design. Next day I saw him wearing a do-rag. The day after that he was brushing his hair at his locker mirror, and his hair had those waves! Yeah, I thought. It's come full circle. Sometimes players made me look like them. Like Ruben, for example. Sometimes I made them look like me! How fitting.

One afternoon Sori came to work with a box and told me he wanted my help. Inside the box was a bunch of blue and white T-shirts imprinted with words that made me stare when I saw them:

40–40 SORI

I looked at them dumbstruck.

"What the heck is *this*?"

"I'm gonna be in the 40–40 club."

I thought about it for a second. Then I realized that he was right. We all knew that he was close. The 40–40 club is a group of players who have forty home runs and forty stolen bases in one season. If he made it to this distinguished group he would join the ranks of Alex Rodriguez, Barry Bonds, and Jose Canseco. But I had never seen a player so eager to jump into history . . . Well, on second thought, I guess I *had* seen it in A-Rod. What I had never encountered before, however, was a player who had such a childish approach to the prospect of getting into the history books. Sori was the opposite of A-Rod, who was always serious as hell about his wins and the possibility of getting another award. Sori, on the other hand, was acting like a six-year-old waiting for Christmas, virtually jumping up and down with anticipation even before winning the award.

"What are you going to do with these shirts?"

He unbuttoned his jersey. Like Superman revealing his secret identity, underneath he was wearing a T-shirt saying 40–40 SORI.

"I want you to wear one," he said. "And make sure the other bat boys and clubhouse attendants wear them, too. And I want you to walk around the stadium and let people see it."

I had never heard anything so silly, but I figured what the heck, and before the day was over I had put the T-shirt on under my uniform and distributed the entire box to our bat boys and to anyone else I could get to wear one. Unfortunately, we waited and waited but he didn't hit the home run he was expecting. He had thirty-nine home runs and needed just one more, but it wasn't happening. The savvy pitchers he came up against knew he was waiting for that home run, and they saw him changing his hitting style in anticipation of the grand slam he thought he would hit. So they changed their pitching style and confused the poor guy! I thought he jinxed himself by getting those T-shirts before even winning the award. He starting acting cocky and arrogant, strutting around with the T-shirt under his jersey like he was already in the club. In the end, he never did make it that year, while he was with the Yankees, though he *did* pass the forty mark with stolen bases, getting forty-one. He also made the 30–30 club, being one of the few second baseman to ever do that. (It would be two years before he finally made the 40–40 club, and by that time he was with the Washington Nationals.)

But after this, having at least had the distinction of making the

30–30 club, he gained a lot of confidence that he hadn't possessed before. He didn't walk with a swagger, but he seemed to have arrived. Now he felt like one of the star players. He had reached the ranks of being a top Yankee. It didn't change the kid in him, though. Nothing could do that. He still did funny things. Like when he hit a home run he would hit hands with all the guys in the dugout, take off his helmet and then say "*Toma,*" which is Spanish for "Here, take that!" Posada and Jeter loved it. It was Sori's way of having fun.

I got to see Sori rise through the ranks, try a lot of different positions, and finally make a spot for himself on second base. It was rewarding to see a player come into his own. But New York is a tough town, and only the best of the best can survive for long in this environment. So I also got to see him decline from grace after he was injured a number of times. He got clipped by a few inside balls, recovered from that, but then his hitting started to get worse and his errors on the field multiplied beyond an acceptable amount. It was like he was returning to his early distractible days.

During the 2002 playoffs with the Anaheim Angels he had twenty-six strikeouts, a Major League playoff record but *not* the kind of record you want. The Yankees figured it would be the perfect time to let him go, and they traded him in a deal for Alex Rodriguez. I, for one, was sorry to see him traded for he had been the life of the clubhouse. I could tell he was disappointed, too. I could see it in his face. It happened that once he went to the Texas Rangers he would come back now and then to peek in the clubhouse and say hello, even in a Rangers uniform! Like he was still part of the team! He was such a friendly guy that we all loved to see him, too. Jeter and the guys would greet him with big hellos and smiles.

After he was traded to the Chicago Cubs in 2007, he got my cell number from a Mets clubbie and called one day. "We're playing the Mets, and I'll be in town and would love to say hello. Why don't you come to the game as my guest?" I was sitting in the stands when he stopped by after the game and asked how I was doing and how my family was. He had that same big smile. I could tell he missed his teammates on the Yankees.

But that's the nature of professional sports, from the lowest to the highest level. It doesn't matter if it's a high school team, a minor league team, or a Major League team. You come together, like one big happy family—sometimes dysfunctional, but more often than not happy—and then, like any family, well, you go your separate ways.

18

The Man in the Iron Mask
Joe Girardi

On July 18, 1999, Joe Girardi emerged from the weight room with a stack of papers in hand and went up to David Cone and started his pregame chat. "Look at this young hacker they have in the lineup. These guys will swing at passing airplanes." Things like that.

Chatting about pitchers and hitters came easy to Girardi. He was a master of the quick wisecrack, too. Upbeat and tough, with muscles in his arms, quads, and behind his ears, he could think on his feet and feed you stats and info faster than you could take it in. David Cone was nodding, listening, absorbing. These two were going to be working together as our point men against the Montreal Expos. Lucky for us, as a catcher Girardi had lots more going for him than fast reflexes and nimble limbs: He also had brains.

Not to mention papers. Ledger sheets. Statistics. The guy amazed me. I'd see him walking around the clubhouse in full catcher's gear, a bunch of papers in one hand, a pencil in the other. He always had notes with him. Ask Posada what he remembers about the 1996 season, for example, he says, "I remember [Joe] looking through notes, going through the hitters, going through our pitchers, their strength, their weakness." Although Girardi might have seemed a little geeky at times, he was basically a technician, a guy who had the facts and figures and who used them for one purpose—to help the *team* win.

On this particular day, however, Girardi and Coney could not have known that their pregame conversation would lead to an important moment in baseball history: a perfect game. Joe was looking from the notes to David and back again, ticking off names: "Orlando Cabrera, Vladimir Guererro, Jose Vidro . . ."

David listened, then began walking back to the trainer's room for his massage, followed by the catcher.

"You never faced any of these guys before," Girardi was saying, two steps behind the starting pitcher. "But they're all free swingers. They're going to be trying to clobber us from the get-go."

Okay, I thought. Okay. Give it a rest.

Then I smiled to myself. Joe never gives it a rest. Once he gets his heart set on something—like winning a game—he goes after it and doesn't stop until he gets it. The guy was harsh the way he went through the Expos' lineup, and I don't for a minute doubt that he was right on the money with his analysis of every one of the opposing batters.

Later in the day as the game wore on, I was out in the field and watched Girardi work. The miracle of it was that *not once* did he go to the mound. Never did he have to call a time out and talk with Coney. Every finger he put down Cone threw. They worked like the most perfect team, as if they could read each other's minds.

Another great catcher, Jorge Posada, who Girardi would train, would turn out to be a better hitter; but Girardi (who also caught Dwight "Doc" Gooden's 1996 no-hitter) might have been more knowledgeable behind the plate. Not to take anything away from Posada—a potential Hall of Fame candidate—but Girardi wasn't just putting emotion and talent on the field, he was bringing a thorough knowledge of the guys we were up against, together with a game plan for how to shoot each one of them down.

The first thing Coney did was fire fastballs at the Expos, showing them that he had it and that he would be fearless about using it against them. Then he widened the strike zone, an inch to the left, an inch to the right. And I could see this tight smile creep onto Girardi's face. The television cameras were rarely on him for a close-up, but from where I was standing I knew that he had something up his sleeve. He looked like he was in seventh heaven. For a catcher, that's a feeling you get when the pitcher and you are working like clockwork. As Coney widened the strike zone, Girardi loosened up, moving left and right to match the incoming artillery. Nothing got away from him.

Girardi was a master of using his knees to twist from side to side as needed to capture pitches. He knew what was coming, but he still had a breeze to contend with on that day, as well as rain, and the fact that the unexpected is always possible. He went left and he went right, and not one ball got away from him. Before the fifth inning was over, David Cone was aware that he was pitching a perfect game, and Girardi knew that he was catching one. The tension mounted as batter after batter struck out.

The slider was probably the most unhittable Cone ever threw, zeroing in on home plate until the last few hundredths of a second, when it would tail in toward the batter's hands. *Strike! Strike! Strike!* Music to Girardi's ears.

The fact is that *pitchers* usually get credit for a win, and most fans remember who the pitcher was, not the catcher. This is because the pitcher is very visible and there is more motion on his part. Granted, the pitcher is also the one throwing the strikes. The catcher, though, is the other half of the equation, and it's his job to review opposing batters in his mind and remember what they did the last time they were up at bat, figuring out which pitch to use next. This is an art more than a science because you can never be sure that the pitch you're calling for is correct.

"It becomes somewhat nerve-racking," Girardi says. "From a catcher's perspective, you go over and over and over the hitters in your head, how you've gotten them out, how you're going to approach them in their next at-bat."

But that smile on Girardi's face told me that he wasn't only thinking and handling the stress well, he was also enjoying the experience—at least some of the time. What more could you ask from an athlete who is part of a winning team? Coney threw a few sliders into the dirt, but Girardi was all over them before they could escape.

When the win came, Girardi rushed out to embrace Coney, who had dropped to his knees in joy.

Of all the players on the team, Girardi was probably the slowest runner, so when he *did* move fast people noticed. He was the first to reach Cone to congratulate him after that perfect game, but the rest of the team wasn't far behind. I remember another time Girardi moved fast, and it was so unusual people commented. On that day he hit a triple, which is quite unusual for a catcher since he has to hustle to get from home to third, and catchers aren't known for speed. I was in the dugout when it happened and Jeter jumped to the railing.

"Look at Yo-yo!" he cried, referring to Joe by his nickname. "Look at Yo-yo fly!"

Tino Martinez sprang forward to see, saying, "Look at Yo-yo go!"

Joe was hustling all right, his feet a blur of motion, head bopping back and forth, pushing his luck and getting all the way to third. Jeter had a big smile on his face and Tino was laughing because they had never seen him move like that. And yet, in those exciting days, during the dynasty years, there were no holes in our lineup. Sometimes when you go to play a team you can count on one or two slackers in the lineup, but in the Yankees, Joe—who batted ninth—held his own. That's how the Yankee lineup was: patient and able to exhaust the opposing pitcher on pitch counts. Girardi might not have gotten as many home runs as Posada would in his career, but he still hit his share of doubles and singles to keep us in the race.

If anything sticks in my mind about Joe it's that no one had a more distinctive appearance in the clubhouse than he did. He wasn't tall, like Paul O'Neill and Andy Pettitte. Instead, he was short and muscular. But there was one other thing that made him stand out: He was always in his catcher's gear, even when eating a snack or reading a newspaper. Why was it, I asked myself, that the man who won three World Series rings as catcher for the Yankees wore his chest protector and shin guards so often? He paraded about like a knight in armor even on days when he wasn't catching. You had to see—and hear—him to believe it: eating and walking around in that getup, making a strange *eeeeeek-unph* . . . *eeeeeek-unph* . . . *eeeeeek-unph* squeaking sound.

Part of the answer must have been that he loved to catch, even on days when he wasn't scheduled to. He wanted to be ready to do his job whenever the call came. The other reason he wore the equipment so much may have had something to do with his military bearing. When I say military I mean he was like a soldier and he towed the line. For example, he loved to shave and he demanded that others be clean-shaven, too. You would see him shaving all the time, feeling his face to make sure it was smooth. With a smile, he would criticize me about having a mustache, instructing me to get a haircut and a shave. He was a mini Steinbrenner. For Joe, everything had to be precise and neat; and everything had only one function and one purpose, even people. *His* function, of course, was catching, so he always wanted to appear ready to do that. You would even see him at team meetings and in the kitchen in full gear.

When I first met Joe he had black hair, but over time it turned gray. I think part of that came with the stress of managing. He was also more muscular and had a rounder face during his early days with the team. Today you can see his cheekbones and I wonder if his diet isn't catching up with him; in fact, he was very strict with that and used to worry about the food he ate. He hated the players' lounge food and considered it junk, especially the soft drinks and cake.

I got a taste of Girardi's military style of running things in 1998 when I was a bat boy and he was catcher. I was covering for one of the other bat boys for a one o'clock day game. Joe saw me at work in the clubhouse and he noticed that other clubbies were absent and that I was doing double duty. He came up to me like a drill sergeant.

"Squeegee, why aren't you in school this afternoon?"

"I'm playing hooky to cover for Tad."

He knit his brows. "I'll have to talk to Robbie about this."

He was so strict he marched me into Rob Cucuzza's office and demanded to know why a high school kid was being encouraged to play truant.

Robbie hemmed and hawed for a while, then he pretended to be angry, saying, "I'll write him a letter to explain his absence."

"But he shouldn't be allowed to continue this behavior," Joe said. He started yelling at Robbie. "This isn't right."

Robbie, of course, never wrote the letter. If Joe had known all the things that Robbie did he would have freaked out. For example, Robbie jumped when certain players wanted a piece of equipment. If Jeter or Andy needed a glove or a bat, the equipment room would be opened at once. But if Mendoza, Sojo, or another less well-known player needed something, they might have to wait days. Some of the guys got annoyed at this special treatment and they turned to me for help. I had to sneak and get an extra key made so that I could do Robbie's job, giving these guys the equipment they needed when they needed it.

One day Robbie told me, "These players aren't your friends. Watch out for them." As if *he* knew them better than I did. Actually, now that I've been away from the team for a few years, I still have a number of baseball friends, like Ramiro Mendoza and Ruben Sierra, and I talk with them and see them when they're in town.

Robbie even used to make me cover for him and say that he wasn't there when a player like Mendoza called. I had to deceive my own friend to save Robbie the trouble of taking a simple phone call.

I'm sure Joe would have hated this kind of behavior as much as I did. He was all for fairness. He never would have tolerated the way pitcher Tanyon Sturtze threw me into the garbage can on Rookie Dress-Up Day. It was just plain unfair. Sturtze's excuse was that he was in a bad mood because he had given up a couple of runs. Making matters worse, even though Sturtze was a veteran, Robbie had taken away his clothes as a practical joke; as if Sturtze had to wear the costume, too. But he was the only one who was upset because the rest of us were cheerfully looking forward to the rookies having to wear Hooters outfits. The media was covering the event, and I innocently went about my job, collecting hats from players to put in the hat box so that we could travel out of town. By coincidence, Sturtze and I both went for the box at the same time, and at just that instant I happened to be laughing hysterically at the costumes. He thought I was laughing at him. "What the fuck are you laughing at?" he said. And all of a sudden he snapped. He grabbed me by the shirt and threw me into a garbage can. I held on for dear life, grabbing his jersey. Two seconds later he must have realized that the media was in there and he picked me up and dusted me off, as if to say, I'm just kidding. That was the first time a player ever put his hands on me. He apologized to me in Boston, and after that we became the best of friends.

Girardi had strong emotions, too, but he never let them get the better of him the way Sturtze or some other players did. He always seemed to have his eye on a bigger picture, and in many ways he was *more* than a player, he was a leader.

Even in those early days I could see the way he prepared himself for the transition from playing to managing. He used to buddy up with Don Zimmer all the time. You could count on Joe to be asking questions in the dugout about why this or that decision had been made. He was being groomed for the position of manager. The funny thing was that Zimmer also taught Girardi to curse. Joe was very religious, but he also had a temper. His religious scruples made him ashamed of using obscenities in front of other people but left him with so much internal steam that when he got angry players thought he was going into cardiac arrest—his neck veins stood out like pipes and his face became red as a tomato.

The odd thing was that the more Girardi associated with Zimmer, the more Girardi would express his anger. For example, Zimmer and he were the first to yell at a bad call. You would see them jump up and run to the railing and even step onto the field to make their point. At first it was just Zim yelling obscene things at opposing players and umpires. But as Joe learned more and more from the veteran bench coach, you'd hear Joe joining in, so that if anything went wrong, you would hear both of them shouting in unison:

"Bullshit!"

"Come on!"

"Terrible!"

"Keep your eyes open, you're missing a good game!"

"Horseshit!"

Joe was a quick study, and there's no question that he learned to curse from one of the best. He was also a patient and dedicated teacher. I was there during the months he groomed Posada to take over as starting catcher. The two men had their gear on—leg guards, chest protectors, face masks—and they would rehearse what Posada had to do to catch baseballs thrown into the dirt, to the side, and straight at him. Joe would give him a few words of instruction and then Posada would practice the moves. During spring training they would work out with the catching coach, and the lessons eventually enabled Jorge to take over as starting catcher.

The fact that he wore his catching gear all the time made Joe appear a little removed from things, but he made up for this by being extra social and outgoing. He was always chatting with players; in fact, he was the only person who could talk with Paul O'Neill, especially when Paulie was in a bad mood. Joe's locker was right next to Paulie's and Joe would chat with the right fielder all the time. They would talk quietly for a while, and then all of a sudden Joe would laugh.

Snnnnnoooooorrrh! His laugh was a loud snort, like the sound of a wild hog. *Snoooooooooooorrrrrh!*

The sound of that snort, together with Joe's friendliness, had a calming effect on Paulie's nerves.

Other times I'd see Joe come up to his locker, and the first words out of his mouth would be, "Hey, *O'Neeeeeeeill*," dragging out the syllables in Paulie's name. This, too, always put O'Neill in a good mood. For some reason, Joe was able to get through to his moody teammate better than anyone. So I wasn't surprised when he eventually accepted a job as the Yankees' manager. He knew how to get along with people, was respectful, and had the disciplined military qualities needed to lead the Yankees.

Every time I see him do an interview on television, though, I can't help thinking he'd be happier if he was talking from behind that mask.

19

The New Ruthless Ruth
Jason Giambi

New York. Darkness gathering round a dismal, damp Yankee Stadium. Short-tempered fans clamping soggy tabloids to their heads, filtering out in dejection and disappointment, convinced *we can't possibly win this one—not in a million years.* More rain than most baseball fans can tolerate. Five extra innings . . . and then in the top of the fourteenth the Minnesota Twins score three runs, sending additional droves of spectators heading for the doors. The score stands at 12–9. *I'm going and I'm not looking back! No way in heaven we can get out of this jam.*

A black squirrel dashes along the foul line and slips under the fence. More drizzle. Twins reliever Mike Trombley stands waiting for the first Yankee batter to challenge him in the bottom of the fourteenth. He's extremely confident since even if the Yankees manage to score two runs in this inning, his team will *still* win. Shane Spencer tiptoes to the plate, uniform clinging to his body, and miraculously manages to hit a line-drive single to left field. But then Alfonso Soriano sends a fly ball to left field for the first out. The win expectancy (the statistical chances of the Yankees winning in this situation) is only 5 percent. Yankee fans can feel it in their rain-soaked bones . . . *Home teams in this kind of predicament lose 95 percent of the time.* Jeter comes to bat with the confidence born of believing he's a clutch hitter . . . and drives a single to center field, allowing Spencer to reach third. A ripple of hope spreads through the small group of fans remaining in the damp stands. New York's win expectancy creeps up from 5 to 12 percent. The next batter is Bernie Williams, who walks, loading the bases and bringing New York's win expectancy up to 21 percent. Still nothing to write home about. No statistician would bet on the Yanks winning now, even as Jason Giambi comes to bat.

With the looks of a California surfer, Jason has the kind of casual manner that makes him a favorite of fans. Probably no one in the stands knows it, but he's got 20/13 vision in his right eye, meaning he's almost got super-vision and can see at twenty feet what others need to be at thirteen feet to see. Naturally he uses this to his advantage in tracking a baseball moving toward him at high speed. Unfortunately there are very few fans left to see him take a mighty swing at Trombley's first pitch. Throwing all his back muscles into the effort, he sends the ball careening clear over center field, where it seems to hang motionless in the air for a while, as if deciding what to do. He stands looking at it disappear, hardly believing what he sees. Then he begins lumbering around the bases, his tongue hanging out of the corner of his mouth. The remaining fans rise to their feet, awestruck at the turnaround that has just occurred. Spencer scores, Jeter scores, Williams, scores—and Giambi comes home for the unbelievable win. Yankees 13, Twins 12. The last Yankee to hit a game-winning grand slam when his team was down three runs was Babe Ruth in 1925. In fact, it has only been done twenty-four times in baseball history.

A raindrop rolls down Trombley's nose. The victory was snatched from his grasp so quickly and unexpectedly he's still in shock.

"This is the setup we've been waiting for since we signed Jason Giambi," Joe Torre boasts to a throng of reporters. "I don't know how many times I've been asked when is he going to have his defining moment."

The Yankees pour out of the dugout to congratulate their hero. However, not many people knew what illegal substance Giambi had ingested before going out to hit that grand slam. I'm going to let you in on that shocking little secret in a moment . . .

Fewer still knew how he got to be a Yankee in the first place. I was in the clubhouse with Rob Cucuzza when the machinery started rolling to bring the big slugger to New York. After the 2000 World Series, Roger Clemens sat packing his things for the summer break. "Get the Big Guy *here*," he bellowed. "Get him on the horn and *I'll* talk to him." Clemens had a keen interest in bringing Giambi, who was a free agent with the Oakland Athletics, to New York. Every time the Yankees played the A's Giambi would humiliate us with upsetting home runs and clutch hitting that turned the tables so often that George Steinbrenner took notice. He must have whispered in the ear of a few of the Yankees' top guys, because Clemens did get on the phone a number of times, and I overheard him talking with the Big Guy. "We'd like you to come to the Yankees," he'd say. "I know you're worried that it's going to be hell, but trust me, it's not. Listen, my worst fears about New York—that they would be bullies and run roughshod over me—never came true." Pause. You could hear the wheels whirring in Giambi's head. "Come on," Roger would say, almost pleading with the Big Guy. "We'd love to play with you."

Few and far between are the baseball players who can resist the lure of the pinstripes . . . or the pleading of Roger Clemens.

Before you know it, we're at spring training in Florida when in walks this six-foot-three, 235-pound giant who intimidates us all . . . until he begins to speak in this come-gather-round-me-boys high-pitched voice. His yellowish-brown brown hair has been trimmed to Yankees' standards, his sunglasses are stylish but unnecessary in the clubhouse, and he's clutching a cup of coffee in one hand. Running up from the elbows of his beefy arms are large blue tattoos of a skull and a dragon. He might have been a rock star on vacation but he sounded like Mike Tyson on ecstasy.

"Yeah, kiddo," he'd say to me. "What's up? Whaddya need?" He's got the most upbeat positive personality of any player I ever worked with. Nothing gets him down—at least not in those early years with the team. He never said no to anything, either. "Want me to sign baseballs for fans? Sure thing. Need me to meet someone and say hello. Let's do it!" And his positive attitude carried over into spring training, where he promptly hit seven balls over the fence. Joe Torre stands by the sidelines, hands behind his back, beaming. A firstborn with a younger brother who plays for the A's, and a younger sister, Jason is like a big brother to us: calm, confident, and well-mannered. Unlike most players, I never heard him curse except a few times if he made a mistake. But it wasn't anything like the string of profanity you'd get from Paul O'Neill,

248 • Clubhouse Confidential

say, or Posada. He was so relaxed that when someone asked him about life after baseball he said, "To be honest, I haven't really thought about it. I live for today and don't look at the past or what's ahead."

Whenever you saw Giambi, you didn't have to look far to see his shadow, personal trainer Bobby Alejo. Resembling an older, skinnier version of Giambi, Alejo is a tall, muscular guy, balding on top. He's such a character that you could see why Giambi liked him: the guy always had a joke, he was kind to everyone, and he was fun to be with.

Despite having Alejo's help, Giambi's career with the Yankees didn't exactly take off like a shotgun blast. He struggled to live up to the reputation of power-hitting Yankee-killer that he had developed with the A's. Like many hotshots dragged almost kicking and screaming out of the environment they started in and brought to New York—where expectations always run high—he had stretches where his batting average would fluctuate wildly. He had won an MVP award with the A's in 2000, but by 2002 he was ranked in fifth place to get the award, in 2003 he was ranked thirteenth, and in the next two years his ranking went from eighteenth in '05 to fourteenth in '06. He struck everyone as cool and laid-back, but there was a motor running in his brain, a demand that he outperform himself, which made him seek out a drink before each game. Beer had been banned from the Yankee's clubhouse, but we still allowed it in the visiting clubhouse. It might have been Steinbrenner's hope that the opposing teams would get zonked and not be able to play up to their usual standards. In any event, alcohol was always available, if you were willing to go over to the other side of the stadium and help yourself.

One day Giambi called me over with a wave of his hand and said, "Hey, kiddo, can you do me a favor and get me a beer from the visiting clubhouse?" I knew just where to look, and I told him I'd be right back. Minutes later I returned with a thirty-two-ounce cup of Budweiser covered with a clear plastic snap-on top. He looked left and right and then chugged it down all at once so that no one would notice. It got to be a routine that I would give him a beer before every game. Apparently it helped him play with more confidence. With a body like his, though, drinking a quart of beer is probably the equivalent for the average guy of drinking maybe eight to twelve ounces. Just enough to give you a little buzz. He had one of those before he hit that grand slam.

His career was wobbly, as I like to describe it. He'd have high spots and then drop into the doldrums. But the Yankees kept him on the roster because his lows were higher than most players' highs, and his highs . . . well, they were magnificent. Take, for example, the summer of 2005, when he hit a high point that few sluggers ever reach. During a fourteen-game span, he had four multi-homer games, something only five players in history have accomplished: Mel Ott, Harmon Killebrew, Frank Howard, Albert Belle, and Barry Bonds. When he hit that last one, he rounded the bases with his tongue out, making Jeter, who was leaning on the dugout fence, shake his head and smile. Giambi's fourteen July homers were the most in a month by a Yankee since Mickey Mantle hit fourteen in July 1961. Some sportscasters, including New York Yankees' radio announcer John Sterling, took to calling him "the Giambino," echoing the famous nickname of Babe Ruth, whom he resembled in more ways than one. Giambi had the same relaxed stride, a similar portly build, and the legendary follow-through on his swing: a loose twist of the shoulders that drove balls out of the park. Like the Babe, he didn't do much roadwork and he liked to smoke. When he rounded the bases he would turn red in the face and he would be huffing and puffing by the time he got home so that you thought he was going to have a heart attack.

He was a prince of a guy to bat boys, too. In an era when money was flowing a little better than it is today, he was still generous by the day's standards and was one of the best tippers, routinely giving us $3,500 at the end of the season.

Giambi happened to be friendly with Barry Bonds's weight trainer, and during a trip to Japan Giambi learned the inside secret of Bonds's weight-training routine. Bonds has been widely reported to have used performance-enhancing drugs from the Bay Area Laboratory Cooperative (BALCO), a sports nutrition center in California. BALCO had been founded by Victor Conte, a former rock musician. With Patrick Arnold, an organic chemist and amateur bodybuilder, Conte had developed a new steroid, tetrahydrogestrinone (THG), nicknamed "the clear" since it couldn't be detected in doping tests. Not surprisingly, it quickly became a favorite with professional athletes. Put a few drops of the clear under your tongue and it enters your cells and triggers muscle growth, as well as giving you a boost of energy more sustained than coffee. Unfortunately, it also causes side effects, such as reduced sperm production, shrunken testicles, and infertility. It was often stacked with "the cream," a testosterone supplement that BALCO sold to athletes.

Before long Giambi was using the clear and the cream, along with growth hormone. At first this regimen helped him gain strength. He was hitting better and running faster. But since he was using powerful anabolic steroids without a doctor's supervision, he was making a number of typical novice mistakes, such as failing to get periodic blood tests to see how his body was reacting to the hormones. Because he wasn't using steroids in a safe manner, he began to suffer some of the side effects that a knowledgeable physician would have been able to prevent.

His body started breaking down in a number of ways. You would see him come into the locker room with his head hanging down as if he had already done a workout, though he hadn't even started. You would see him take off his T-shirt and pants and notice an unusual amount of flab instead of the cut profile you expect from an athlete. Then things started going wrong with his joints, his knee, his stomach, even his brain. There were rumors he was suffering from a pituitary tumor, which turned out to be true. Luckily it was benign and he received treatment for that and his other ailments. One good thing about the Yankees is that they take care of players—provided, of course, that the guys reveal what their physical problems are. But during this time, when his body seemed to be failing him and his playing got worse, the Yankees took him off the postseason roster.

He apologized to fans in early 2005, sitting in a room with reporters and revealing that he felt bad about having used steroids. "I'm sorry, but I'm trying to go forward now," he said. "Most of all, to the fans, I'm sorry . . . I know it's going to be hard and I understand how they feel." His straightforward confession put him heads and shoulders above players like Barry Bonds, who denied steroid use despite plenty of evidence to the contrary. Giambi had given grand jury testimony in 2003 in which—unlike many players who used steroids—he candidly admitted what he had done. By the time that secret testimony became public, he was ready to admit his use to the mass media.

Despite his open confession, or maybe because of it, the Yankee organization came down hard on Giambi. They made him an example and started applying pressure to force him out. It's true that George Steinbrenner had said that Giambi was "a hell of a big man to stand up and apologize"; but even while the owner was patting him on the back, the front office was working behind the scenes to shoot the Big Guy down. One of the first things they did, and probably the meanest, was to fire Bobby Alejo. They did it in a sneaky way, too, instituting a new policy prohibiting the use of personal trainers who weren't part of the Yankees' staff.

The loss of Alejo took a terrible toll on Giambi. He was now missing his closest buddy, the man who had helped him through thick and thin. He looked like a lost boy in the clubhouse, and not just because his former personal trainer had disappeared or because he was suffering from physical injuries. The blow to his pride was probably the biggest slap in the face. The Yankees' administrators are masters of this indirect form of psychological torture, and they were actively working to make him feel unwanted. Walking toward the batting cage one day, he had a bat in one hand and a beer cup in another and I was right beside him as he took a drink from the cup and said, "I feel unwanted. I'm being treated unfairly . . . Don't wanna be in New York, kiddo." I knew he was referring to the organization, not to the fans and his teammates. All I could say was, "You'll be okay, Jason." But at that moment I felt so bad for him. The Yankees pressured him to leave, to go down to the minors, and to take other actions that made him feel less than welcomed. But he stayed strong and refused to let the organization send him away. After all, he had signed a seven-year contract in 2002, and three years remained.

Jason tried to keep up appearances, and from what I could see he was successful in keeping the fun going, even on the road. One time we were in Baltimore and staying in a beautiful suite. The players had paid for my accommodations and I didn't have to work. I was just there to vacation while they did the same, although, of course, they occasionally had to play a baseball game. That's the way he seemed to live, like a man eternally on vacation, a man of leisure, a member of the elite. I was in his suite around six o'clock when the party started. Joe Torre's personal cook, Theresa, was there, as were a couple of blondes, Rob Cucuzza, and a few members of the training staff. We were all drinking and having fun, waiting for Jason to show up. He finally arrived and saw the crowd in his suite, but instead of looking annoyed, his face brightened and he came in and said a cheerful hello to everyone, making us all feel like honored guests.

We retired into one of the rooms and sat on the floor passing something around. I saw smoke go into his mouth and come out, but I can't say whether he inhaled. A little later, though, he started laughing at everything and seemed to have an increased appetite. As for myself, I didn't know what we were smoking, despite the aroma of the burning leaves. I had associated with so many Panamanian players and guys who chewed tobacco and smoked cigars, that I honestly thought this might simply be a new blend of tobacco. I realize that may sound hard to believe to some, but you must remember that I was only a teenager at the time, and a straitlaced one at that. The truth is that I wasn't sure what we were doing. One thing I *was* sure of, however, was that it was getting late . . . very late, especially for an athlete who had to go to Oriole Park at Camden Yards the next day and play ball.

At about four in the morning there was a loud knock on the door. Fearing that hotel management had called the police, we jumped up, shut the stereo, and opened all the windows. "Just a minute!" we were calling. "Just a minute!" Then we sat in the living room and picked up magazines and pretended we were reading. When the door finally opened, a black butler was standing there in a red uniform and white gloves. My heart sank. This guy looked like an official with bad news. I prayed we weren't going to get hauled away in a paddy wagon. But before my confused mind could adjust to what was happening, he wheeled a red and white cooler into the room and flipped back the lid to reveal a case full of beer and wine. Jason's face broke into a smile. The party was far from over.

I wandered into the kitchen where a blonde in khaki shorts was sitting on the sink nursing a tumbler of whiskey. She talked about how much she liked Jason. Yeah, I agreed, he's a great guy, and a terrific party organizer, too. This get-together didn't break up until five in the morning. Next day, Jason was in uniform, playing his heart out. I was popping hangover pills.

Back at the clubhouse in New York he started getting relaxed about things as his physical condition slowly returned to some kind of normalcy. While most players, including Mariano and Posada, have only one locker, Jason needed two in order to hold the bags of fan mail he received. Most players also take good care of their things, and a few of them, like Posada and Matsui, are exceptionally neat. Giambi's locker, in contrast, was a mess. I'm convinced that you can tell the state of a man's mind by the state of his locker. Jason's mind was often unfocused. Even scouts would comment that he had a glazed look in his eyes. I went over to hang his uniform up after the game one day, and I couldn't get closer than four feet from his locker, there was so much junk in front of it. I was standing on one foot, leaning forward like a ballerina, when Giambi, who was sitting taking off a sock, looked up and said, "Do you need space, kiddo?" He gave me a good-natured chuckle. "I have a lot of junk here, don't I?"

Jason had an amazing ability to bounce back, especially considering all the ups and downs he experienced. He was made the designated hitter after he sustained a number of physical injuries, but it wasn't so much a demotion as an acknowledgment that he might not be the most graceful and talented of fielders. It was also an acknowledgment that he was a powerhouse of a hitter when he was on his mark. Still, he sat out a lot of games and looked glum, his head drooping and his hair slicked back with styling gel. He was waiting for things to change, for injuries to heal, and for the Yankees to warm up to him again. Derek Jeter was about the only one who supported him during this time, conceding that we all make mistakes and that Jason was a good guy for the team. Finally, Commissioner of Baseball Bud Selig decided that the Giambino wouldn't be kicked out of baseball after all. That announcement sent waves of euphoria through the Big Guy. Unfortunately, it only solidified the Yankees organization's determination to get rid of him. There was no loyalty to a player, no recognition of the fact that you should do something for those who did something for you. It was all take, take, take. The more I saw the front office in action, the more I disliked them.

One day Jason walked into the players' lounge and stared up at the television where a young tennis player was being interviewed. "Holy mother of God," he said. "Look at the body on her!" He had bounced back from the dumps, all right. We all knew he had a strong sex drive because he was always surrounded by women and he never complained about how they hounded him. These women were sometimes older, sometimes younger, sometimes darker, sometimes lighter, but always flattering and flirtatious. And he was always a ladies' man. During rain delays they would call to him from the sidelines, waving their arms and tossing their long hair, "Giambi! Giambi! Giambi!" He was happy to oblige, running over to say hello and chat before batting practice.

In fact, girls may have played a part in his recovery from the difficulties of his rocky later years. He signed autographs for them during rain delays. That went without saying. They flocked to him in his hotel rooms and after games. He had initially entertained the idea of getting girls by being a rock star, but he couldn't sing. "So, I'm just living a similar lifestyle," he said. He even tried to get in shape to become more fetching. Like his hero Barry Bonds, he developed a thirst for creatine shakes to gain muscle. His huge body, already swollen from years of reduced aerobic exercise and increased weight lifting, seemed on the verge of betraying him. To compound matters, he also drove a small purple Lamborghini

Diablo. The two-seater was low and sleek and every day Jason appeared more massive and bloated next to it. At some point—it was in late 2004—it became nearly impossible for him to fit into his own car. A friend and I used to watch him struggle to squeeze behind the wheel. He had bulked up so much with creatine that one night he got in but looked as if he would be stuck in there forever. And that's how I remember him: no longer getting out to open the door for girls, just waving them in beside him and driving off into the sunset.

20

Red Alert!
George Steinbrenner

One day I was folding towels in the clubhouse in preparation for an afternoon game when George Steinbrenner surprised us by walking into the room. The arrival of the owner was always cause for alarm. Every one of us—from bat boys to coaches to multimillion-dollar players—wanted to look like we were doing *real work* when he was around.

El Duque was putting on cleats in front of his locker. The muscles along his neck and arms rippled as he tied his laces. He was the only one who didn't appear concerned about Steinbrenner's arrival; I guess because he *was* doing work—getting ready to be the starting pitcher.

Decked out in a cream turtleneck, blue cashmere blazer, cream slacks, and cream-colored leather shoes, Steinbrenner looked the complete businessman. His hair was plastered down with Brilliantine. You could smell the old-time pharmacy fragrance as he stepped up to El Duque.

Without warning—without so much as uttering a word—Steinbrenner raised his thick palm and slapped it down in the middle of the starting pitcher's back.

Orlando's jaw fell open and his tongue popped out as if he were choking. He didn't even have time to straighten up before Steinbrenner pounded him three more times in quick succession. I stood looking in horror. Orlando's face turned a weird shade of purple. As if he were a trainer, Steinbrenner kept his hand on the man's back, moving his palm in heavy circles, clenching and un-clenching his fingers. This massaging continued while George said, "Are you READY?" Then he smashed El Duque yet again—BAAAAAAAM! The flat palm thudded down dead center on the pitcher's spine. "Now you GO OUT AND GET 'EM!"

Nodding in self-satisfaction, the man we affectionately called the Boss strolled out of the room. After he was gone, El Duque turned to me, his face dark and twisted.

"FUCK!" he said in Spanish. "Doesn't he have anything *better* to do!"

I put my hand to my lips to prevent myself from bursting out laughing, afraid George might somehow hear me.

El Duque shook his head. This was a guy the Coast Guard had picked up during his escape from Cuba and thrown into jail—a man able to handle himself in political battles, tense MLB games, and shark-infested waters.

"But he's the Boss," he said, his mouth moving in an involun-tary twitch. "He pays the bills."

This unenthusiastic acceptance of the man in charge was shared by all of us. It was, at best, a love/hate relationship. We had this fear of the man ingrained so deeply in our blood that we could smell trouble a mile away. When the clubhouse door opened you would sometimes see Jeter or Paul O'Neill. But sometimes the door would open, and for a fraction of a second—the time it takes a fastball to travel from the pitcher to home plate—*you would see no one.* During that short silence, a dark breeze would blow in from outside, and players as far away as the players' lounge or the weight room would feel the hairs on the backs of their necks rise. In the next second you would see a security guard step through the door, behind him the shadow of a giant. That's when the trembling in the boots would begin. For we knew, just by the way that door had opened, that HE WAS HERE.

George Steinbrenner in the house! RED ALERT! Get your asses moving, you loafers, you.

I have *never* experienced such a rush of emotion when anyone entered a room—not A-list movie stars, not Yogi Berra, not even the president. Everyone was instantly on their best behavior. Guys who in the previous few seconds had been lounging with their hands behind their heads or watching television would be transformed into busy bees, picking up their T-shirts, folding uniforms, arranging their lockers . . . The Boss was here! Things had changed, and you damn well better be on your best behavior.

If Robbie had advance notice, he would holler to us, "Get lost! Go! He's coming!" Clubbies and bat boys would scatter like cockroaches.

That's why we eventually developed a system to alert us when George arrived at the stadium, so that we would have at least a few seconds' notice. I'll get to that system a little later, but first I need to tell you a few things about Steinbrenner that have never been revealed before, and which stand out in my mind because they paint a picture of the man that has rarely been discussed. I'm talking about his very human and almost silly side.

One afternoon I was carrying a jumbo garbage bag out past Joe Torre's office, and George Steinbrenner happened to be walking down the hall toward me. I gulped, praying I wasn't going to drop the goddamn thing in front of him. I was extra careful to make sure nothing leaked out because George was a clean freak.

When he saw me he said, "Hey, son."

I stopped and said to myself, Oh, my God!

George walked up to me.

"You need some help with that?"

"No, Boss."

He loved being called Boss.

He dipped into his pocket and pulled out a wad of cash and peeled off a hundred-dollar bill and handed it to me.

"Thank you, Boss."

I wasn't the only one who got the willies when George Steinbrenner appeared, and, let me tell you, we saw *our* owner a lot more than other teams saw theirs. Ted Turner, owner of the Atlanta Braves, for example, had a reputation as a guy who *never* stepped into his clubhouse. Well, George was *always* showing up—unannounced—and it drove guys off their rockers.

I'll never forget this one time I was in Tampa and he appeared during spring training. On that occasion I happened to be sitting in Lou Cucuzza's office with a few other clubbies and Rob Cucuzza. We were all in a relaxed frame of mind; in fact, Lou had his feet up on his desk. We were talking about having a tournament for PlayStation *Madden NFL*. Suddenly Lou's ears pricked up like a cat, and I swear he looked like he had seen a ghost. His antenna was always attuned to trouble, and off in the distance he had detected George's voice. As if he had received an electric shock, he jumped up and pretended to be yelling at us.

"Get back to work!"

A second later Steinbrenner popped his head into the office. Lou was still yelling at us, and, believe me, the Boss loved it.

"Way to go, Lou!"

We were all red in the face, but not because we were afraid of George or afraid to be caught talking about a game. No, we didn't want to laugh out loud and make George lose face. Because if he knew that Lou had been giving us a fake scolding, it would have made him feel terrible. Thank God he hadn't come in one second earlier or he would have hit the roof because he hated it when you sat around doing nothing on his time. You always had to be doing *something* productive when he was around.

After George left, Lou stopped pretending he was working. "Whew!" he said. "That was a close one."

I used to think that George was only a taskmaster around Yankee Stadium and that we'd be safe when we traveled to other stadiums. But that wasn't so. Oh, did I have a few things to learn about his controlling nature! In fact, when we were away from home he became even *more* protective of his team, and I soon saw to what lengths he would go to make players comfortable—even if it meant breaking the backs of his support staff.

———

The worst example of this mother-hen behavior happened during the 2000 World Series against the Mets. The day before Game 4 Steinbrenner showed up at Shea Stadium in the Mets visitors' clubhouse. That was the beginning of the nightmare—the fact that he was scouting out the location where his team would be working.

True, the place was a shambles: the ceiling was low and dilapidated, the floor was torn up, and the only place for players to sit was on tiny wooden stools with no back support. George was horrified by the condition of the room, and before long he got an idea so unusual that it had never occurred to a baseball manager before. He told Robbie to bring the truck to the Yankees' clubhouse and haul our tables, couches, and chairs to the Mets' visiting clubhouse!

Next day I was commissioned to help move the furniture out of the clubhouse, but when the truck arrived I knew I was in trouble. A skinny nineteen-year-old, I had never lifted a weight in my life. Although I pitched on a Summer League, I never trained; I just went out and winged it. Now, as I stared at the couches and tables, I wondered how my back was going to feel once I lifted these deadweights. Meanwhile, Craig Postolowski, who was the strongest bat boy, was intrigued by the challenge. Robbie started barking orders.

"Pick up that couch! Move that table! Lift those chairs! Bring 'em out to the truck!"

I curled my fingers under one end of a couch. Craig took the other end. When we lifted it, my back made a sound like a rubber band snapping. Craig was fine with the weight, but because of me we struggled past a flurry of activity in the clubhouse, knocking against lockers, chipping paint off walls, and scraping our fingers.

Once we got it into the truck, we had a short rest as we wound our way through traffic. The fun continued as we unloaded at Shea Stadium. I had come to work expecting to carry a few thirty-three-ounce bats and to fold a few fluffy white towels. Instead, I was breaking my back hauling furniture because the Boss wanted his players to be comfortable.

Little did I know it, but this was just the first part of the nightmare that was about to unfold.

When he had initially arrived and eyed that Mets' locker room, Steinbrenner could not have known that directly above was an ancient standpipe that was just waiting to cause trouble. Like a ticking bomb, pressure in that standpipe built up during the game. Unaware of the danger above him, George was in the lounge watching the game on television. (Many players, especially Paul O'Neill and Tino Martinez, hated the fact that he hung around because it cramped their style. But George preferred to be as far from the prying eyes of the media as possible.) Unknown to any of us, a small fire had broken out on the third deck of the stadium, and when firefighters opened their hoses to extinguish the blaze, they contributed to the buildup of pressure above the Yankee locker room. During the eighth inning, the standpipe burst, sending gallons of water pouring down on us. Someone ran to tell Joe Torre, but he had no time to focus on the flood. Even though the Yankees were leading 3–2 at that point, all his energies were needed to manage the game.

"I was in there when it happened," Jeff Nelson, the Yankee reliever, said. "All of a sudden . . . it was like Niagara Falls . . . [Then] the ceiling collapsed."

Steinbrenner ran to the locker room and joined a group of firefighters trying to contain the situation. He sloshed through the water as if wearing fishing boots, not caring that his blazer and dress pants were soaked.

"I tell ya, they did this on purpose," he was saying. "The Mets will do anything to try to win a World Series."

Parts of the drop ceiling were hanging down, and George maneuvered his way below the debris. He was using a broom to push green water aside. Light fixtures and broken air grilles dangled overhead.

"That they would stoop to something like this is outrageous! I'm going to bring it up with the commissioner."

But in those magic days, the Yankees couldn't be stopped by problems with furniture, fires, or floods. We won the game 3–2.

It seemed like the fun with Steinbrenner never stopped. Before Game 5, Fox News was setting up wires and microphones in the Mets' visiting clubhouse. If we won that game, we would win the series, and it would be big news. I got there early, as usual, to take care of my chores, and I was tripping all over these guys, they had so much equipment. By the time they had everything squared away, however, they had done a professional job of using black tape to conceal all the wires so that nobody would get hurt.

After the seventh inning, George came out of his television room, looking pink in the face and nervous. I always knew when he was nervous because his eyes would blink and there was a knot in his brow. The score at that point was tied 2–2. It was a tense time for him, as the outcome was uncertain. David Cone, who wasn't pitching that day, happened to cross through the room. There was a mischievous twinkle in his eye. Cone loved to ride George. Like a prankster, he seemed to tag after the Boss, looking for opportunities to poke fun. Spotting a microphone taped under the table, Cone stood looking at it. "Oh, my, my my," he said, as if speaking to himself.

Steinbrenner approached.

"What's the matter?"

Cone didn't reply. Like the undeniable actor he was, he simply stood with one hand on his jaw, peering under the table. His curiosity roused, George tottered closer, the game largely forgotten now. *What in God's name was Cone looking at?* George was bending down, too, both of them peering under the goddamn table.

"Can you believe it?" Cone said. "Can you believe they'd do something like *this*—"

"Like *what?*"

"Don't you see it! They taped a microphone under there."

"Who? Who taped a microphone?"

"The Mets."

"Are you ser—"

"They've got the room *bugged*."

"Holy crap!"

George stood up, bumping his head on the underside of the table. He was red in the face. The prankster had him going now, for sure, and Cone was having fun. For Cone, this was almost as good as winning games. He lived to ride George. The two seemed to be made for one another. Strict and controlling, George needed Cone to provide occasional ribbing as a way to let off steam, and, just as surely, the fun-loving Cone needed the stern presence of George to playfully taunt.

In the corner, Robbie was looking on with a grin. Lou Cucuzza put his hand over his mouth to prevent himself from laughing out loud.

George went nuts. He had taken the bait—hook, line, and sinker. He started looking around for something, then turning to us, he yelled, "Somebody get me a pair of scissors!" He wanted to cut the wire!

He was tough to work for, yes, but funny at the same time. One day I walked into the clubhouse to drop off some cleats that I had finished cleaning. When I was done setting down the last pair at players' lockers, I decided I wanted a drink. But when I walked over to the kitchen I discovered that there was a meeting going on in the players' lounge. Tino was sitting by the entrance, his face red, squirming like he wanted to escape. I slowed to a standstill and looked into the room. My heart jumped when I saw what was happening.

George Steinbrenner was on his hands and knees—in his dress clothes—trying to crawl behind the refrigerator.

Intending to make things quieter in the room, he wanted to pull the plug to prevent the refrigerator's hum from distracting players. But his desire to have them focus was distracting everybody even more. He couldn't find the outlet, so finally he asked Mitch to unplug it. Once the humming stopped, there was an awkward silence in the room. George's scheme had backfired: instead of helping people focus, his actions had made everybody uncomfortable. A few minutes later, the meeting broke up and Tino exited quickly. Tino and Paul O'Neill were the most spooked by George's annoying habit of sitting in on meetings, but none of the other players really liked it either.

The Boss had a few other annoying habits, including his custom of criticizing players not to their face but through the media. He had brought Hideki Irabu to the team at a cost of $12 million. Naturally, he was heavily invested in the man's success. Irabu was a terrific pitcher on the 1998 team, but during spring training he made an error and failed to cover first base. The runner got to first and Irabu was left with egg on his face. But George wouldn't let it rest. The first opportunity he got, he criticized Irabu to the press.

"He's a fat . . . TOAD!"

Sputtering disgust with the guy he was paying millions, Steinbrenner was referring to the fact that Irabu was out of shape. But of course! He never worked out. He was more portly than anyone. When he stepped out of the sauna you always knew it was him since his silhouette was unmistakable. He never set foot in the weight room. Half-American, half-Japanese, I never saw anyone with a head shaped like Irabu's. It was formed like the figure 8: round on top, narrow around the eyes, and round again at the cheeks and chin. Like Matsui, who would join the team five years later, Irabu always had a translator with him. The next day when Steinbrenner's remark hit the papers, the translator was trying to explain it to him. "Toad," the guy was saying. "*Kare wa anata o norowa* . . . He called you a bad name." Finally, the light went on in Irabu's eyes.

Next day Irabu was out there practicing the run to first over and over. He rehearsed it in PFP until he got it right. Not long afterward, in a game at Yankee Stadium against the Red Sox, he got a chance to show his stuff. In the sixth inning a ground ball was hit away from first base and Tino Martinez jumped toward it. Instantly Irabu was chugging over to first. When Tino snagged the ball and turned to throw, Irabu was right where he was supposed to be. The throw to first and . . . runner out! Happy with this turn of events, the New York crowd cheered. Steinbrenner's comment to the media had worked. Harsh though it was, it caused Irabu to improve his fielding. Later, George apologized to Irabu for the remark, telling the pitcher that *he* was his biggest fan.

One evening George showed up in the clubhouse before a night game. He hated to see newspapers in the clubhouse, especially if they featured stories about the Mets on the front or back covers. It just so happened that the *Daily News* was opened to a big spread about a Mets win, and George flipped out.

"Robbie!" he cried. "Get rid of these papers."

Rob Cucuzza hustled to pick up the offending papers. Then he ordered the bat boys to comb through the entire area looking for any other copies.

"I don't care who they belong to," George said. "Throw them out! I don't want my boys seeing this propaganda."

George reacted to Mets cover stories the way Andy Pettitte reacted to centerfolds. He would scream and yell and order Robbie to get rid of them. Of course, Robbie always passed the buck and the order got relayed to us to clean the place up. But when Steinbrenner wasn't around we still bought the newspapers: two

*Post*s, five *Daily News*es, four *New York Times*. The guy at the corner store thrived on our business.

This love/hate thing between us and the Boss took its most outrageous form with the system we called the "Red Alert." We had been surprised by the Boss so many times, caught with our hands in the cookie jar so often, that we needed to find some way to defend ourselves. Well, the Red Alert was our way of doing that. It worked like this:

If George Steinbrenner was coming in from out of town, he would arrive at the airport, and from there he would take a limo to the stadium. If he was coming in from his suite at the Regency, he would arrive in the back of a blue Lincoln town car. You knew it was his because it always came up slowly and the license plate said NYY. The car would park in the players' parking lot. Then George would enter through the press gate of old Yankee Stadium, wave to the security guard, pass through the press gate lobby, and push the button for the elevator.

Unknown to him, the Red Alert system had already crashed into high gear as soon as his car had appeared. Rob Gomez, the manager of stadium operations, had picked up his walkie-talkie and punched in the code for the security officer on duty downstairs. As George got out of his car, Mr. Gomez relayed a message to Craig Foley, the security guard standing in front of the clubhouse.

"Red alert. Boss in the house."

"Is he in the elevator?"

"Not yet . . . Stand by."

Gomez would calmly turn, smile, and wave to the Boss. Then he would wait for him to enter the elevator. As soon as the doors closed behind Steinbrenner, Gomez would relay the message to Foley, so that there was no risk of being overheard.

"He's coming down."

"Check."

Robbie was the mastermind who had set up the Red Alert system, and it usually worked like clockwork to protect us. Upon receiving word that Steinbrenner had entered the elevator, Mr. Foley would stride down the hallway, open the clubhouse door, and sound the alarm.

"RED ALERT!"

Whoever was in the room—whether it was bat boys, coaches, trainers, or players—would spread the word to everyone else.

"RED ALERT!"

"RED ALERT!"

Called from man to man, player to player, room to room, the alarm would spread like wildfire. Within seconds of Mr. Foley's announcement, a sweeping transformation would take place throughout the clubhouse. You would see clubbies jump out of chairs and hang up the same piece of underwear six times, waiting for the door to open. You would see coaches put down newspapers and start scribbling notes on clipboards. Bat boys would snap out of inactivity and deposit those newspapers in trash cans.

"RED ALERT!"

"STEINBRENNER IS HERE!"

George would get out of the elevator and walk down the hall. When the clubhouse door opened, everyone would be working—and George would love it. You could tell by that big smile. At his side, the security guard would smile, too, but for an entirely different reason.

The Red Alert system had worked again.

After the day was over we used to reward those security guys, too. We would let them come in and eat all they wanted in the players' lounge. They looked forward to it because it was a free meal—and it was good.

Yes, we were like a big family, and George was the father figure we all feared. Joe Torre used to take a lot of guff from him, but he never really let it interfere with his game plan. "This is what the Boss wants," he would tell players in closed meetings. "But this is what I'm going to do." And there would be smiles. It was like us versus George. Torre used his conflict with the owner to bring the team together.

Don Zimmer, the bench coach, was less careful about his rebellion. In fact, he was the only one who really had the balls to stand up to Steinbrenner. Popeye—as players sometimes called him because of his resemblance to the cartoon character—was a feisty guy, especially as he got older. He would openly challenge Steinbrenner if he felt the Boss was wrong. For example, after Steinbrenner called Irabu a toad, he apologized to him and told him he was going to be the starting pitcher. But Zimmer had already selected Ramiro Mendoza. Zimmer thumbed his nose at George and used Mendoza, who pitched eight nearly flawless innings. Furious, Steinbrenner refused to talk to Zimmer for months.

"I'm sixty-eight," Zimmer would say. "The worst thing I can

do is go home. What are they going to do, shoot me? While I'm here, I'll do the best I can."

Eventually the contest between the owner and Zimmer came to a head. I was there in 2003 on the day seventy-two-year-old Don Zimmer left the team for good. He was wearing a brown sweater and cleaning out his locker.

"Chief," he said, "can you carry this box for me?"

I hoisted his belongings onto my shoulder, and we walked up through the tunnel. When the media caught sight of us upstairs in the parking lot, they gathered round for a final interview. Zim talked about his fondness for the team and his sadness at leaving. I was still holding the box when he fired his parting shots. During his remarks he referenced the fact that the Boss had called the coaches "a bunch of assholes" a few days earlier.

"This is one asshole they don't have to worry about being fired," Zimmer told reporters. "He don't have to worry about that 'cause I won't be back. I'm a human being, and I ain't been treated like one in eleven months." Zimmer's lower lip quivered and tears started to form in his eyes.

Let me tell you, I've heard plenty of interviews with coaches, managers, and players, and I've even been a translator for some of the guys who didn't speak English, but I never heard an interview like that. By the time Zim had finished, I was all choked up, too. Then I followed him out to his car with his box of clothes. It got heavier with each step because I knew he was going for good. When we got to the car he turned to thank me. "Okay, Chief," he said. He handed me thirty dollars and got in the car and before I knew it he was gone. I walked back alone into the stadium. At that point I was the only one who knew that our bench coach had left.

I didn't know who to tell. For some reason I didn't feel like working. I just looked around at the empty lockers as if I were seeing ghosts.

Good-bye, good old Zim! You had the guts to challenge even the Boss. The rest of us, well, we pretty much towed the line under George's heavy-handed rule. Still, I learned a good deal about discipline while working for the Boss. He was the most demanding employer I ever had. And yet . . . he had his soft side, too.

I'll close with this story from when we won the 2000 World Series. George was with the team and happy to celebrate. At this point he became emotional and he was crying with happiness. The media was there and the players were in a silly mood. Jeter— the only one who had the guts to do it—poured a bottle of champagne over George's head. It soaked him from head to toe, making his suit jacket stick to his body. At first the Boss's face turned dark, and we thought he was going to explode. It got very quiet in the room. Then suddenly the commissioner of baseball started giggling . . . and—thank God—so did George.

When all's said and done, that's my favorite memory of the Boss: drenched in champagne at that World Series victory party; crying, laughing, and enjoying the hell out of baseball.

21

In the Blink of an Eye
Mariano Rivera

One day in October 1998, a thin, broad-shouldered man walked down a flight of stairs in the old Yankee Stadium, turned a corner, and made his way along a damp corridor, at the end of which he entered a large, dimly lit room. Six men sitting along the far wall glanced up at him with worried expressions. They were looking at Mariano Rivera.

The room smelled of ozone and decaying plastic. For a while the only sound was the *hissssssss* of a malfunctioning ventilation duct. But if any fresh air was entering the room it was impossible to feel. Instead, players sitting along the wall were heaving difficult breaths. The look on Mariano's face said that today's business was deadly serious. His eyes were dark as he surveyed the group of men watching him, and when he sat in a chair at the front of the room the closing pitcher's lips were tight and bloodless.

In the corner behind Rivera, a heavily built young player with a fleshy round face was busy wrestling with a mop. Luis Sojo, eyes narrowed in concentration, twisted the cotton mop head off the stick. Then he adjusted the straggly mess until it sat on his head like a barrister's wig.

No one was smiling, but when Mariano Rivera looked up from his notes, his lips curled into a frown.

"Huh!" someone said in the back of the room. This word was repeated by the other players: "Huh-huh-huh."

"Quiet," Rivera snapped. He banged the mop stick on the table.

"Huh-huh-huh."

I have to admit that I was more than a little frightened to be sitting on the floor just a few feet from Rivera with him in that mood. I could smell onions and garlic on the breath of the players behind me. I didn't really think any of them would do physical harm to me on purpose, but uncertainty and claustrophobia had me wondering whether Mo might accidentally hit me with that stick.

Before we go any further I have to sneak in a little departure from the subject here and explain exactly why I was so jittery in that room with these guys, watching Rivera play the part of a judge. It was because it was Mo up there with that batlike gavel and not someone else. From personal experience I knew that he had playfully attacked his own teammates on numerous occasions up in the clubhouse. He would grab them, like an older brother wrestling younger siblings to the floor. I had seen him jump over a chair and spring across the clubhouse like a wrestler leaping from the ropes onto an opponent; but Mo's actions on these occasions were never prearranged, the way a wrestler's might be. No, he never gave fair warning or rehearsed his attack, he simply flung himself at the other player, landing on top of the guy and grabbing him by the neck, tackling him to the floor and then wrapping his long throwing arm—that band of highly muscular steel—around the poor guy's throat, holding him in a full nelson. I saw him do this to Doc Gooden one day, surprising the tall black pitcher with the fury of his attack. Two or three other players had been equally astonished, but did nothing to aid their teammate. Instead, they looked on from the sidelines, even going so far as to step back to give Mo extra room so that he could pin the struggling Gooden, who was gasping like a fish out of water. I never saw a black man turn blue before, but Gooden managed to do it, his tongue hanging out of his mouth and saliva dripping onto the gray rug. He knew he was a beaten man, and he was saying, "Okay, Mo! Okay, Mo!"

This was just before a game, too. Why would the Yankees' closer exert so much energy in horseplay when he had to go out and pitch? He also risked injuring his pitching arm by the way he had pinned Doc, but it seemed a necessary part of his warm-up on certain days. It was as if he needed to let off steam by horsing around.

You could never predict what Mo was going to do. Playful and impulsive, he was a man of many moods, few of which, other than his extraordinary self-control under pressure, are ever visible to baseball aficionados. How could I forget seeing him in the whirlpool room adjacent to the Yankees' locker room, eating junk food with "Flash" Gordon! It was a funny side of Mo, but it also revealed his stern nature, which could erupt at any time into horsing around. That whole episode had started when reliever Tom Gordon asked me to pick up some hamburgers from a fast-food restaurant across the street from the stadium. I began doing this regularly for Flash. When I returned to the clubhouse it would usually be empty, except for Mo, who would be getting ready to go out and pitch. I would see him in his shorts and T-shirt, but I would always avoid him because by bringing junk food into the clubhouse I was breaking team rules. At this time the trainers had players on strict diets. There was plenty of health food available in the clubhouse, but players weren't supposed to eat burgers and fries.

One day Mo followed me down the hallway, past the window to the trainer's room. I quickened my pace but he easily caught up with me and stuck his nose down to the paper sack I was carrying. I had hidden the McDonald's bag in there, but now I felt like I was cornered. Mo looked up, frowning.

"What's that you got there?"

"Nothing."

"Don't lie to me."

"I'm not."

"You got food in there?"

"No."

I continued walking. His curiosity roused, Mo followed me into the whirlpool room where Flash was lounging with his shoes off. Gordon got up and grabbed the bag out of my hands. Mo took one look at the steaming food and his eyes grew wide. "You lied to me, Squeeg." He put on his baby face. I knew that he never laid out cash for snacks and that he would want some for free. Sure enough, he came closer. "Is there anything here for me, guys?" Before we could stop him, he began munching one of the burgers, and I was ordered to run across the street and fetch more. This became a regular thing, with me supplying them with cheeseburgers and fries before games. Flash always laid out the cash; Mo never paid. The two of them would eat secretly in the whirlpool room so that players and coaches wouldn't criticize them for their rule-breaking diet. On those days Mariano was demanding but nonviolent, and I was counting on that to be his disposition today.

Still, I kept worrying about the times he had gotten physical in the clubhouse. Like when he and Jeff Nelson used to throw grapes at each other in the players' lounge. You would hear the grapes exploding—*Splat! Splat! Splat!* El Duque, Mike Stanton, and reliever Jason Grimsley used to horse around even more than Mo on occasion, pitching black grapes at each other like fastballs. Bat boys would get caught in the crossfire. Mo loved throwing grapes, and he'd hide after hitting someone.

He was pacing now at the front of the video room, the players sitting behind me watching his every move. Posada entered and took his place beside Ramiro Mendoza, Raul Mondesi, Enrique Wilson, El Duque, Ruben Sierra, and Miguel Cairo. Only Hispanic players had been summoned to this kangaroo court. It occurred to me that this was their way to relax before a game.

Because they knew him better than I did, these guys treated Mariano like Doctor Jekyll and Mr. Hyde. He could be calm and personable one minute and snap the next. When they were tackled, for example, they knew that they had no chance of getting up without a fight. Smart kids that they were, they didn't want to struggle with him. Why lose all that energy before a game? So they begged and pleaded with him, knowing that by doing so they would get him off their back more quickly than by fighting.

Slowly but surely, I had come to think of Mariano as an impulsive jokester. The same explosive power he unleashed in a pitch was directed backstage at teammates in half-humorous, half-serious attempts to release pent-up energy. He was a walking time bomb, and you never knew what was going to set him off. Fans never see this side of him since when he's in the public eye he channels all his energy into that cut fastball. When he's on the mound he appears to all the world like the king of calmness and control. I loved watching him pitch against the Red Sox, our rivals. He would take deep breaths. He would never sweat. Icy command. Total control of his emotions. And he would save the win. You loved him then; we all loved him. But when you were on the other side of the curtain you would see another face of the great pitcher: you would see the inner child that needed to tease and taunt. But it wasn't a normal child, like Jeter (who can tease along with the best of them), or Joe Torre (who has a dry sense of humor and loves practical jokes). No, Mariano could be a bit of a roughneck and sometimes he needed to physically triumph over those closest to him. That's why I was sweating in that video room—less because of the heat than because of what I was afraid he might do.

Which isn't to say he was mean and nasty to *every*one. Plenty of times I had been asked to get two-dollar or five-dollar calling cards for him. He'd give me exact change and I'd buy the cards. Then he'd storm into Rob Cucuzza's office and shoo us all out to make his call. "Everybody out!" Robbie would look angrily at him and complain, "This is *my* office, brother." But Mariano was insistent and he'd kick us out so he could make long-distance calls in the privacy of that little office. *Who was he calling?* Was it family, friends, a woman? Nobody knew.

All I knew was that he was close to *some*body, and it wasn't me. The first defendant Mo called to the witness stand—which was no more than an aluminum folding chair placed at the front of the room—was Bernie Williams.

"*Silencio todo mundo!*" Mariano said. "Silence in the court!"

"Huh-huh-huh." Players were laughing now.

"Quiet in the court or you'll get thrown out," Mo said. He sat at the table behind Bernie and rapped on the desk until people quieted down.

Sojo came forward and addressed Bernie Williams. "We have it on good authority that when you arrived at the clubhouse last Thursday you told one of the bat boys, who is present in court today, that you needed to take a nap"—the Mop gave me a sideways glance—"and you asked him to wake you in half an hour. Your turn to bat was 4:35 P.M., yet you were seen sleeping by your locker in your uniform with a bat in hand. The bat boy has submitted a sworn affidavit indicating that he woke you up, as requested, at four P.M., with plenty of time to get up to the field, but that after you thanked him, you closed your eyes and dozed off again. As a result you missed your turn to bat. What do you have to say in your defense?"

At this point in the procedure, players who had been accused of infractions of team rules would be allowed to plead their case and tell why they should not be fined. Most defendants relished this opportunity to give excuses, and like kids caught doing something wrong they would come up with the most far-fetched reasons you could imagine for their bad behavior. But not Bernie Williams. The man was always at a loss for words.

Bernie looked up and said, "But, um, but, but—" He seemed to be thinking hard. His face was beaming with innocence, yet all he could say was, "But, um, lemme see, uh—" The other players were laughing, hands over their mouths, trying not to laugh too loud. It was always the same with Bernie. Unlike other players, he never came up with any excuses.

Sojo leaned down toward Mo and grit his teeth, strands of his wig brushing the table.

"What's the verdict?"

"Guilty!" Mariano cried. He rapped on the desk. As he pronounced the sentence he knit his brows. "You're fined the sum of one hundred dollars."

Bernie shook his head like a defeated man, peeled two fifties from his wallet, and laid them on the table. This action was greeted by cheers and laughter. The Mop pushed the cash to the side and turned to the next defendant . . . which was me.

"Luis Castillo, please take the stand."

I walked to the front of the room and sat in the chair Bernie had vacated.

"It has come to our attention that you failed to ship a FedEx package that the honorable Mariano Rivera asked you to send for him," Sojo began. "It wasn't until three days after the request was made that the item was finally shipped, despite repeated inquiries from Judge Rivera about the status of the shipment and after numerous false promises by yourself about how you were going to do it 'Right away.' So, what do you have to say for yourself?"

Unlike Bernie, I was perfectly capable of defending myself, even in front of these star athletes. I knew that I better tell them something or I'd be found guilty.

"I had a lot of other things to do that week," I began. "But I never forgot the FedEx request, I just put it down on my list until I finally got around to it. You see, I *did* send it after all."

"No, no, no," Mo said. "You sent it *late*. I asked you three days ago to send it and I kept asking you, 'Did you ship it yet?' and you kept putting it off, promising that you were going to do it that afternoon, or right after you got off work. But it never got sent for three days! What good is it for me to ship something FedEx if you're going to hold on to the package for three days before you even bring it to the office!"

"It doesn't look good for you, kid," Sojo said.

"Guilty!" Mo cried. "Fine: one hundred dollars."

I stood up and said, "I don't have it!" I fished in my pockets and came up with fifty cents. I placed two quarters on the table. "That's all I've got."

The room echoed with laughter. This was exactly the kind of silliness they all wanted and needed to set their spirits free. That video room, which had been filled with anticipation, had served its purpose, taking the guys away from the pressures of the game they would be playing, and for one magical hour we were all one big happy family.

But how the tide can change in the blink of an eye! Anyone close to Mariano Rivera can tell you about the violent changes in his behavior during the course of a typical day. You only had to observe him at batting practice with Jason Grimsley to see one of the more dangerous examples of his conduct on the field.

Allow me to pause before I get to that little scene of needless violence. You see, I'm afraid I've painted a picture of a man who is completely out of control, and that's not the case. No, he only goes wild now and then. Most of the time—such as when he's pitching or warming up—he's Mr. Control, and he knows exactly what he's doing. When he goes out to pitch and his theme song pours from the stadium speakers—that familiar DUM-da-da-DUM-DUM, DUM-da-da-DUM-DUM riff from Metallica's "Enter Sandman"—you get goose bumps and your heart goes out to him. You know he's going to save the game the way Superman saves the day. I know, from working with him, that he has emotional control as well as control over that cutter. He used to warm up by throwing that cutter to me, and if you've ever wondered what it's like to be on the receiving end of a pitch from the great closer, let me tell you, it's scary. He has one pitch, his trademark 92–94 m.p.h. cutter. We would set ourselves up in right field, sixty feet apart: the distance from the pitcher's mound to home plate. He would practice for location, location, location, aiming to place the ball to the right or left so that it would be impossible to hit. Before throwing, he'd give me a signal so I'd know what to expect. Imagine squatting down, glove in hand. Mariano signals you: the ball is going to cut right. You set. He winds up, *annnnnnnnd* . . . FIRES. It comes in fast and blurry and it's making an evil little hissing sound—*Fffffsssssss!*—as the seams shear off the air molecules in front of the ball. You can't move, you can't breathe, you don't have time. Then—*Bammmmmmm!*—it hits your glove so hard your finger is numb.

We would do this ten or fifteen times before a game. Then the fun would start for real. I mean fun for *him.* Before games, each team is allowed forty-five minutes for batting practice. Players who aren't scheduled to hit—such as pitchers—go onto the field and catch the balls. But instead of throwing them back to pitchers, which would slow things down to a standstill, they throw them into buckets carried by bat boys on the field. We return them to the pitchers, replenishing their supply to keep practice going.

Mariano enjoyed playing shallow center field, and he was better at it than most outfielders. I got a chance to see him in action and it always amazed me. In fact, he was such a good outfielder that reporters used to ask him why he never made a career out of playing there. This question would bring a smile to his lips. A skill he rarely used on the mound, he had mastered the art of shielding his eyes from the sun with his glove so that he could track a ball with eagle-eyed precision. Like Joe DiMaggio, he was poetry in motion, gliding under fly balls and snatching them out of the air. His buddy Jason Grimsley would patrol the outfield with him. Making matters worse for us, they happened to be two of the hardest throwers on the team. To our shock, and for their own amusement, they would play the game of who-can-hit-the-bat boy.

Every day they would throw balls back to us so fast, and in such hectic patterns, that they crisscrossed the field in a blur. We carried plastic buckets to collect the balls, and we scurried around the field trying to make sure that the balls went into the buckets, not our heads.

Mariano loved throwing in competition with Grimsley—and I'm not kidding when I say he had terrific aim. Baseballs would bounce once or twice, but if you weren't fast enough, or if you misjudged the angle of approach, you could get zonked. When he connected, Mo's lips would part in a grin and he would point at you. *Gotcha!* On more than one occasion he clocked me in the body. Once I got hit in the ankle and was limping for days. But of course, none of us complained; they were just fooling around, and it was all part of the game.

After batting practice Mo would laugh like a demon and retire to the kitchen for his favorite reward: fried chicken. Meanwhile, bat boys would limp back to the clubhouse and nurse their wounds with ice and Band-Aids.

Epilogue

Oh, how I remember those days! For eight years I had fun, worked my butt off, and rubbed shoulders with legends, finding inspiration to do my best no matter what the obstacles. From George Steinbrenner, who taught me persistence, to Derek Jeter, who taught me humility, to Joe Torre, who showed me how to get along with all types of people, I went to school with the Yankees from 1998 to 2005. Nowadays I don't go to the stadium on a daily basis, but I still feel its attraction like a hunger that, for me, can't be satisfied by watching televised games or attending as a spectator. Because for one never-to-be-repeated time in my life . . . I was part of it all.

When I left, nobody gave me a World Series ring, despite the fact that during three World Series wins I worked just as hard as other clubbies who *did* get one. But why should I be bitter? They didn't give me a cap or a diploma, either, but I had graduated nonetheless. The lessons I learned about teamwork will stay with me forever. Of course I'm proud to say that I had an opportunity to work with the Yankees, and even prouder to think that I met some of the most talented athletes and managers of my generation.

I've often thought about what I would have missed had I never written that letter asking for a job with the New York Yankees. I would never have seen Paul O'Neill catch the last out of David Wells's perfect game from twenty-five feet away. I would never have met Derek Jeter, or heard him singing in the clubhouse, and would never have been given the nickname Squeegee by the Yankees' most famous player. I would never have warmed up with my idol David Cone for his historic perfect game in 1999. I would never have been able to stand next to home plate and listen to future Hall of Famer Roger Clemens's fastball whiz by me into Jorge Posada's glove.

But . . . I *did* write that letter and as a result, in my own small way, I'm honored to have been part of baseball history.

Acknowledgments

In one way or another, many people contributed to the creation of this memoir, and I wish to acknowledge the kindness of those who have helped me in bringing it into your hands. To name them all would be impossible, but I wish mostly to mention how grateful I am to Tina Lewis, Queen of the Bleachers, for helping me become a bat boy in the first place. Thanks also to Sonny Hight in this connection.

I feel a special debt to Donald Antonetty, Heriberto Martinez, Vernick Alvarez, Joe Alvarez, Carlos Escobar, and Victor big brother Butchy Martinez. Thank you for your emotional and consultant help. The feedback, advice, and guidance of Steven Vice Gracia has been a great help to me.

In New York, I would like to express my gratitude to the Central Park Yankees, including Barry Bowen, Fidel, Victor Morales, Paula, Deivy, Juan and Danny Almonte, Jochi, Bombi, Chupa, Solmo, Beezie, Iona, Juansito, Goldo, and Nelson. For their encouragement and suggestions about various chapters, I would especially like to thank the Bleacher Creatures, including Big D, Midget Mike, Tom, Larry, Evelyn Hayes and family, Milton, Big Joe, Bald Vinny, MTA Joe, and the late Ali. If I missed anybody I promise to drink a beer in your honor.

In Cincinnati, Los Angeles, Tampa, Miami, Baltimore, Boston, Phoenix, Chicago, Atlanta, Detroit, Kansas City, Denver, Houston, St. Louis, Minneapolis, Milwaukee, Oakland, Philadelphia, Seattle, Pittsburgh, San Francisco, and Washington D.C., I gratefully thank the many bat boys and clubbies I've worked with in visiting clubhouses and Yankee Stadium in the American and National Leagues, many of whom have extended assistance to me that went beyond the call of duty.

For discussions and advice over the years, I'm very grateful to the many players, coaches, trainers, and staff that I have worked with. I would particularly like to thank David Cone for sharing with me the perfect-game moment and telling me "No one can ever take this away from you"; Derek Jeter, for giving me the name Squeegee; Bernie Williams, for playing catch with me in the outfield; David Wells; Paul O'Neill; Raul Mondesi; Darryl Strawberry; Michael Coleman, for his friendship; Homer Bush, for bowling with me (and letting me win); Ricky Ledee; Luis Sojo and his brother, for playing dominos with me; Marino Rivera, for preaching the word of God to me; David Szen, for being my good buddy; Gene Monahan; Steve Donohue, for taking care of me when I was sick; Mike Borzello ("Lets go, Lakers!"); the late Arthur Richmond; and the late Bobby Murcer for mentioning my name during a Yankee live broadcast.

I want to also mention how grateful I am to Reggie Jackson,

for talking Spanish with me; Don Zimmer (Thank you, Chief!); Felix Heredia; Jason Giambi, for being down to earth; and Roger Clemens, the Rocket Man. Thanks to Jorge Posada and his wife, for the kindness they extended to me when I had questions about catching and their charitable work. Thanks to Joe Torre, for being a guy who was easy to talk with and work with. Thanks to the late George Steinbrenner III, for the lessons he imparted about hard work and dedication to the task at hand.

Special thanks are due to Ruben Sierra, for taking me under his wing while I was a bat boy. I'm also most grateful for the continued friendship of Ramiro Mendoza, who not only took me on vacations and fishing trips while I was a bat boy, but who continues to be an inspiration and friend to this day. Special thanks to his wife, Cynthia, and to their children for their kindnesses.

I think it would be hard for me to express how grateful I am to my literary agent, Steve Harris, for his help shepherding this project through the publishing process. He's experienced, full of helpful ideas, and a pleasure to work with. Thanks also to the contributions of Adam Chromy during the initial stages of the book proposal. And thanks to psychologist Philip D. Cristaniello for supplying research and insight into the mind-set of the players. A special word of thanks is due to our editor at St. Martin's, Marc Resnick, whose invaluable suggestions made the book easier to read. Few publishing professionals have the savvy, tact, and patience of this man. Every time he cut a word we cried, but in the end we saw that he was right. If there is any clarity in this book, any organization in its pages, any lightheartedness in its lines, he is the man responsible for the way it all hangs together.

I would like to thank my father, the late Luis A. Castillo, for instilling in me a love of baseball, and my mother, Milagros Reyes, for her support from the time I became a bat boy through the entire grueling process of writing of this book.

My collaborator, William Cane, deserves a standing ovation for the time and energy he put into working with me on this memoir, day after day, month after month; for three years we talked, wrote, revised, and revised again. He appeared with me and former Yankees players on radio shows, went to editorial meetings with me, and in every way fully entered into the subject of the book. But I don't think I need to tell him how grateful I am because, as the manuscript demonstrates, he clearly knows my thoughts.

A large number of friends and relatives deserve special thanks, including my sister Marylin, brother-in-law Blas, nephew Andy, nieces Gina and Kiani, cousin Albenio, Aunt Iladia, cousins Jerry, Javier, and Christine, the late Doris Ocasio, godson Angel, cousin Mayra, the Antonetty family, Raul and Anita, the Martinez family, Sandy, Spanky, Vicky, Stephanie, Titi Sonia, Joeyito, PJ, Brandon, Felisha, Jaylen, Jessica, Pilly, Margie, Suezette, Eliezer, the Gracia family, Xavier, my goddaughters Genesis, Tiara, and Tabitha, the Alvarez family, Jojo, Jaden, and Reina, the Pacheco family, sister-in-law Madelin, brother-in-law Manny, mother-in-law Margarita, godson Xavier Gomez, Brian Meijas, Hawky, Lou Colon, Cim Ortiz and family, Tdi, Gilly, Marcus, Nilda, Uncle Ray, Paul Lulaj, Oates, the Santana family, Carlos and Leslie, Fat Mike, Anthony Maldonado, Keith Jones, Alberto Big Al, Little Mikey, Sondy, Robert Felix, my barber Jay, Jason and Earth, Triple Seis, Jaysun, Cuban link, Gorilla Tone, Rizzo, Griffin, Chino, little Danny, Deshaun Green, Tommy Rodriguez, Jimmy, Future, Nick Newsome, Tony Newsome, Josiane Espinal, Yolanda and family, Juan Rodriguez, Nephty, MTA Richy, Mario's Grocery store, Wings Academy (my high school), David Defensor (thank you for helping the family), Millie, Longwood Ave., St. John Ave., Beck St., and Fox St.

Finally, I don't know if I can adequately express my gratitude toward my wife, Margarita Pacheco, for her understanding while I worked early and late for three years on this manuscript. Last but not least I would like to thank my children, Luis A. Castillo III, and George Santiago, for staying away from my work room, except to run in and ask for cookies while I worked on the manuscript and wrote these words about a game that changed my life in so many ways.